28

Witch in the Bedroom

proven sensual magic

About the Author

Stacey Demarco is a businesswoman, witch, writer, and horse rider, although not necessarily in that order. A workshop leader, consultant, and teacher, both in Australia and the UK, she is recognized for her humor and practical style of magic. Stacey has a weakness for long hot baths, shoe shopping, and sleeping in on Sundays. Australian by birth, she lives by the sea in Sydney.

For personal or corporate consultations with Stacey Demarco, to learn more about Career Covens, or for recommendations for Wiccan resources close to you, visit www.themodernwitch.com or write to The Modern Witch, P.O. Box 1373, Mona Vale 1660 NSW, AUSTRALIA.

Witch in the Bedroom

proven sensual magic

Stacey Demarco

Llewellyn Publications
Woodbury, Minnesota

First Edition
First Printing, 2006

Author's photo by Jennieann Jones
Based on book design by Connie Hill
Cover design by Gavin Dayton Duffy
Cover image © Getty
Editing by Connie Hill

Llewellyn is a registered trademark of Llewellyn Worldwide Ltd.

Library of Congress Cataloging-in-Publication Data
Demarco, Stacey
    Witch in the bedroom : proven sensual magic / Stacey Demarco. — 1st ed.
      p.   cm.
    Includes index.
    ISBN-13: 978-0-7387-0844-7
    ISBN-10: 0-7387-0844-5
    1. Witchcraft and sex.   2. Magic.   I. Title.

BF1572.S4D46   2006
33.4'3—dc21   2006040924

Llewellyn Worldwide does not participate in, endorse, or have any authority or responsibility concerning private business transactions between our authors and the public.

All mail addressed to the author is forwarded but the publisher cannot, unless specifically instructed by the author, give out an address or phone number.

Any Internet references contained in this work are current at publication time, but the publisher cannot guarantee that a specific location will continue to be maintained. Please refer to the publisher's website for links to authors' websites and other sources.

Llewellyn Publications
A Division of Llewellyn Worldwide, Ltd.
2143 Wooddale Drive, Dept. 0-7387-0844-5
Woodbury, MN 55125-2989, U.S.A.
www.llewellyn.com

Printed in the United States of America

For the two A's,
and P.

Contents

Section Three: Witches in the Bedroom

Section Four: Passing On and Extending Your Tradition

Recommended Resources

Spells, Meditations, and Rituals

Acknowledgments

The relationship I have with the Divine is the relationship that is closest to the center of my being and the one with the most impact on the care of my soul. I am grateful that the Goddess has lived through and within me yet again as teacher, muse, model, and co-creator. Goddess, you have shown me that at every ending there is always a beginning . . . even though I may not see it at first.

And again, as with my first book, a big thank you to all those people who participated in the case studies for this book. Your honesty, faith, and sheer guts are astounding and inspirational. I am sure your stories will inspire others who read this book. Without your trust in me, this work would not have its foundation.

Angela Heise, thank you for being the best of friends in every way. You somehow always know what I need. Your intelligence and your friendship light up my life!

Phyllis Tsolakis, the stunning Greek Goddess, thank you for allowing me to try out some rather audacious, live, on-the-spot experiments and for being joy incarnate!

For those close friends who have supported me during the cycles of writing and relationships over the last year, I am deeply grateful and honored to have you so active in my life. These include the gods: Dr. Pete Prendegast, Todd Crooks, David Garland, Shag, Guinness, Wookie, Ghengis, Goog, E, and the goddesses: Vasudha, Kathy, Honor, Pam, Indie, Ro Markson, Dolores, and the CC girls.

To my parents Bev and Ted Laing, who have done more house minding than anyone really ever should, I heartily thank you and promise that you should be able to spend more time at your home from now on.

I would also like to thank the Australian fertility specialists who kindly advised on the procedures in the Fertility section and gingerly suggested subjects for my case studies. I understand what a big leap of trust that was for you. I'm happy to say that perhaps our techniques are more complimentary than we first thought!

Special thanks to the wonderful Elysia Gallo, Connie Hill, Natalie Harter, and team at Llewellyn Worldwide.

Finally, it has been said that when the opportunity comes to learn a new way, the Goddess provides a catalyst. She sent me you, Adam, as a surprise gift, as an unmistakable reminder of how easy, difficult, wild, solid, frightening, courageous, cerebral, physical, exhilarating, and grounded this whole love, lust, and relationship business is. Thank you from the bottom of my heart for walking beside me and not behind me. Thank you for being both a crash test dummy and a thorough inspiration. And most of all, thank you for the ice cream.

Stacey Demarco, 2006

In the Beginning

I remember running. I remember running fast, laughing, dancing. Then I found my place in the forest. I put the flaming torch on the stone and waited, eyes straining in the darkness. I felt everything: the moisture of the leaves at my feet, the breeze lifting the hairs on my arms, the way it carried away the light mist of sweat I acquired from racing there . . .

I can smell the lush blossoms I picked that day woven through my hair. I look down at my own chest and can see the surface of skin vibrating in the flame; swirling symbols painted in gold, glowing as if tattooed on my breasts and stomach, visible through my simple sheer shift.

Far away, I hear the voices of men in chorus and in solo. They sing and laugh, and then with a shout that could have been drums, or drums that could have been a shout, all goes silent.

I smile, but I am very still.

I listen hard. I feel I can hear many footsteps, many hands blindly pushing through the night. My heart pumps faster and faster.

And then I hear him running toward me to my right. A quick thump of feet faster than a heartbeat. A wave of adrenalin stings me. This could be my God, my chosen one.

A man runs to the center of the clearing. He is carrying a flaming torch too. He is naked and ready. His eyes glow and this is not just the flame reflected in them. He is magnificent, virile and beautiful. I feel a huge attraction. But he is not my God here tonight.

He stops before me and says: "Goddess! Will you accept me here tonight?"

I answer: "Pass on, God. There is another Goddess waiting for you. Be fruitful! Run hard!"

And he does, passing by, giving me a brief kiss, and giving a yell of pure power.

I listen again with the ears of my heart and I know that my chosen one will not be far. I am aware that around me there is delight being taken in fertility, and it is being sown back into the earth.

I look up to Mother Moon and she is orange and heavy in the sky.

Then . . .

He is steady, fast, and stealthy. I see only a flying trail of flame before he stops, a mere half step from me. His strength is palpable. He is naked, painted with the same golden spirals. His eyes are laughing. I can almost taste the heady mix of sweat and sage smoke, and I know that he is erect without having to look. I notice he has a fine scratch on his shoulder, the dark blood smeared over the curve of his collarbone. I think: he got that running to me.

"Goddess! Will you accept me here tonight?"

I feel my power as a Goddess as I answer: "Yes! You have run hard. Let us be fruitful!"

And worlds collide.

This is a description of a traditional Beltaine.

Beltaine is a Pagan ceremony that can be traced back to ancient times celebrating the coming of Summer and the importance of fertility to the cycle of life. Men and women would come together to joyously celebrate and re-enact the natural creativity of the Universe and to give back the fertility to the soil. Then, women saw themselves as Goddess, the creatrix, and would choose one or many Gods to sew fertility back into their fields and forests, not only continuing the cycle spiritually, but ensuring a bountiful crop and plenty of game.

Yesterday's Beltaine* is today's May Day, which is still celebrated in England and Europe. A little less dramatic, but equally as symbolic, people still dance happily abound maypoles, weaving different colored ribbons in and out of each other. They still feast and party, light bonfires, and wear blossoms and herbs in their hair.

What I would like to ask you is how you feel about the story of the Beltaine above? Do you feel it is of academic interest? Perhaps a little titillating or romantic? A little erotic perhaps? A bit of good fun on a Saturday night for a bunch of hippies? Or alternatively, does it disturb your sensibilities? Is it a little too wild, does it make you uncomfortable? Wouldn't this type of thing be dangerous or too promiscuous? Does it sound like trouble? The rational part of you may even begin to ask logistical questions like, "How could you run in the dark and find someone out there anyway?"

The big question I would like to pose to you is whether you believe the story above is a piece of fiction? By this, I don't just mean whether it ever happened, or even when it happened. What I mean is whether you can accept that something like this would be of benefit to anyone at any time? Could you consider that some of the intentions of the old ways may indeed inject new life into the place where we find ourselves now? Whether or not you can suspend your disbelief long enough to consider all the possibilities contained in this book may well be the difference between your taking something useful or even vital from it. Whether or not you can step beyond the concrete walls we live in and go back to a time when pleasure was not steeped in guilt, when creativity was a miracle, when power was shared between the masculine and the feminine, and when chaos was just one stage of the science of building relationships is up to you.

This book is not some mere spell book where I get to tell you how to turn your wife into a cow or your boyfriend into a toad. It's not going to show you how to curse a man who has cheated on you or trap into bed

---

* Beltaine is from the ancient Celtic *bel tan*, which literally means "good fire."

that woman you've been hot on. Hey, I won't even give you graphic details of some of those sexy witchy orgies that you have probably heard about. So if that's the kind of thing you are after, perhaps you ought to shut the covers now and spend your time with another author.

What this book testifies to is that the ancient principals of the Witches Way are equally effective and relevant today as they were since before written history. Yes, they simply still work.

What this book offers is a different model to work with when it comes to improving relationships of all kinds. Its keys of attraction, creation, and focus offer a set of tools that empower those who choose to utilize them. Witchcraft turns ordinary relationships into extraordinary ones, as it also makes us, as individuals, more extraordinary than we could ever imagine. It encourages us to concentrate first on ourselves and get clear about what we want, and then when we are on-purpose we can attract and co-create with another with spectacular results.

What this book will give you are proven techniques, with many case studies demonstrating that this form of magic is real. Woven throughout the latter three sections are many case studies of real-life people, pagan and nonpagans, who have tried and tested the witches' techniques that are suggested. This is so you can benefit from real magic, the stuff that makes logical sense as well as heart and spiritual sense.

This book is written with the presumption that readers will have little or no prior knowledge of Wicca or the Witches Way. I believe you do not need to call yourself "Witch" or even "Pagan" to benefit greatly from the principles proposed in this book. You do need to embrace the rationale and techniques enough to try them and record your progress. For those who are more experienced with the Craft, or for those who are familiar with my earlier work, *Witch in the Boardroom*, there are advanced techniques for you to try and you may wish to skim over some of the power building exercises as you may already be at a stage where your personal foundation is strong, as is your ability to raise power.

When I first let it be known I was researching and writing a book on love, lust, relationships, and fertility, I got one of two reactions. From those who already knew of the effectiveness of the kind of techniques I usually employ in my work, the reaction was one of great anticipation and curiosity. "These case studies are going to be great reading if you can get anyone honest enough to tell you their love life sucks. Or magically gets better!" said one client. Another giggled, "Great idea—just show me how to get a decent guy for a change and I'll be a case study."

The second reaction was more of a worry. It was one of great nervousness. It was mostly a fear within the pagan community that the general public might not be ready for a book that discussed the witch's principles of love, the rational choice of lust and pleasure, and raising the more sensual and sexual parts of some witches' practices. Misunderstanding and controversy could make it worse for everyone. Even my intention to show ways to support those undergoing unnatural invasive fertility techniques such as IVF was seen as controversial and perhaps a sellout.

To those in the latter category, I have done my best to be of service to all. It is my belief that witches have always been called upon to be of help in the bedroom, whether it involves fertility, attraction, the sustaining of intimacy, and/or even healing the wounds of these things when they go wrong. I am a modern witch and, as such, wish to evolve the tradition to be of use in today's world against today's problems for today's people. The tradition of the witch is a rich and truly useful model, but I never forget it is also one of profound beauty and depth.

This book will give you a glimpse of an alternative that allows you to be empowered yet connected with those around you, whether they are lovers, partners, or friends. I ask that you open up your heart and mind to real magic—the brand of magic that clears away old scars, that gives us real possibility, that creates a level of ease, understanding, support, excitement, and ecstasy that we have only dreamt of before.

I urge you not to say Pass On.
Run hard. Be fruitful!

Stacey Demarco
P.S. By the way, the Beltaine story is real and recent.

Section One

The Way of the Witch

The Spark

Recently I visited a museum that housed some very beautiful prehistoric art. Some of this art was over 30,000 years old, yet it spoke to me eloquently as a woman, as a witch, and as a human. There, under glass, were some tiny stone figures of the female form, with exaggerated breasts and hips. Some with rounded pregnant bellies, and some with tiny waists and rounded buttocks. Even the most cursory of glances could determine that these were symbols of fertility and of the spark of creation. These were the most ancient deities; they were female and they celebrated fertility.

Why venerate and celebrate creation and fertility at all? In our complex world, it is hard to put ourselves in the footprints of our more simple ancestors and imagine what was important to them. Without the understanding of biology we have now, what a miracle pregnancy was or the birth of a child? Without the sophisticated farming methods developed over the last two hundred years, how difficult would growing food be or obtaining vital herbs for medicine? Growing something consistently to eat or use could be a fairly hit-or-miss affair unless Mother Earth was listened to and her cycles respected.

I do not use the term Mother Earth lightly. The Earth herself became the first deity as it was her, like a mother, that provided everything that humans needed to live. Early humans knew that there were distinct cycles and seasons, and the better they understood this environment the more chance they had of living plentifully and surviving. The closer they observed the land and the habits of game, the closer they came to the everyday beauty, bounty, and miracles that she provided. It was also to her arms that humans went when they died. Buried or burned, humans knew that their time alive was limited, and that death was as great a miracle as birth. Nature or Mother Earth was a true source of inspiration, magic, and devotion.

It is rational to suppose that the more fertile the land, the more food and the more game to hunt. The male developed as the hunter, the one who ruled animals and game. If pleasing or honoring the Mother in simple or ritualized ways enabled the earth to offer more edible plants and medicine or to encourage conception, this seemed a rational method to ensure survival. Doing the same to Father Hunter, if this yielded more meat, even one more stag at tonight's feast, was the natural and right way to act.

It is thought that Pagan beliefs started in such a way. The word "pagan" refers to "one who dwells in the country." As these were the people who had the most intimate relationship with the land and its inhabitants, it is no surprise that rituals that ensured high levels of fertility and creation should develop and be strongest here.

As the ideas of creation and fertility were so important, rituals with these themes were often of a sexual nature or featured nudity. This demonstrates one of the earliest principles of magic, that "like attracts like." If you want to catch a stag, *be* a stag in the ritual dance. If you want to secure the fertility of your land or your tribe, *show* fertility in a shameless way. Having large families to hunt, work the land, and care for each other was also important, so being able to conceive and bear children easily was also a pagan need.

As societies and cultures grew and became more complex, the idea of gods and goddesses evolved to meet the needs of the time. Gods and goddesses, the basic masculine and feminine energies, were equally important and began to evolve into particular faces or character traits linked to the realities of being human, and were assigned to typical problems. For example, goddesses developed to protect the home or those who assisted in childbirth. There were gods who gave courage to those involved in war and other gods who ensured a successful hunt.

Most of these gods and goddesses were created in our likeness. They looked like us, and we had a direct relationship with them. It was natural to believe that as we were created by them and we looked like them, then we would have some spark of their divinity within us. They were our mothers, sisters, daughters, lovers, or fathers, brothers, sons, all at once, and as we were touched intimately by them, we too were gods and goddesses.

The Relationship Breaks Down

It is important to note at this time that there was no one religion as we would define it today, but many traditions or belief systems to view and communicate with the gods and goddesses. This period lasted for thousands of years, until a new model of spiritual practice emerged.

The nature-based style of living was drawing to a close in the modern world just around the time of written European history. In its place, the idea of one god (monotheism) began to form. This new belief system was far removed from the issues of creation and fertility and the importance of the balance of the masculine and feminine energies. Within the new system there was a god only and no goddess. The emphasis was on control *over* the land, not collaboration *with* the land. The idea that a balance of masculine and feminine divine resided in each person was rejected in favor of the militaristic power of the masculine only, and instead we took a subservient position to this god.

Typically, when we find a spiritual belief system that omits the representation of one gender completely, that particular gender is generally treated in an inferior way in that society. In almost all modern religious practices, barring Hinduism, there is an uneven balance between the importance of male and female deities. Here we find the beginnings of a systemized denigration of all that is feminine.

The personal relationship that pagans had with their gods and goddesses was also discouraged by the new ways. The idea of "control over" was a key theme in this new patriarchal system, even to the extent of how someone spoke to this god. Control was also necessary in defining who and how one had direct communication with this god. Co-creating one-on-one with such a god was impossible and one's wishes or intentions could only be communicated by and through an intermediary, such as a priest.

As cities and trade grew, a wider gulf formed between the Pagan people from rural areas, who relied upon the earth for their living, and those city dwellers who had alternative means far removed from the cycles of the earth. The new monotheistic religion, Christianity, grew out of this disconnection and separation, and first took hold in the cities.

An Uneasy Marriage

For some time, both systems existed side by side, with the majority of the old ways still practiced in Pagan areas. However, law and the government were controlled by city dwellers and it was a directive to spread this new faith all over the country. The continuation of the old ways threatened the success of the new religion—there was little enthusiasm among Pagans for a spiritual practice that did not connect with their needs. After all, the old ways were geared to their problems; the gods and goddesses co-created with them, they celebrated pleasure, and it worked! Why would anyone wish to swap all that for a practice that did not venerate the land, had only one God who had lots of rules and regulations, no Goddess, who didn't like sex, and who you had to go through someone else to talk to? Forget it!

In an initial effort to make the transition between the old and new ways easier, many of the new Christian ceremonies were linked to the existing Pagan ceremonies. Although many Christians today do not like to admit this historical fact, important festivals such as Easter and Christmas are actually overlays of older Pagan festivals.

Easter, the time of Christ's death and resurrection, was overlaid on the festival of Ostara, the Pagan day of spring, birth, and renewal. Ever wonder where the idea of the Easter bunny fitted in with the death of Christ? It doesn't. The hare and the egg were Pagan symbols for fertility, sex, and new life. The intent of eating eggs was to increase fertility—we still celebrate Easter that way.

Similarly, Christmas was overlaid on the mid-winter Yule festival. Yule signified the longest night of the year and the idea that even through the darkest, longest night comes light and hope. Christians celebrate the birth of the Christ child—for them, the embodiment of light and hope. These are more than coincidences; they were deliberate moves toward integration. The fact of the matter is that Christianity has Pagan DNA.

The Ugly Divorce

As pressure to convert to the new religion grew more intense, it also became lethal. Aggressive tactics were first the norm, then gradually were accepted as law. By the fifteenth century in Europe, abandoning the old ways became a life or death choice. In countries where Christianity had the most precarious hold, hysteria and inquisitions were most brutal. Germany and France were particularly fierce, with the killings likened to genocide.

Over three centuries, Pagans lost their faith, their land, their friends, their herbal traditions, and for a great many, their lives. Greed, paranoia, and fear ruled both the city and country. Those who were loyal to the old ways chose to go underground and practice at night, hidden away in secret. They performed their old rites only with those they could trust, and elaborate levels of secrecy were formed to protect this precious knowledge (and their lives), lest someone expose the rest of the group.

Bit by bit, the Pagan ways began to be ground down, left to blow away like the ashes of their dead practitioners.

Mythology vs. Truth

It is often said that the angels of one religion become the devils of another. When the purveyors of the new religion realized that the old ways were not dying quickly enough, they began to use some dirty tricks to ensure that they won the battle for souls.

Fear is a powerful weapon, but there are other ways to convince.

As a former public relations professional, I know it is a common strategy to find strengths and something newsworthy about the person or product you are trying to promote. It is also a common strategy to exploit the perceived weaknesses (or create one) of your competitor. By making up stories and creating fears about some of the very innocent aspects of Paganism, doubt and fear were created in the minds of those who hadn't really made up their minds. Some of the mythology that arose regarding witchcraft, although based in absolute nonsense, survives today.

Let's look at some of these myths as they apply to lust, love, and relationships, and we will see how the Goddess has had a bad PR day for a very long time!

Myth: Witches Interfere with Free Will: The image of a witch casting a spell to control the actions of her victims is still a potent one today. In the past, witches were often accused of controlling the minds of their victims; in the burning times it was easier to not take responsibility for one's actions and to blame a witch for making one do something. Those accused who made confessions would blame the Devil, which is also a breach of free will and a surrender of personal responsibility. The idea that witches commonly cast spells to ensure that someone falls in love with them or their client is an everyday fallacy. Asking a witch to assist you to make someone love you, or fall in love with you again if love is lost, is impacting the target's free will. It also breaches our central tenet of Harm None.

Truth: Witches Empower Themselves and Their Clients: One of the central guidelines of Wicca is the idea of Harm None. By interfering with free will one changes the natural way of things and enforces his or her will over others. Real witches do not engage in this behavior.

For example, no matter how desperate the case, one should never cast, or assist anyone to cast, a love spell that involves a specific target. Instead, ask the person to refocus their intention on what they want, list the attributes of the ideal partner they wish to attract, and cast for that, not a person they know. That way, no free will is being affected. If the person someone desires is in fact the person that the Goddess sees as ideal for them, the person will be attracted. Wonderful! If not, someone else more suitable will enter the scene. Wonderful! A win/win situation.

Myth: Witches Control Your Mind: There are pages and pages of transcripts from trials involving the testimony of suspects who blamed witches for controlling their mind and therefore their behavior. To ensure a conviction, witch hunters often called for witnesses to a supernatural crime; if no one came forward it was presumed that a witch was controlling the witnesses rather than that there was no real crime. It is a simple stretch to presume that if a witch can grant wishes, she could also control minds, and so this twisted notion of dangerous mind control entered the culture.

Truth: Witches Focus Your Mind: When a client comes to me with a problem, it is important to first clarify exactly what they want rather than what they don't. Being very clear about what we want is imperative to casting an effective spell. If we aren't sure about our purpose and intention, our end result, then how can a spell work? Witches assist you to focus your unconscious mind on what you want, rather than taking a shotgun approach. The empowering nature of the Craft allows you to gladly take personal responsibility for your actions and concentrate on creating the future that you desire without blaming others.

Myth: Witches Are, or Employ, Sexual Demons: In many of the recorded testimonies against witches, there is an element of the sexual. In the new order of complete sexual control, it was important to wipe out any remnants of the pleasure-loving old ways through a combination of law, fear, and shame. Like parents using the idea of the boogieman to frighten children, many fantastic stories were generated about sexuality. One such myth was that of sexual demons, referred to as succubi or incubi. A succubus was a female sexual demon who would prey on unsuspecting and innocent men using their feminine wiles and turn them to sin and the devil. An incubus was the masculine equivalent. In a climate of sexual repression where people still committed adultery, had sex before marriage, or even enjoyed the sexual act, having the scapegoat of a sexual demon that "made me do it" was a handy thing.

There is a delightful English transcript where a farmer accuses his next-door neighbor, a very comely wench, of being a succubus. Apparently the two had a number of months of quite satisfying sexual encounters in the pastures of his land. Of course, he told no one until all this was revealed after his wife caught them *in flagrante* one day among the daisies. He jumped up, wide-eyed and afraid, pointed at the woman, who was a second before giggling underneath him, and proclaimed "I don't know what I am doing. She is a succubus!"

He further testified that he was unable to resist her seductions and she was so desirable that she had to be a demon. Although this does sound amusing to modern ears, unfortunately the woman went to jail for three months for her trouble and only escaped further physical torture by confessing her crime and accusing another older woman of bewitching her.

Truth: Witches are Attractive: The more you follow the Witches Way the more attractive you will become in body, mind, and spirit. This is a broad statement, but it is true. There is nothing more attractive than someone who is confident, comfortable in themselves, vital, and authentic. All of these attributes can be achieved via the witches' principles. As for lust, love, and desire, the Witches Way guides us to love our bodies more, and reduce shame and guilt. If things do go wrong, the Witches Way provides us a solid personal foundation that can give us more resilience, more self-respect, and faith that, no matter what, we will never be alone. The chances of co-dependency and unhealthy neediness are lessened and the expression of healthy anger and grief is encouraged and honored. If you follow some of the case studies in this book you will see how ordinary men and women have transformed their relationships, their bodies, and their connection with life through these techniques.

Myth: Witches Engage in Orgies: Groups of witches were said to meet naked in fields and forests and by drumbeat have wild orgies involving themselves and the devil and his demons. These escapades were used to create evil energy that could pollute whole villages and recruit innocents. Human or animal sacrifices were said to be part of this scenario, as well as the spreading of blood on the soil.

Many people in today's society also believe that these kinds of rituals are commonplace with today's pagans. When I am interviewed by media I am often asked whether I belong to a coven that has ritual sex and whether I take part. Some of the more educated journalists may refer to the idea of the Great Rite, and ask if anyone I know regularly has sex in front of others. This question pops up in interviews where sex really isn't the topic so I know it's pretty much something that is still on peoples' minds!

Truth: Some Witches Engage in Sex Magic and Creation-based Rituals: Many of the ancient rituals invoking and honoring creation and fertility involve the reenactment of the merging of male and female energy. Pagan rituals that had as their intention the continuation of the fertility of the land, such as Beltaine, did involve highly ritualized sex, but between consenting adults or between a nominated priest and priestess. The rituals were performed skyclad to show that there is no shame in our bodies and no fear in our hearts. Going skyclad is always optional anyway. Plus, the devil really isn't on our dance cards!

The Great Rite is a highly ritualized expression of the creative powers of the Goddess and God. It represents the natural process and cycle of fertility, and the balance between the Masculine and Feminine energies. The Great Rite is mostly a symbolic process involving joining the traditional tools of chalice (representing the feminine) and athame (representing the masculine). In some Wiccan traditions, the Great Rite is performed between a consenting priest and priestess. Their coupling is highly ritualized and mostly does not culminate in climax. It is penetration only, symbolizing the union of the masculine and feminine. This rite is always performed within the confines of a coven, which of course is made up of a small, tight-knit group of people who have built up a high level of trust from many years of training and working together. At no stage is this a titillating or pornographic act. Again, this practice is performed by a minority of Witchcraft traditions and is no means the norm.

Sex magic is more common, though, and can be defined as using the sexual act as a way of raising power for a particular intention. Usually, intention is released at the point of orgasm, although this depends upon the ritual. Sex magic can be performed alone or with another consenting adult. For those who regularly perform sex magic with a partner, there are a number of benefits including a certain synergy of intention, increased bonding, and a high level of sexual satisfaction.

Myth: Witches Killed Children: The older women of the villages were the keepers of the traditional knowledge of childbirth. It was these older crones who were the midwives, the healers who knew all the special herbs and remedies to assist in pregnancy, labor, breastfeeding, and for general postpartum care. In fact, pregnancy and birth was truly women's business, an area in which male physicians were not welcome. There was true power in their wisdom and in their midwifery of creation. However, any kind of female power was not in keeping with the new patriarchal order and midwives were easy targets.

Truth: Witches Are the Midwives of Creation: With birth comes death, and in early societies the death of either baby or mother in childbirth was common.

Midwives were always present at such a tragic time and as they were older, often respected, and experts with herbs, they were easy targets in the new order. Rumor and innuendo became rife when a grieving family needed someone to blame. The Christian Church further propagated stories that reduced feminine power, such as how midwives killed babies at birth to provide ingredients for various potions, including the infamous flying ointment they needed to go soaring on their broomsticks at night. Many women were tortured and killed during the inquisitions simply because they were doing their jobs as midwives. Today we know that witches are not responsible for deaths in this way, and that they acted only as midwives for creation. Unfortunately huge amounts of valuable herbal knowledge were lost with the women who were burned. As for the stories of flying ointment, there are recipes floating around, but the authentic ones did not contain any body parts, infant or adult. They were more likely to contain herbs and fungi that promoted either sexual energy or hallucinations—perfect for flying.

Myth: Witches Are Satanic: Possibly the most damaging and still lingering bit of mythology that witches have had held against them is that we are satanic. Witches do not believe in Satan. Witches do not even recognize the idea of Satan, which is, in fact, a Christian construct. Satan is a fallen angel who rules hell, tempts humans to sin, and is featured in Christian stories. We are not Christian so we do not buy into the idea of Satan or even the concepts of sin and hell.

The idea of a horned man, wildly and inappropriately sexual and evil, can be traced back to the Pagan masculine entity, the God. The God was the partner of the Goddess. He typically was depicted as the powerful figure of a stag, fully realized with huge protective antlers. His sheer life force was one of vitality, virility, and fertility. This beautiful, inspirational masculine face of the Divine was soon tarnished and denigrated by the new religion into a horned, hoofed, sex-crazed figure. The horned devil was born and he was bad to the bone.

Truth: Witches Are Educating Society in Regard to Satanic Labeling: No doubt there are Satanists out there. Some of them may even choose to call themselves witches, but these groups or individuals are not the majority, and they differentiate themselves from Wiccan or other Pagan groups.

Although Wicca is the fastest-growing spiritual practice in Australia, the United Kingdom, and the United States, we still battle Satanic stigma. At this writing, in Australia, we have just had some very archaic anti-Witchcraft laws repealed, enabling witches to have the same legal rights against religious vilification as any other spiritual practice. Some who objected to the repeal argued that it was not a true spiritual practice and that society needed to be protected against the spread of Satanism. The overturning of this law was the result of three years of intense lobbying by the Australian Pagan education group Pagan Awareness Network. Even as we celebrate this victory, we know that our work is far from over.

Myth: Witches Are Part of a Cult: It is easy to see how it could be misunderstood that a coven is a cult—all that mind control, all that chanting and clandestine meetings—and what about all the secret magical business that no one knows about?

Most witches in today's world would describe themselves as solitary. This means they do not belong to a coven or to traditions that require this kind of training. Covens are groups of likeminded people who come together to focus and release energy for specific purposes, and to worship.

Truth: Witches Are Part of a Legitimate and Evolving Spiritual Practice: The Witches Way is not evangelistic in nature. We do not recruit members nor do we ask others to. There are many different paths to the Goddess and we believe all are valid as long as they Harm None.

The Pagan path in its many forms is a legitimate one and is recognized as such by many official channels. Wicca is officially recognized as a religion by the U.S. military, and in Australia and the U.K. its members are protected against discrimination on the basis of religion. We do have a long way to go, however, before the average person on the street is comfortable with the idea of having a witch in the family, in the workplace, or next door.

I believe that as more and more people decide that the Witches Way is for them, the more important it becomes to educate society on what we are and what we believe. As such, I am often asked how to best break the news to relatives or friends. My advice is always to not make this a dramatic thing. Ensure your own motivations for wishing to share what your spiritual practice is, unmotivated by grandstanding or self-promotion. You don't have to wear a pentagram or tell everyone about your latest ritual to proclaim your faith. Instead, you may choose to allow the positive effects of the Craft to become apparent in your life, which will soon become obvious to those around you. Allow the magic to work and others cannot miss it!

The New Relationship

The Goddess went underground, but amazingly didn't disappear. Although her followers and those who were accused of being her followers were murdered and vilified, the Old Ways did not perish. They evolved instead and waited quietly until society seemed safe enough to again resurface.

There are many theories about where and how the old religion resurfaced in popular culture and if, indeed, there has been an unbroken line of some rituals. There are many wonderful books that provide a modern history of the Craft, and the religion of Wicca in particular. Many Pagan paths grew into prominence in the free and experimental sixties where the idea of earth-based religion seemed again rational and timely. Women were reaching out and reclaiming their power through feminism as a political movement. Looking for a spiritual practice that gave them a positive role model and empowerment in their own image, Wicca and other Goddess-orientated traditions fit the bill. The Goddess was able to breathe again in this air of change and creative chaos. It seemed that the circle had continued, with the Divine Feminine being honored above all again.

Over the years, as participation grew, so did the number of traditions. We are diverse in our beliefs, yet many common themes (such as those regarding creation and fertility) run through our practices. I will touch on just two of the many paths. One, the Reclaiming Tradition, is headed up by eco-feminist witch Starhawk of the United States. Starhawk is a model of an eco-witch/warrior in action, and her open tradition has attracted many modern women and men to her community.

The second tradition is that of the solitary witch. Author and witch Scott Cunningham was one of the first practitioners who wrote about the life of the solitary witch rather than those within a coven. A solitary witch is one who is not part of an organized coven and does not follow an established tradition that involves a hierarchy, or they may create a tradition of their own. Cunningham certainly inspired me to understand that my practice alone was as valid as any practice within an organized coven environment, and that I could choose to have whatever relationship with the Goddess and God that I wished.

This ability to co-create in such an intimate fashion has drawn me and many others to the Way of the Witch. The idea that I could be my own priestess, channel divine energy, and have direct conversation with the Divine was extremely attractive. There was no pressure to adopt any particular process, although discovering and building my knowledge about all traditions was encouraged. After conducting my own research through books, with teachers, and by performing practical magic, bit by bit I built a very solid practice that felt right and holy to me. I soon found out what worked and what didn't. I avoided the distraction of having to fit into a particular tradition, but was able to pick what suited me best and what gave me the most power. Being a solitary allowed me to progress in my own time, without restriction, and to initiate myself when I knew at a deep level that I was ready.

I would encourage any budding witches to do the same research and investigate what is right for them. This is why traditionally no one can initiate themselves unless they have studied for a minimum of a year and a day. Explore whether the faith is for you at all and whether a coven or a solitary path fits your purpose.

Being a solitary witch doesn't mean that you are always solitary. I have the best of both worlds, a strong, evolving solitary practice that I am able to share with others through my books, TV appearances, teaching, and workshops. I am invited to covens and large gatherings and love the interaction and the charge of sending out focused power generated by numbers. There is much choice available in deciding to follow the Witches Way—this has been both our strength and our weakness.

The fact that there is such freedom to practice and so many paths to the Goddess enables us to be flexible and nimble and change to suit the times. Unlike inflexible religions such as Christianity, we do not exclude anyone from fully participating or becoming priests or priestesses, whether they are gay or straight, married or single, male or female. This tolerance and respect for diversity is perhaps why we are growing and other religions are hemorrhaging members.

It could also be said that this diversity could be a disadvantage with some older traditions proclaiming that theirs is the real Witchcraft and anything deviating from this is simply new age. This is a common belief of witches who are from an unbroken hereditary line. There is also some current controversy that there is too much emphasis on the Goddess and not on the original idea of a Goddess and a God. I believe that this attitude is a form of fundamentalism that does not have a place in the organic style of Paganism. As long as practitioners hold to the key tenants of the spiritual practice and transform their lives through the manipulation of the force of magic, it matters not what the label is.

Now, our numbers are growing more rapidly than ever before. In the last Australian census, one percent of the population described itself as Pagan, but this percentage is considered low due to the reluctance of many Pagans to step out of the broom closet. Wicca is the fastest-growing spiritual practice in the United States and the United Kingdom. In the United States alone, over one million people admit that their religion is Wicca.

As a group we have become fertile in our expansion and creative in the way we communicate yet again. Google-search the Internet and you can see just how enormous our web presence is and how connected witches of all kinds are all over the world. Books such as my first, *Witch in the Boardroom*, discussing the links between business, career, and the Witches Way would not have found a legitimate market until recently and certainly would not have been reviewed seriously by mainstream financial press. We are at last beginning to make progress in demonstrating that the ancient principles are relevant and effective today, whether it is in the boardroom or the bedroom.

Witches Have Always Been Good in the Bedroom

The Witches Way is a spiritual practice that has themes of creation and fertility at its core. The Goddess created humans in her own image of beauty, intelligence, and dignity, and in turn, required them to create as she had.

Sex, then, was never shameful. Guilt was never used as a bargaining tool in relationships. The body was always beautiful and a vessel for pleasure and creation. Desire fostered a feeling of being fed and nourished. Relationships were encouraged to grow and evolve in a synergistic way between individuals, rather than be constrained by societal rules and regulations.

Witches were consulted on many matters of this world and the next, making clear recommendations and weaving the mysteries into reality of creation and fertility. For millennia now, the Craft of the Wise in its many forms has been used to solve problems with lust, love, relationships, and fertility. With their great herbal knowledge, witches could assist the physical parts of us to be more vital, more potent, more fertile, and even more virile. With their knowledge of mind magic, witches could assist with the process of building a robust personal foundation that allows great relationships to be attracted and to magically happen. How well we actually relate to each other depends upon how we relate to ourselves first, and witches have always emphasized the importance of ensuring we have our own backyards in order before we can expect a satisfying exchange from anyone else.

Our modern problems are not all that much different from those of our ancestors. Singles still want to find a mate, for one night or for life. Finding a balance of power between couples is still a valid goal. We still want to be desired and feel comfortable about being thus. We still want to find ways to keep our relationships with long-term partners happy and fruitful. We still want to experience great sex. We may even want to conceive a child easily and quickly, should we choose to do so. We still want to be able to recover well from our pain should relationships break down.

We can look to the Witches' lore and principles for guidance in action. The Five Ancient Laws, as they apply to a relationship, give us a good start to the answering of this question. The exercises in Section 2 introduce some proven techniques that will give you greater connection, more pleasure, and more choice when it comes to love, lust, fertility, and relationships. I invite you to allow the witch in you to awaken and power up for the bedroom!

The Five Ancient Lores that Apply to Love, Lust, and Relationships

As effective and relevant a thousand years ago as they are today, the belief system surrounding the Goddess offers guidelines that give us a firm foundation in creating the relationships we all dream of having. These five ancient lores and how you can avail yourself of their active wisdom are explained in the following pages.

I. Harm None

The Wiccan Rede is the central tenet of this Pagan path. A concept and guideline for right living, it states: "Harm None, do what thou wilt." It sounds like a deceptively simple statement on first examination, but perhaps on the second, impossible. However can you go through life, hurting nothing or no one?

Simply translated, it is asking us to have the intention to do what we like, create as we wish, but without harming each other or the earth. Yes, it is an almost unattainable covenant to live by, however the key word here is *intention*. If you start your day, every day, with the intention to Harm None, your unconscious mind will guide you toward just that.

Harm None starts from the inside out like many Witches' traditions. We must be mindful about how we treat our Selves. If we over- or under-eat, don't exercise, work long days, have an addiction, ignore pain, or even don't get enough sleep, we are harming ourselves. If we don't get our needs met, don't have any idea of our purpose, are the victim of any emotional or physical abuse, if we numb out, act out, or settle for anything less than our hearts truly desire, we are also ignoring the Harm None rede. To achieve wholeness, and to attract great relationships of all kinds, we must love ourselves enough to choose not to harm ourselves by making poor decisions, and to be with the kind of partners who will nourish us.

Once we have made the conscious decision not to harm ourselves, then the magic of attracting and keeping a magical relationship can begin in earnest and with great success. If we begin to be mindful of treating others with the Harm None intention, whether they be a lust or love partner, we will achieve greater connection, pleasure, and intimacy.

There are countless ways to consciously live the Harm None principle and all will be unique to your circumstances. The intention to Harm None can be integrated into all manner of relationships:

- Create and develop your own Power Circle (page 122) to boost your self-trust, self-esteem, self-knowledge, and self-care.

- Deliberately activate self-care on a daily basis.

- At the beginning of relationships clearly state what your intention is so that there is no confusion. If your intention is in fact to have only a short sexual encounter (a "one-night stand," perhaps), let the other person know so that there is no pain or confusion.

- Forget stereotypes of what your relationship needs to look like.

- Have a joint vision.

- Know the attributes of your ideal partner, and attract for this.

- Be open to the fact that everyone has different perceptions of how they see the world. Take a breath before jumping in to disagree with someone else's point of view. Find a point of similarity, not of difference.

- Do not gossip about others or share intimate secrets with others.

- Put family before work.

- Be purposefully present with your partner and family.

- Practice active listening.

- Get clear about your purpose. Not knowing your purpose, at least the vision you have for now, can be harmful to you and those around you.

- Put pleasure on your daily agenda—enter it on your calendar!

II. Pleasure Is Your Birthright

As we discovered earlier, the old ways celebrated life, which included the functions of fertility and celebration in creation. As the new religion needed to control all aspects of life to gain total power, even pleasure was restricted. At its most fundamental, simple, innocent pleasures such as dancing, playing drums, and wearing sensual fabrics were outlawed. The idea that sex, even marital sex, could be pleasurable or recreational was abhorrent.

Witches believe we were born for pleasure. Why have we been given this exquisite instrument of our bodies if we were not meant to feel, see, heal, and move? To experience pleasure is to dance with the divine and refill the creative well drained by day-to-day mundaneness and difficulties. It is a prayer to the Goddess to joyfully accept pleasure with open arms.

These days, we are so ground down by the complexities of life—long work days, strenuous mind gymnastics, financial worries, mortgages, study, career ambitions—that we often forget that pleasure is a key part of the magic of life. Without it we are dull, dead, and listless. We make knee-jerk or inappropriate decisions. We get bored, we get angry, and we get resentful—not useful states in which to interact with partners or prospective partners in a satisfying manner. Including healthy levels of pleasure in our lives brings great fulfillment rather than just a hovering at the survival level of existence.

There are those who get addicted to pleasure and the balance swings too far the other way. Sensual addictions ranging from over-exercising to spending too much time and money at a spa, or process addictions such as gambling or drinking to change one's state of consciousness ensure that the addict does not engage in connection of a real kind by over- or under-stimulating themselves to override anxiety or pain. More subtle, socially acceptable pleasure-seeking addictions such as shopping are on the increase all over the Western world (obvious by our credit card debt). Again, building power from the inside out through self-knowledge enables us to identify such addictions and the reasons for them, and to actively do something about them.

It seems odd to have to advise people to take time to look at whether pleasure plays an active and refreshing role in their lives. After all, it's a pleasant thing, isn't it? Should it not come naturally, this urge to experience pleasure or even ecstasy? Certainly, with most people who haven't experienced trauma, seeking pleasure is a natural thing. It is our minds that generally get in the way of prioritizing pleasure's importance, either switching off from it totally, giving it an "irrelevant" rating, or withholding it as punishment in some way.

Look at the following questions and see whether you are rating pleasure as important in your life:

- When is the last time you had a belly laugh? Too long ago?
- Do you *know* what you find pleasurable?
- How far up the chain of priorities is experiencing pleasure regularly?
- Do you see anything worth achieving as hard won?
- Do you have enough touch in your life? For example, if you live alone, do you have friends or family who you regularly come in contact with,

with whom you share a hug?

- If you have any guilt or shame connected to sex or pleasure, are you taking action to eliminate these obstacles by gaining professional and spiritual assistance?

- Do you allow yourself to have fun and to experience pleasure alone?

- Do you allow yourself to experience pleasure with your partner?

- Do you withhold pleasure or sex with a partner as a form of punishment? Are you aware if you do so that you are withholding it from yourself too?

- Do you buy into beliefs such as "Life is meant to be hard work," "pleasure is sinful," "pleasure is like laziness," and "I don't deserve to have pleasure"?

If you are finding your answers less than satisfactory, you may wish to come up with a pleasure plan over the next few weeks and begin to act it. This is a list of pleasurable activities or remedies to heal your lack of pleasure over the next few moon cycles. Below are a few suggestions of the kind of things that you could add to your list:

- I love baths, so I will have one at least once a week and it will be undisturbed, fragrant, and have all the trimmings like candles and music.

- I will go to that wonderful restaurant I know with my partner and have that great dish that delights my taste buds so!

- I will go shopping for a new fragrance. I can just try them all—I don't have to buy one!

- I will get a massage or a reflexology treatment.

- I will enroll in that painting class.

- I will not let work get in the way and allow me to be late tonight, and will just relax and spend time with my partner in bed.

- I will negotiate my needs with my partner until we get a win-win solution. I will not show my resentment by withholding pleasure from myself or my partner.

Add your pleasure plan to your Book of Shadows (BOS) and ensure you track your progress over time and see how refilling the well with pleasure enriches your relationships. You might also wish to add a joint pleasure plan, including some pleasurable activities that you could experience as a couple. Be creative and remember to try out new forms of pleasure—not just the activities you have always done.

III. Attraction: Like Attracts Like

One of the oldest Witches' principles of magic is that like attracts like. In some of the most ancient societies, to attract prey you dressed and acted like the prey. To attract the person of your choice or to keep the person that you feel is right for you, you must demonstrate some of the attributes you would wish to attract.

For example, let's imagine I wish to attract a partner who is better and more suitable for me than the previous ones I have had. Let us say that I have determined that previously my pattern has been to attract men who weren't all that interested in my life and were unavailable in some way. So that this pattern will not repeat, and I will not attract the same kind of man, I will need to learn how to be confident, to love my life with or without a man in it, and actively encourage the man to take an interest in my life. I will also ensure that the man I choose demonstrates an ability and capability to take an interest in someone else s life other than his own—and that I can demonstrate this ability. As Mahatma Gandhi said: "Be the change you want to see in the world." The truth of this in relationships is that we can't expect someone else to fill in the gaps we have.

How can we rightly expect our partners to love us, respect us, take an active interest in us, encourage us, support us, and so on, if we have little capacity to do this for ourselves? If we know clearly that we have certain attributes that we wish to attract and foster within a relationship, we can tell earlier if the partner is capable or willing to encompass these attributes. If not, and these attributes are important enough, we can more easily end the relationship and make room for someone more suitable, rather than hang on to something that will never work.

What can we do to increase attraction? Let's look first to the Witches' Power Keys.

By building our self-knowledge, self-trust, and self-esteem, and by exercising self-care, we are well ahead of most people in developing a healthy, connected, relaxed, vital, engaged, and loving mind, body, and spirit. Being the best we can be enables us to attract better and better things into our lives—including people and relationships. We can then step up into what we want, rather than settle for what we falsely think we can only have.

Rose, a thirty-six-year-old solicitor, continually attracted men who within twelve months had cheated on her. Attractive, intelligent, and therefore never short of men pursuing her, she came to me asking for a love spell that would bring her a faithful man. After speaking with Rose and eliciting some history, I discovered she had some deep beliefs about her own value and had poor self-esteem. Her problem was threefold. First, she felt that since she was getting older she had less choice now and therefore she was less selective. Second, she was unclear about the kind of man she ideally wished to attract, and third, she felt there was little room in her life for a partner who really deeply engaged with her as she worked six days a week and long hours.

I advised Rose to concentrate on her own internal power levels first. She would continue to attract cheating men if she allowed that kind of man into her life. I also asked her to put into action immediately an alternative to the long days she was working. Her love life needed to take priority. This was a huge change for Rose and it took six months before she had created enough space in her busy schedule for the possibility of a partner. This was a vital step in having her attract someone who was worth it: if Rose could not devote enough time to the relationship to keep it alive there would be a high possibility that even her ideal mate would eventually tire of this and walk. She also performed the Spell to Attract an Ideal Partner on a trilunar cycle, which gave her a clear idea of what and who she wanted.

What can you do to increase attraction?

- Concentrate on yourself first.
- Establish self-care, self-trust, self-esteem, and self-knowledge so you can be authentic and who you need to be to attract who you wish.
- Be proudly authentic and gentle in your execution of your uniqueness.
- Know your purpose and have a vision.
- Don't settle for partners who do not fulfill your criteria and with whom you do not experience a combination of biological chemistry

and spiritual chemistry (page 54). If there is no spark, there is no lasting combination.

- Engage in life.
- Continue learning.
- Create room in your life into which you can welcome a relationship. Creating a void means that nature will fill it. If you know what to fill it with, there is a high chance you will achieve it.

Later in this book there is a section on attraction that gives more detail on how to attract different kinds of relationships. The Spell to Attract Your Ideal Partner is on page 69 in this section.

IV. Know Thyself

One of the most beautiful and relevant pieces of ancient wisdom comes from the ancient Greek Oracle at Delphi. The Delphic Maxims, the sixteen guidelines for living believed to be given to man from the God Apollo through the channel of the Oracle of Delphi, were recorded by historians of the day. They still remain intact for our view in the second millennia. The maxims cover many topics, from aging gracefully to advising a middle path, and one of the most enduring maxims states "Know Thyself."

Witches have always known the importance of developing self-knowledge as a key part in power building, but also in assisting and encouraging problem solving in their clients. Our prescribed techniques, spells, and rituals are often designed to stimulate the person's own inherent sense of knowing and wisdom. This way the person can wake up to their patterns and heal themselves, much like the body can be stimulated to heal itself or build its immunity, rather than by using harsh medicine.

I often invoke Goddesses like Sophia, whose message encourages us to listen and seek our own deep wisdom as a guide to life and to solve problems and dissolve obstacles.

She whispers to us quietly and we often call this intuition. If we listen, she is reassuring us that "You know, you know," and she invites us to act on our own keen wisdom.

When it comes to relationships, if we know ourselves well we know what (or who) will be nourishing for us. We know the kinds of patterns to avoid, the kinds of attributes in others that do not serve us, and a match to the key values that we have.

Every person should be aware of his or her values and needs in life. Values are things that we hold highly and are almost themes in our life. If we are not living to our values we are rarely happy, comfortable, and content. Needs are those values that we need to fulfill to be at our absolute best. Needs are rarely negotiable and cause big trouble if we don't understand them and take steps to fulfill them.

Let's take Tina, for example.

Tina is a thirty-four-year-old woman living in a country town in rural Australia with her partner Mick. She came to me feeling very little direction in any area of her life and her six-year relationship was on the brink of breaking down.

"Mick had really had enough of me. I was so unhappy and depressed, and I wasn't even sure why. I just didn't seem to have any direction any more.

"I worked with Stacey on developing my self-knowledge. One technique was to list my values and needs in order. I got my top three and they were needs. In some ways I wasn't surprised at what they were. Just surprised that I wasn't *living* them any more.

"My top three needs were honesty, freedom, and learning. My partner and I had not been completely honest in a number of ways for many years now, and I realize this was contributing to my indifference to him. Honesty was so important to me, but I had just let it slide out of fear. As for freedom, I felt very trapped in the town I was in, since our farm really kept me close to home. I loved the vastness of where I lived, I mean I had plenty of space physically; it's just that I felt closed in. We hadn't taken a real holiday in years. With the learning value, I was doing an agriculture degree, but because of the birth of my child I deferred it, never picking it back up or anything else. I haven't done any learning since, although I absolutely love it and always have done well at anything I have tried."

Tina spent some time discussing openly and honestly the issues she has with Mick. This was a huge step for both of them, bringing up much fear and taking a number of counseling sessions to sort out. However, what resulted was a clearing of the air and a new level of intimacy between them.

As both partners could not take time off at this time in the growing season, Tina negotiated a two-week holiday overseas on her own. Killing two birds with one stone, she did a short course in organic farming methods in the UK, beginning to fulfill her other values of freedom and learning. Additionally, she began to build in many other ways to fulfill the values she held so highly over the longer term.

Magically, her relationship with Mick moved back from the brink of oblivion and they are now "happier than we have been in five years."

If you are still unsure about what your values or needs could be, look at this list of examples:

Excellence	Creativity / creation	Uniqueness
Beauty	Animal companions	Connection / connecting
Intimacy	Originality	Expression
Understanding	Fun	Flow
Respect	Generosity	Intelligence
Entrepreneurship	Knowledge	Helping
Healing	Learning	Recognition
Stimulation	Solitude	Community
Status	Trust	Integrity
Justice	Adventure	Choice

If we do not know what our values or needs are, how can we know who and what to attract? We may choose partners who totally do not suit us, as they may not respect or embody those things that we hold so highly. We do not have to have a carbon copy of ourselves (life would be very boring!), but one common factor of long-term successful relationships is a core of shared common values. This may not even translate to wanting the exact same things, but respecting that the other has a need to fulfill and this need is not directly opposite or abhorrent to us.

A good example of this is Bec and Jez, a couple in their late twenties who have known each other for two years. Bec loves to be connected with the community and loves nothing better than to be organizing dinner parties, having friends over, and she is the social club co-coordinator at the big company where she works. She does enjoy her solitude, but it isn't a high value or a need for her. Jez is an articulate and interesting man, yet doesn't have a need for the high levels of interaction with groups that Bec has. He needs sufficient quiet time to refuel and prefers to have enough time to just think and process internally. In the beginning of their relationship, Jez quite enjoyed the newness of having all this buzz around him, but after a year or so began to realize it drained him, and he began to disconnect at these functions rather than just say no, he didn't want to attend. Bec was puzzled at why her normally pleasant partner would be grumpy with people or just go and watch the television rather than sit and talk. Jez tried to explain to Bec that he needed some downtime with her and some solitude, and could she perhaps consider cutting back on social activities or do some of these things on her own. Bec was devastated at this and took it that Jez didn't want to be with her so much. Although he reassured her that wasn't the case, Bec could not respect Jez's need for solitude, and took it as a personal affront. This incompatibility and the inability to negotiate through it eventually saw the end to their relationship.

Neither Jez nor Bec are wrong in their needs here. Needs are never wrong, they just *are*. Witches recognize it's *how* we get our needs met that matters. A need for recognition or stimulation could easily be met by quite destructive means, yet they are valid needs to have. It is a fair thing to wish to be recognized for one's hard work or achievements. It is a fantastic thing to have the drive to be exposed to many new experiences and be open to being excited by ideas, although if we choose to have our need for recognition met by sabotaging someone at work or our need for stimulation met by continually being unfaithful to our husband, then we are choosing badly, as well as breaking the law of Harm None.

At the beginning of many relationships the idea of opposites attracting does add a spark to things, yet it can give you the false illusion that in front of you "is my other half." Expecting someone to complete you is a very big mistake.

We cannot expect relationships to work as optimally as we would wish if we do not take the time to know ourselves as much as we know our partner. Often, we think we know our partners more deeply than ourselves as we pay little attention to our selves, our needs, and our lives compared to them. This can be a massive blind spot for many. Psychologists call this condition co-dependency.

The cure for co-dependency is an unrelenting focus on one's Self, and the Witches Way encourages this. At first this may feel to the co-dependent like being totally selfish or self-indulgent, but it is a false feeling fostered by a habit of being totally disconnected from the importance of the self. You may wish to answer the following questions. If you respond to a number of them positively you may wish to look seriously at your levels of self-knowledge and assess further whether you are co-dependent.

- I know what my partner wants most of the time.
- My partner has an addiction (alcoholism, smokes, drugs, food, sex) but I can help them control it.
- I like saving or fixing people.
- I like to know where my partner is all the time.
- I call my partner on the telephone constantly.
- I like it that my partner organizes everything for me, but sometimes I feel quite smothered and rebel (but the cycle continues).
- I know my partner's vision for the future but I'm not sure about mine.
- My partner's career is more important than mine.
- My children's lives are more important than mine.
- If I didn't have a partner I would be very uncomfortable.
- I would rather have a partner who treated me badly or wasn't really suitable for me than no partner at all.
- I have a secret suspicion that I could never get anyone better than who I have, even though he or she is not right for me.

Look at the exercises in the power building section of this book, such as Power Circles, the Invocation to Artemis, and Spells for Purpose, to begin to uncover what a unique gem you really are. Knowing yourself allows you to know someone else with more depth, more flexibility, and with more heart. As the ancient Greeks knew, the more you know yourself, the more connection and flow and less drama would fill it.

V. Three-fold Law of Return

The three-fold law of return has often been called the witches' equivalent of karma. The law can be seen to describe the idea that if you do good you will be rewarded many times over and if you do bad you will suffer the consequences of this many times over.

There is some argument in Pagan circles about how literal this law is. I do not subscribe to the idea that you will be punished three times over for any bad deeds that you do. This is a little too patriarchal and Christian for my liking. My interpretation is that we reap what we sow, and that we are all interconnected.

A friend of mine is a very dynamic and handsome man in his thirties. He has basically been the stereotype of the sexy-man-about-town ever since I have known him. He flits from one woman to another, which actually is just fine, as long as he makes this known to his lust partners. He has never done this—in fact, he took great delight as part of the conquest in promising the world and radically underdelivering. Until he met Judith.

Judith rocked his world. Equally dynamic, equally beautiful, she challenged him like no other woman before her, and he fell hard. After a fantastic six months he began shopping for a diamond engagement ring, only to find her in bed with another man. Shocked and shattered, he asked her why. She shrugged and simply said, "Why not? I thought you understood I would rather not get tied down."

A classic case of reaping what he sowed. My friend now has learned the hard way how it feels to be the one left behind and tricked, and will probably not exhibit quite the same kind of behavior again. He is clearing the way to a more balanced relationship for his future, rather than being punished for his sins.

Here are some simple ways that you can be mindful of the three-fold law of return.

- Be honest about the nature of your relationships as early as possible.
- Have clear intentions about what kind of relationships you are seeking.
- Know yourself and act accordingly.
- Do not play games with people.

- Flirt all you want, but be mindful not to hurt anyone.

- Try to stand in the other person's shoes before making decisions.

- Take steps to break the cycle of codependence if you have this happening.

- Know your shadow side and be aware of its destructive patterns.

- Understand on a core level that we are all connected.

As witches understand the world, we are all connected, and this includes being connected to the Goddess. If we believe, and act on the belief that we are all equal, purposeful, and precious, then it is not a big leap to understand that choosing to be connected in positive ways is beneficial. If we choose equality over judgment, collaboration over domination, multiple views over a single inflexible view, empathy over mind-reading, and a deep belief that we are all Divine, created with love and care individually, we can develop a better initial rapport with everyone we meet and a relationship with those we choose to love that goes beyond sex or friendship.

These five ancient laws lay down a series of solid touchpoints as a guide to our relations with other people. Although these laws are very ancient, they are extremely relevant to the needs of today and offer real guidance to enriching and improving our intimate relationships. When you begin to examine these principles closely and begin to actively live them, you will see how effective they are at reshaping the areas of lust, love relationships, and fertility into something that is more satisfying and connected than you would ever have thought possible.

Section Two

Before You Put Your Broom in the Bedroom . . .
Preparing for Power

Magical Thinking vs. Thinking Magically

I was sitting in a club one night with a close friend of mine—let's call her Rachael. As we sipped on our cocktails, we eyed the crowd. Among the so-hip-it-hurt couples and singles, we spotted a hens' night group (bachelorette party) there; all giggles and squeals in the corner.

We soon identified the bride. She was the one with the veil. Suddenly the whole group began to sing a drinking song to her that included her name, Tina. Soon most of the room was yelling "Tina" as she threw down yet another glass of champagne.

Rachael sighed, her eyes locked on the wobbling figure in white.

"Ah," she sighed, "That takes me back."

"How so?" I asked.

"Let me tell you a little story. I remember when I was nineteen; I was head-over-heels in love with a shaggy-haired, snake-hipped, slightly older guy named Michael. He was in my class at the university and it was love at first sight. Well, from my side, anyway!

"He ended up in my tutorial class and we became friends. I thought he was quite shy and secretive, but really bright, and I would dream about him day and night! The problem was, of course, he never tried anything other than the friend routine and I became obsessed with trying to find ways for him to fall in love with me. In fact, I was trying so hard that I began to search for clues for a reason that he wasn't already in love with me.

"One day, we were lying on the grass between lectures, eating the sandwiches that I had carefully prepared for him at 5:30 A.M., before early tutorial. We are just generally checking out the lunch hour crowd and he comments on a girl in one of our classes.

"He says, 'That's that Gina girl isn't it? Man, those pants don't look good on her. She really has let herself go since beginning of term, huh?'

"I look at her and yes, her pants are pretty tight, and she probably has gone up a dress size.

"Interesting.

"I decide on the spot that his comment is a blessing, because it is obvious that Michael likes skinny girls. It's now likely the reason he hasn't hit on me is because of my weight. It has to be this, it couldn't be anything else. I mean, I thought back then that my backside deserved its own zip code.

"So, Stacey, over a three-month period I went on a savage guerrilla campaign to lose weight. I hardly ate anything! I remember eating lots of apples and cutting out everything, absolutely anything I loved. If I got tempted, I would just imagine being in his arms, and my appetite magically disappeared."

I was startled by Rachael's story. Rachael is a very attractive woman. Curvy and long-legged, with a mane of jet-black hair, she turns heads wherever she goes. I told her I couldn't imagine her losing any weight.

"I was a little rounder, but I wouldn't say fat, by any means. I developed into my bones late. At this age I had a little baby fat and I hated it. All I knew was that if I lost weight and became skinny, Michael would be mine.

"Months went by and I did lose a couple of pounds, but it seemed to no avail, until one day Michael pulls me aside in the shadows of the cafeteria.

" 'Hey, I'm having a party in two Saturdays' time, and I would really like you to come. It's kind of a small party and I would love you to be there.'

"I remember every bit of blood running to my face as he leaned closer to my ear and said 'Don't tell everyone, I don't want *everyone* coming.'

"Oh my God! He wanted me! My first thoughts were that starving myself had worked! He had finally seen me for the absolute beauty that I was and that this would be the beginning of the rest of my life.

"So I buy the new outfit, get my hair done, and borrow my brother's car so I could arrive in style. I don't even bother going to lectures for the days beforehand as I am sooo excited!

"I walk into Michael's house that night and it's all decorated in sweet little paper lanterns and there is food laid out on pretty tablecloths. I walk out to the garden and there he is. I can see him now, wearing this beautiful white shirt and the coolest jeans, brushing the hair away from those big brown eyes. He spots me, smiles slowly, and walks over. Time stood still. I remember just taking the biggest breath and holding it."

" 'Glad you could come!' He says, grabbing my hand. 'Come over here with me, there's someone you should meet.'

"We walk toward a group of girls with their backs to us. He taps one on the shoulder. A girl about my height, in a yellow dress, smiles brilliantly at me.

" 'Rachael, this is Tina.' Michael says, pushing this girl in front of me squarely. I shake her hand.

" 'She's my fiancée, we are announcing our engagement tonight!'"

"My face must have registered my horror as he quickly said, 'Oh Rach! You must be so shocked. I was keeping it a secret from all the jocks at school. I'm sorry I didn't tell you but I thought I'd surprise you! You're not angry with me?'

"I must have mumbled a 'no, not at all' and kissed them both 'Congratulations.' I also noticed that this girl was more rounded than I was and I think this just was the most painful part of all. The waking up bit! I was so stupid!"

Standing there in the nightclub, I felt sad for the young woman who was Rachael back then. Here was someone who believed that if she simply lost weight, and hung around enough, the boy of her dreams would automatically love her. How devastating for her. How disappointing!

How naive to think that you just do something and then ask for something and magically you will receive it! A typical teenage mistake that we would never make when we are older and wiser, would we?

But we do. All the time.

Most of us, at some stage, have engaged in this same magical thinking.

Have you or anyone else you know voiced or thought the following or something along a similar theme?

- If I get married my life will be happy.
- If I just find the right partner my life will be complete.
- I need a child to be happy.
- If I do everything perfectly I will get that promotion.
- If I marry a man with money I'll never have to worry again.
- If I just lose weight I will be confident and attract a boyfriend.

Any of these sound at all familiar?

Magical thinking is when you believe that if you do one particular thing, then there will be a particular result . . . just like magic . . . with no other involvement.

Let's examine the first example on the list:

If I get married my life will be happy.

Absolutely. You may very well meet someone wonderful and get married and end up extremely happy in all ways. Anything is possible. Just like Michael could have fallen in love with Rachael only because she dropped a couple of pounds. But what about the other person and their needs? What about the other parts of your life, such as work, your family, your health, your spirituality? Do these have any impact on your happiness or is it just by finding that person who will marry you that everything will magically change, fall into place, and you will be happy?

Do you see that merely getting married is no guarantee that your life will be happy? This is magical thinking.

You have to take action to move toward what you desire, no matter how small that action.

This is *participation*!

Participation is the key difference between Magical Thinking and Thinking Magically.

Magical Thinking: Action + Desire = Result?

Thinking Magically: Intention + Participation X Time = Result!

This is particularly relevant to you as a modern witch because spells and rituals do not work in isolation. You can set in motion a powerful intention that can seem to work instantly. It appears that events have happened magically. However, in reality this only occurs when you have already done the groundwork and are ready for the change.

When you perform any of the spells and rituals contained in this book, you must be prepared to follow up with appropriate action. This is thinking magically. It is not enough to merely talk the talk; you must also walk the walk!

This is why the concept of your personal Book of Shadows (learn how, page 77) is so important. In any real system of change there is always a record of progress. In traditional and contemporary magic, this record is referred to as the Book of Shadows. Your Book of Shadows will list the intentions you have set, the rituals you have performed, and, most importantly, your progress. The entries in your Book of Shadows will be stepping stones forward, a catalyst for your momentum. One of the most magical feelings in the world is when you have achieved your intention! Looking through your Book of Shadows is a powerful reminder of how far you have come, the successes you have experienced and, most of all, a record of how you did it so you can succeed again and again!

Many witches and non-witches fail in achieving their goals because they fail to follow through and continue to participate! That does not sound like the easy way out, like perhaps the advice in some spellcraft books you have read, but my methods are not meant to be flowery—just proven and effective. It is one thing to perform a beautiful ritual, but it is a more difficult thing to ground yourself and move back into the *real* world. It is one thing to make a wish, but another to actually take the steps to make it a reality, even when those steps may scare you.

I look forward to introducing you to doing both, setting intentions and participating, exceptionally well.

Welcome to the world of thinking magically and to increasing your personal power to get the relationship that you desire.

The Creation of a Personal Foundation of Power

Inside Out vs. Outside In

It was a public holiday Monday, and I was lying late in my bed, cuddled up and pondering the nature of love. All the case studies and research for this book were tumbling lazily through my mind, like laundry in a dryer. There was the scientific research about love and attraction, heavy and clumping but real like a pair of sand shoes thumping around. Then there was the spiritual side, fine and floating like a silk scarf, but still strong and very beautiful in its making.

The biology of attraction, the science of it, tells me that love is nothing but a chemical cocktail. If falling in love is then mainly chemical, a series of body-made potions released in sequence that trick us into staying put long enough to mate, is that all there is?

Could thousands of love songs and ads in classifieds looking for soul mates be wrong? Could all those greeting card poems, valentines, teddy bears, and death 'til us parts be, for a better word, unrealistic? Or even in psycho-speak be labeled rabidly co-dependent?

The truth has come out somewhere in the middle. Yes, unmistakably, scientifically, the chemistry of love sets the scene, our family background and culture shapes this recipe of attraction, and we need to be aware of the brutal and awesome power of this. But there *is* something more. It is a connection of beings that have something to share, say, and learn on a deep level, in order to forward the individual's journey.

Please be aware of the subtle discernment in what is put forward here.

We meet, share, and love in order to form partnerships that will enable our own journeys, and possibly assist theirs, but it is ours that comes *first*.

This is not a narcissistic or selfish point of view. Without satisfaction of our own Goddess-granted purpose, our relationships will never be as close, intimate, or connected as they could be. If we don't know who we are and what we want, how can we offer something truthful, real, and lasting to anyone else? In fact, we may never form quality relationships at all because we have never bothered to form a quality relationship with ourselves. This is why I place such huge importance on self-knowledge and knowing what we want.

It is very common for me to see clients who believe they are cursed because the same bad luck seems to be plaguing them. I always ask them to explain these situations in detail because here is where a pattern is revealed, and frankly it is not because someone cursed them. It is because there is a pattern or a blind spot in the way the person sees themselves or, more accurately, doesn't see themselves.

It is easy to want to just skip the hard work of looking at ourselves, warts and all. Let's face it, if we are awake enough to want to know ourselves, or in pain enough that we know we have a problem, we can perhaps glimpse the seemingly dark and twisted path before us. However, that path is also littered with the most delightful surprises, glittering rewards, and happy endings, should we choose to venture tentatively down it.

Witches believe that power is built from the inside out rather than the outside in.

Building internal power has always been a priority for us, due to the fact that it could be quite dangerous in the past to rely on getting our recognition or power externally. Additionally, without a high level of physical, mental, and spiritual strength, spellcraft and making effective magic is almost impossible. In covens, where the priestess is the conduit to the power raised by the rest of the members, it is imperative that she has an incredibly solid personal foundation to be able to channel and control that power so that it is directed accurately. As a solitary witch, this ability to be a clean and strong conduit to power is equally as important.

We believe that without a strong personal power base or personal foundation nothing lasting and strong can be built. This includes relationships of any kind.

The Witches' Keys to Power Building as Applied to Relationships

There are four key areas that witches choose to concentrate on in order to build internal power. Each is as important as the other in building a more connected, happier, more resilient, and frankly, more attractive person. It is vital in order to get the strongest synergy that we be mindful of developing all and not just the ones that seem obvious to us.

The four keys are:
Self-knowledge
Self-esteem
Self-care
Self-trust

Self-Knowledge

Knowing yourself well enough is integral to your purpose. Your purpose could be defined a number of ways, but could include:

- Why you are here.
- What your core competency or life theme is.
- What excites you, makes your heart sing, makes you feel focused and on-purpose.
- How you are of service to the whole of life.

If we are fuzzy about our Selves it is virtually impossible to connect with what it is that we are here to do. That familiar nagging feeling that something is missing is usually a symptom of not knowing who we are enough to flush out our purpose—and live it!

The consequences of not knowing our purpose can most easily be seen when it comes to career and business. We all know of someone who has had a midlife crisis in their twenties and thirties, well before the old norm of late forties. There are more and more of us who wake up one morning, look at the jobs we have created for ourselves, look at our belief that we need more and more stuff to be happy, look at our externally full but internally barren lives, and, in utter shock, recoil at our own choices.

These uninformed choices are often the direct result of an uncovered, unlived purpose, affecting the way we react, respond, attract, and connect with other people. Our relationships become at best satisfying, but strangely restless, and at worst, totally destructive or co-dependent.

In *Witch in the Boardroom* I revealed how living an unauthentic life by ignoring the signals of purpose and taking jobs one after another to gain external power left me spiritually bankrupt. It wasn't until I dared to dig and uncover what was under the layers of security fear that I began to rediscover what it was I was here to do. What I didn't talk about was what the cost of burying myself was when it came to relationships.

Like many women of my generation, I wanted more than my parents had. I worked hard for my education, I had more opportunities, and wasn't going to let that go to waste. However, no matter how focused I was on my own life (or the life I thought I wanted), as soon as I picked a man, my focus ended up on him. Why? The long answer is because I didn't know my Self or trust my Self. I would concentrate on and actively build up the businesses, careers, and even lives of these men rather than my own—anything rather than look at myself and my life. The short answer is that I was avoiding uncovering my purpose because it seemed so unreal and unattainable, so it was easier to concentrate on helping someone else get theirs.

This also extended to problem-solving behavior and "saving" partners—in particular if they had addictions of any sort, lack of motivation, or money problems. Or all! Classic co-dependence.

I totally take responsibility for my actions here. These things did not just happen to me. I was no victim. I consciously chose this behavior. The costs of this, although not immediately obvious at the time, were huge. By negating my own life and purpose, I got into debt, I felt empty, I felt lonely, unfulfilled, angry, and resentful when I didn't get appropriate gratitude, and got to live with the roller coaster of mood swings of partners who had addictions. I let go of real friendships and made others that were based on the status I could offer, rather than who I was. And I would come back for more, one relationship with greater destructive power than the next.

Now that I have a deeper knowledge of myself, both my strengths and vulnerabilities, my shining lights and my blind shadows, I can make better, more informed decisions about my relationships. At first learning to do this feels clumsy and unnatural. When I began to date again after these realizations, I asked myself a set of questions before I accepted a date: Does this man need saving in any shape or form? No. Tick! Does this man seem to like his own life? Yes. Tick! Does this man have any addictions of any kind that he is not dealing with? No. Tick! Does he need me to complete him? No. Tick!

And then I would bite my tongue every time I was tempted to offer a piece of advice, or help him with a proposal. If I discovered that he had an addiction of any kind, I would walk, no negotiation. This is a balancing act; real support is something you want to share with your partner, but not if it stops you from fulfilling your purpose because you are *only* focusing on them. I worked with Artemis energy (see Spell for Selfhood) regularly to enable me to stay connected yet revel in my selfhood. I also ensured that I continued to follow the Five Ancient Laws, which gave me considerable impetus toward a healthy balance.

Now I do this more instinctively in my unconscious competence. Needless to say, there is a lot less pain in my relationships, and not just the love relationships. My relationships with family and friends are unrecognizable to what they once were. I now have a level of intimacy and trust with them that is bred from deep acceptance and wisdom. I know they stand with me solidly in times of trouble, and I with them unquestionably. They know who I am and what I am because I do not hide it from them, and so they can engage with me all the more honestly.

Not knowing your purpose can also affect long-standing marriages as well and not just individuals. It can jeopardize whole families if not diagnosed early enough.

I recently consulted with a thirty-five-year-old man named Arron who was an airline pilot. Arron came to me purely on the urgings of his wife of ten years, who was complaining that the relationship was dying due to Arron's neglect. He complained of feeling flat, bored, and depressed, and explained this by saying that it was his job causing this.

Being a pilot seemed like an interesting job, I ventured, so why was he bored? The fact was his boredom was a symptom and a signal of his confusion over what he really wished to do with his life. Question after question delved deeper until I discovered that Arron really didn't know what he wanted to do or why he was here, but he did know that being a pilot was perhaps only part of the picture.

"I know there are some things I get from being a pilot that I like. I like the freedom, I like the technical aspects, but there is something missing. And it's big. It's affecting everything else, including how I connect with my wife."

Arron performed the Spell for Purpose on a full moon. What he learned from this didn't surprise him. "I realized I had forgotten a real love, let's say a real passion I had for helping, for being of service. I remember as a teenager wanting to do search and rescue, or even work in the extreme wilderness. I always looked at the guys who worked in the Antarctic regions as having my ideal job.

"I forgot about all this with my exams, then my flight exams and building up the hours I needed. And then I met my wife and we got married and we had kids and I had to earn a certain amount and everything just rolled along. But it rolled along without me really being a part of it."

I asked Arron how he could weave his purpose into his current job. He suggested a number of alternatives including working for aid agencies, working for the air force, and even contacting the Arctic/Antarctic services.

With renewed vigor, Arron began to search for where his purpose could more readily match his talents. He found a wonderful job working for a large aid agency in a third world country. This seemed to satisfy all his criteria. However, his wife didn't want to go or take the children to what she thought would be a dangerous place.

It is here that we see the unpleasant consequences of leaving your purpose buried for so long. In Arron's words: "If I had only looked at this earlier I wouldn't be having all this hassle with my wife. In fact, I don't know where I would be. It really isn't fair to her to want her to share my passion for this, but it's not fair for me not to go either."

Arron was coming to the realization that he may well have married someone who doesn't really know him or what his deepest dreams are because he hasn't known it himself.

Arron and his wife made a compromise where he took the job for three months to see how he felt about this role. Of course, Arron loved it. He also realized that he loved his wife and family too. He was able to negotiate a contract where he did six weeks on duty and six weeks off, which was an acceptable situation for both parties.

Self-knowledge begins by answering and asking the easy and hard questions. Take a look at this list below for starters. Can you answer these questions clearly or do they need further investigation and consideration? How many can you answer clearly without mentioning your traditional roles or using labels such as wife, mother, sister, husband, job title, profession?

- Who do I believe myself to be?
- What do I really love?
- Do I experience what makes my heart sing?
- What are my strengths?
- What are my vulnerabilities?
- What do I fear?
- What am I attracted to?
- What do I value?
- Why am I here?

Answering these questions carefully and truthfully may lead to further enquiries such as:

- What kind of relationship do I really want right now? (love, lust, long term, short-term, gay, straight, married, defacto, etc.)
- What beliefs do I have around my external appearance or my body and does that hinder me in any way?
- What patterns do I see emerging time and time again that sabotage real connection and satisfying relationships?
- In what or whom do I have faith?

If you can answer these kinds of questions clearly, keep delving as you evolve and progress. Participation and movement are the rewards of superior self-knowledge.

Self-Esteem

Witches believe that we each have a spark of the Goddess and God within us. In natural return, the Goddess and God have a spark of us within them. Knowing intimately that by having a spark of Divinity within you, you are indeed Goddess or God, tends to change reality. It is difficult to experience self-hate if you know that you have the Divine within you. Self-esteem comes flowing back, flooding into us with positive change if we come to this realization.

Having solid levels of self-esteem is considered by psychologists as one of the keys to building successful and resilient relationships. It is an area of psychology that has been well-researched, and there are large amounts of data showing that at younger and younger ages children are aware of themselves, their bodies, their intelligence, and how this compares against others of the same age and by societal standards, and we know how this affects their self-belief and behaviors. For example, many children as young as kindergarten age begin to exhibit negative changes in behavior, such as becoming more withdrawn if they believe they aren't as attractive as their peers. This is magnified with children who are overweight or clinically obese, and unfortunately one of the key behaviors as a consequence is more self-loathing, and, moreover, eating to comfort these painful feelings. The story ramps up another level by the time children with low levels of self-esteem hit puberty.

If self-esteem is not experienced or learned by either methods, these young people have a higher than normal incidence of addiction, truant behavior, health problems, self-isolation, and unplanned pregnancy. Adults who experience chronic self-esteem problems experience a lack of resilience and poor societal, educational, and career development—all of which are factors in experiencing satisfying personal relationships. Women, in particular, develop eating and body disorders that naturally impact sexual function and enjoyment, and their initial selection of a suitable partner.

Some of the questions that you may want to ask yourself to evaluate the levels of your self-esteem would include:

- Do I lack confidence in making new friends and relationships?
- Do I feel that I am somehow less than others?
- Am I unhappy about who I am?
- Do I need to continually prove my worth to others including my family, friends, and close intimate partners?
- Do I avoid social occasions because I don't like the way I look or feel?
- Do I avoid sex because I don't like the way I look?
- Do I automatically think learning something new will be difficult?
- Do I exhibit inappropriate emotions at times when I feel uncomfortable or am lacking in confidence?

- Do I get involved with partners who I know are unsuitable for me so that I can feel better about myself comparatively?

Self-esteem can be developed, even if we have missed out during our earlier development. The sources of poor self-esteem should be identified and the Witches Way actively honors individual gifts, bodies, minds, and spirits. Know that your uniqueness, your differences, and even the parts about yourself that you consider worthless are the very things that make you powerful and special in this big wide world.

Self-Care

It is truly a difficult job to write a section on self-care without sounding like a worried mother. But bear with me. I'll try not to tell you that you aren't looking after yourself enough.

Take yourself back to the last time you felt sick. Maybe it was a while back or maybe it's right now. Think about what being sick costs you. By this I don't mean in dollar terms but in opportunities missed or happiness gained. You may not have been able to avoid being sick, but perhaps if you had been looking after yourself, you might not have become ill.

Self-care isn't just about not being healthy, though. It concerns everything that we do to honor (or not honor) our Selves.

Some simple questions you might like to ask yourself about the issue of self-care:

- Do I experience enough genuine moments of pleasure in my week?
- Do I feel vital?
- Do I regularly put work ahead of sleep, eating, family, pleasure?
- Does my body get sufficient amounts of movement?
- Do I have a partner or close relationship that I know will support me unconditionally in times of crisis?
- Am I overweight or underweight?
- Do I consider times of play as important as times of work?
- Do I get professional assistance promptly, be it medical, psychological, or spiritual, should I require it?

- Do I consistently put the needs of others ahead of my own?
- Do I find it hard to say NO to requests that I really don't want to do?
- Do I find it hard to say yes to activities that I think would be great, but feel guilty about it?
- Do I believe or have faith in something bigger than myself?

One easy way to begin to introduce the concept of self-care into life is to simply ask upon waking and just prior to sleeping, "What is it that I need to care for myself more?" Or perhaps you could ask: "Please tell me what is best for me right now." And listen.

These will be very short answers, and don't allow yourself to think about this for long or edit . . . these are short, sharp messages from the subconscious. Record the answer each night in your BOS or another journal, and of course act on these.

Here is a random sample of my answers over a week as an example for you:

- Sleep more
- Go dancing with the girls on Friday
- Chinese vegetables
- Talk to Athena
- Spaghetti Bolognese
- See the accountant
- Bath tonight
- Workshop August, not June

A fairly innocuous list on first look, isn't it? With a little explanation you will see how much this small communication improved my self-care during that time.

Sleep more—obvious, but a great reminder, since I was working and traveling long hours.

Go dancing with the girls next Friday—besides letting off a lot of steam and having a lot of fun, I met someone who has since become a relationship that has made a big difference in my life.

Chinese vegetables—I realized I had not been eating many vegetables at all as I had been traveling, and was feeling very lethargic and tired. I changed my diet.

Talk to Athena—Athena is the goddess of wisdom and strategy. I invoked her and she gave me a very obvious answer to something I had been struggling with and worrying about for some time. Thank the Goddess!

Spaghetti Bolognese—I have a friend who does the best version of this dish. Catching up with her is always a restful and mutually beneficial thing to do.

See the accountant—when I phoned my accountant, he said he was just going to call me with a great suggestion, which has cut down on a lot of paperwork.

Bath tonight—that bath ended up as part of a ritual that was vital in getting a useless old belief beaten once and for all.

Workshop August, not June—I had been stressing that I would not be able to organize a June workshop as planned due to other commitments that had arisen. Reluctantly I moved the date. The result: more time to prepare, less stress, and more participants were attracted.

Listening, recording, and participating make this a powerful yet simple daily reminder of how important it is to exercise self-care.

A time of extreme pressure is the time to exercise extreme self-care. To be at your best, knowing what you tend to let fall away in times of stress, such as nourishing food, clear communication with friends and family, or adequate sleep, can be the canary in the coal mine. Establish a clear plan of extreme self-care prior to times of pressure and then you (and often those close to you) will have a better chance of getting through this more demanding time in better shape.

Self-Trust

I love to ride horses, but as I learned to ride as an adult I don't possess that complete lack of fear that the gorgeous girl children have at the stables I visit. There they are; literally tens of them, aged between five and fifteen, confidently leading, galloping, jumping, and maneuvering animals that are literally half a ton in weight.

I watched as one eight-year-old girl spoke to her friend as she faced a new jumping height on her mare, Red. She examined the height intently as she led her horse to it. Both circled it like prey, and then with simple ease trotted back up to the starting point where her friend was waiting.

"Yep, we can do this," she said to her friend.

"Ooh, it's a bit higher than the last one. You better be careful," her friend replied.

The girl smiled at her friend with shining eyes and said, "Yes, it is higher, but I can lead Red to that, and I don't need to think about being careful. Red does that."

Off she went, sailing over the jump like she had been doing it all her life. A huge smile and cuddle for her horse followed, and as I watched I knew that I had witnessed the unerring power of self-trust, rather than lack of fear.

Self-trust is a surety that we can rely upon ourselves, that our decisions are valid, that we ourselves matter, that knowing ourselves combined with trusting ourselves leads to better, more informed decisions about all aspects of our life, including love, lust, and relationships. Witches believe that when we put our trust in ourselves, as we are connected with the Goddess, we put trust in her, and vice versa.

Self-trust is far more than a flashy show of confidence. It is deeper and farther-reaching than that. It is the security at the very core, that no matter what, our wisdom matters and it is best. It allows for flow and for faith in ourselves and the way we do things.

I remember the first time I met Richard. Richard was considered brilliant at what he did. He had a sparkling personality and a heart of gold, and he was the new man in my friend Jane's life. I am generally a very good judge of character, not just on intuition but based on a number of skills honed through years of business, training, and techniques and of course through the Witches Way. So when some of the answers Richard gave to some of my questions seemed at best evasive and at worst incongruous, all my alarm bells began to go off. Richard also had a business that could supply my business at the time and when he suggested that we should consider buying from him I felt another red flashing light go off, but thought I should consider the offer, partly because of his relationship with my friend and partly because I thought I was imagining things about him.

My accountant discovered in a routine credit check that the man was a total fraud. My girlfriend wasn't so easily let off. The man had a different name, a family, and to top it all off, had sweet-talked my friend into *lending* him $6,000. Bravo for my accountant, but why didn't I act upon my first suspicions? Because I had a small (not!) blind spot called "people pleasing" at the time—I wanted to please my friend by liking her new partner and not spoiling her pleasure, no matter what. I didn't trust myself enough to take the rebellious position of telling her honestly, as a friend should, what I thought. I allowed one of my best competencies to be railroaded by fear of upsetting someone. Lesson learned!

Self-trust is a full acceptance of self. As accepting one's self becomes easier, self-trust will begin to shine, giving great momentum to anything that we choose to tackle or do.

Check your level of self-trust now by answering the following questions:

- Do I let my partner or family make all my important decisions for me?
- Do I believe what people say about me—negative and positive—without checking it with myself internally?
- Do I worry that someone will find out that I am not as good/loving/happy/sad/talented/as they think I am?
- Do I worry that someone will find out that I am not perfect?
- Do I believe that I am not beautiful/good/talented enough because someone told me so?
- Do I fear obstacles of any kind?
- Do I wait to hear what others have to say before expressing my own opinion?

If you have answered yes to some of these questions, your self-trust could do with strengthening.

I would encourage you before you put your broom in the bedroom and begin to practice your own brand of proven relationship magic that you choose to create for yourself a solid personal foundation of power by participating in the development of these four Witches' Keys to Power Building. Without this unshakable core, any internal power we may possess cannot radiate cleanly outward, obliterating obstacles, bypassing distractions, reducing fear, and creating connection after connection. If we are constantly trying to glean all our power from sources external to ourselves and the Goddess we are reliant on what others are willing to give. Unfortunately, what they are willing to give may not be enough, nor what we need.

In its simplest form, the formula for internal vs. external power sources is:

Power Built from the Inside Out:
Witches' Keys to Power **x** Time + Solid Core Self = Power Full

Power Built from the Outside In:
Lack of Witches' Keys to Power **x** Time = Fragile Core Self = Power Less.

It is an easy choice to be power full. Take a leaf out of the most ancient of witches' books of shadows and create for yourself a more empowered, flexible, yet stable future by building the power from the inside out through the techniques, spells, and rituals crafted for you in this section.

Health and Vitality Ritual

Preparation

Perform this spell on any night where the moon is full. Ensure the room is warm. Ensure that you will be undisturbed. Decide on the location for the spellcraft. Have your intention clearly in mind or written down.

Welcome the Goddess and thank Her for being with you here tonight in this beautiful place.

Gather

Orange or white candle
Matches
Jasmine or rose petals
Essential oils: 2 drops rose geranium and pine, 1 drop bergamot mixed in
    5 ml of carrier oil.
Moon-charged water
A comfortable robe that you can slip out of easily for the skyclad elements
    of the ritual

Sea salt

Focus

Cast and open a Circle if you wish. Light the candle, dim the lights and relax. Take several deep breaths.

Run a bath. Add some of the potion to the bath—no more than a teaspoonful and add the other to a bath sachet. Soak and relax for at least fifteen minutes. Visualize how good each part of your body feels in that soft warmth. As you come out of the bath, gently towel off.

Then take almost all the remaining oil and massage your body from the feet up, keeping a few drops in the bottle. As you massage your body, say this to each part of your body as you massage and move up:

My feet are healthy, my ankles are healthy,
my calves are strong, my thighs are supple, etc.

Use your own words. The idea here is to infuse positive qualities to each part. If you feel a hesitation somewhere, notice it, but still say something positive.

Slip into your robe or dress comfortably and go somewhere right away to do your spell.

Building Power

Bring your candle and the bottle with the remaining oil into another room, or outside if it is warm enough. Face the moon if you can. Ask that you receive the Goddess, she who embodies health and vitality, to bless you this night.

Look at the candle or close your eyes and go within.

Look back in your mind now. Look back in the harvest of your life . . . the riches you have gathered.

Look to your strengths. Look to a time when you felt vital in a positive way. If you cannot remember a time, that is OK. Just recall another scenario where you felt good about yourself.

See this and *feel* this time clearly in your mind and body. Feel your personal vitality. Feel it warm you, pulse through you. Notice how you feel and what thoughts enter your mind. If your thoughts or feelings are negative, note this, but decide you will put this aside until a later time.

Now light your herbs and incense. Breathe in deeply. As you breathe in, you are inhaling even more power from the earth, the trees, the moon, and the sky.

The Goddess is still with you and sharing with you her attributes of focus, health, and vitality. Accept these gifts in your own body. Allow these energies to begin to mingle—yours and those of the Goddess. Feel your own strength and that of the Goddess course through you. Now focus on the feeling of that power in your hands.

In a loud, firm voice, chant:

> *I allow my body to shine*
> *Health and vitality are mine*
> *My body is a source of beauty*
> *Blessed Be the Goddess within me!*

Repeat the chant faster and faster, at least three times, feeling your strength, health, vitality, and energy grow.

Release Your Intention

Now hold your oil bottle and infuse into the oil that powerful energy of strength and vitality. Never fear, you will not run out of power—you will be channeling it now. Keep chanting—even shorten the verse if it helps power building. At the height of your energy hold your oil bottle in your hands and *shout*:

MY BODY WORKS FOR ME, NOT AGAINST ME!
MY BODY WORKS FOR ME, NOT AGAINST ME!
MY BODY WORKS FOR ME, NOT AGAINST ME!

Offer Your Gratitude

Know that the Goddess has heard your intention.

Thank the Goddess. Be grateful in the knowledge that all is as you have asked it to be, if it be Her will and for the greatest good of all.

Know your mind and body are already responding.

Complete the Ritual

Close your Circle. Take the energized oil with you. Extinguish and bury any remaining charcoal or herbs/incense in the garden or yard. Ground yourself by eating or drinking something, exercising, or dancing!

Participation

You now have highly energized oil. Take just a drop and anoint your heart or even take a quick inhalation, every morning, until it runs out. Carry it when you feel the need.

Let no one else touch it. Keep your oil close at hand or even on your desk, ready for use.

Book of Shadows Entries

Chart your progress by recording your feelings, behaviors, actions, and results, paying close attention to coincidences and details even if they seem insignificant or unrelated at the time.

Remember to date all your entries.

Chemistry vs. Soul Mates

The Case for Chemistry

There are so many powerful chemicals released in the body during attraction (and even more during sex) that it's a wonder they haven't made falling in lust or love illegal!

We have chemicals that slow us down, speed us up, change our emotions, kill pain, and make us deliriously happy. Let's start with the dynamic neurotransmitting duo of dopamine and noradrenaline, which get released into the body from nerve cells and turn on other nerve cells. Dopamine, through various actions, is involved in memory, pleasure, problem solving, motivation, and some circulatory function. Noradrenaline is primarily responsible for maintaining blood pressure, but is implicated in everything you could imagine in the central nervous system, emotional pathways included.

We can then add PEA (phenylethlamine) to our body cauldron, which stimulates the body to speed up and release even more dopamine and noradrenaline and thus up the ante even further.

Allow all of these potions to run around your body and the results are blushing, a huge energy boost, feeling nervous, anticipation, heart palpitations, and a general increase in awareness and vitality. If that isn't enough to get you going, then the endorphins kick in.

Endorphins are the pain killers and pleasure-delivering chemicals in our bodies. You know that feeling in the gym when you are just about to give up halfway through a big workout and then, magically, you get a second wind? That's endorphins. Similarly, many an eager lover has tried some adventurous position enthusiastically only to feel the painful consequences later after the natural drop in endorphins occurs! Endorphin functions also involve stopping anything that inhibits dopamine and noradrenaline so we have a pretty big open door here to fun and painless pleasure.

And all this is just foreplay! When we actually have sex, our body is flooded with endorphins and a highly studied chemical called oxytocin. Oxytocin is one of the key enablers of orgasm in both men and women and in the process of bonding. It is really the *trust* drug.

A recent study also showed that those of us with naturally high levels of oxytocin are able to form relationships more easily, but, on the flip side of the coin, can get taken in by lies and cons more often. Women have naturally higher levels and this is thought to be because of the role oxytocin plays in ensuring attachment between mother and baby.

Let's summarize our potions list then. We feel like superman or woman. We feel stronger, more aware, more alive, more attractive. At the same time we feel nervous, anxious but strangely happier, more inspired, and ready for anything. When we do come together we have another set of hormones that keep us together, enjoying each other as long as possible and as painlessly as possible. Frankly, we have chemicals racing around the body that put us in a state that would fail us on most sidewalk sobriety tests.

So the facts are that our bodies, and our minds, for that matter, have evolved to bring us together to mate (like just about every other organism on earth), and keep us together as long as possible. And even though it's agony and it's ecstasy at the same time, we want to do it again and again. It's a pretty powerful and, at times, addictive combination.

Doesn't all this evolutionary bag of tricks just fool us into falling in love, lust, or reproducing? Is this truly what we call chemistry? Or is there something else? Something that brought us together in the first place or keeps us together long after the chemical party wears off?

The Case for Soul Mates

The concept that there is just one special soul for each of us permeates most modern Western cultures. This soul will offer us deep friendship, wonderful companionship, and a life-long dedicated love—and we back to them. We need to find them, and we will certainly know when we do.

My next-door neighbor, a man in his seventies, was talking about his recent sailing holiday. He had sailed all around Australia's Whitsunday Islands with his buddies and all their wives.

"We had a great time," he said. "Of course our better halves made sure we didn't get too out of control!" Whether or not his wife kept him out of trouble or not is incidental here (although amusing). What is interesting is the concept of a "better half." It is common to describe a marital partner in particular as the better half. Take a look at Internet dating sites. Plenty of people are looking for that "person to complete my life" or "my missing other half." This is one of the strongest features of the idea of soul mates, that we are one-half of a whole that, once connected, will change our lives for the better.

Most Western marriage vows would validate this view, generally mentioning words such as "'til death do us part" or "together for eternity." Whole industries are based on the romance of soul mates. Listen to the radio or think about your favorite love songs. Generally they feature a message of love with one specially chosen person, who makes us feel better than we can ever alone, and this connection will never die. (Even if we have, in fact, lost them or done them wrong!). Look in any card shop (particularly around Valentine's Day) and you will find a variety of views with the core message that "you are my chosen one, and our love will last forever."

Where do these soul mates come from? There are many spiritual theories. Some say that the higher power has created them especially for us and we just need to wait and watch. Some say they are part of our karma; this time around we are getting the mate we deserve. Others are of the opinion that this is just the natural way and that we are meant to be with just one mate long-term, and that the force that brings two people together in the first place is the very force that keeps them together forever.

So we wander through our lives searching for that other half, our best friend, our soul mate, this one person who will change everything—and then, when we meet them (or think we meet them), we expect the instant romance and deep intimacy that we would expect from this one person, created especially for us. This soul almost automatically knows what we want, what we need, and they will support us in getting what we want (even if we aren't sure). They may even save us from our own vulnerabilities, insecurities, and shadows, such is the strength of this other half. They will, in all ways, make us whole.

Magical Relationships: The Witches' Middle Ground

Witches believe the Goddess has created us with everything we need to fulfill ourselves in our purpose in life. We are powerful. We are Goddess as She is us. We are full of possibility, even in our vulnerabilities. That means we are perfectly imperfect in the fact that we are whole, but evolving. That we are only one half looking for the other half to make us whole indicates that we in ourselves are not enough.

As you read in the previous section, Witches choose to focus on building themselves a firm personal foundation so that they need no one else to make them whole. The fact that they are working toward being the most authentic, resilient, genuinely happy, and vital person they can be means that having a partner to walk the journey with is the icing on the cake rather than the cake itself. Having high levels of self-knowledge, self-trust, self-esteem, and self-care, they know that they sell themselves short should they believe they need someone else to complete them. Synergy between two whole people is greater than two needy halves.

This does not, of course, mean that we should not desire someone to walk beside us on our life journey. To the contrary. However, what it means is that we will have high levels of charisma (spirit runs through) and we will attract more of the partners that more completely fulfill our current needs. What this also means is that we will be able to recognize the kind of person we want and don't want in a clear way. We have the sight and courage to reject those who may be detrimental to us, where in the past we might have accepted them rather than be and feel alone.

The huge numbers of men and women who are in co-dependent relationships illustrate the fallout of the soul mate idea. Rather than feel alone, unfulfilled, and continually experience abandonment pain, co-dependents will stay in destructive relationships when those who feel whole would have long ago flown the coop. Often there is a continual push-me-pull-you style in relationships where one partner treats the other poorly until they finally get pushed away when things become totally unbearable. The first partner then is alone and knows unconsciously they need the other half that they have treated poorly previously to make themselves feel good and *better* again. They apologize. The abandoned partner feels vindicated, takes them back only for the whole cycle to begin again six months down the track. This kind of dysfunctionality continues when we do not have the self-esteem to be able to walk away, or when we feel that this person we are with is the *only* one for us, almost no matter what may happen.

If you have ever experienced the sheer exhilaration of being in or close to a relationship that is a fantastic balance between two strong, authentic people, you will certainly feel the power of it. There is absolute magic present. There is an individual energy that enables them to continually strive for their own goals and purpose but also support the other's endeavors without detracting from what is important to them. There is a creative power between them that, when activated, is greater than the two individually. This synergy between two whole people is greater than two needy halves will ever be.

Our culture propagated "someone forever" as a method of control. We know that the Christian Church needed to contain and control sexuality, and fidelity through marriage was one way to do this. Prior to this, marriage was either not official or undertaken for the protection of estates and property. Then, women were inheritors of property, as were men, and often a more official sanction was needed only to protect or join together assets rather than for any romantic reason. Evidence shows that our ancestors lived much more sexually open lives than we would expect, unbound by laws to make them valid.

The concept of one-life–one-marriage is a recent development particular to our longer life expectancy and less war. In the past it was virtually unheard of for someone to live past forty, let alone the ages we do today. We married early, reproduced, and died early. Women outlived men, often due to their not being casualties of tribal warfare, and they often married more than once. Therefore, being with one person for life meant maybe twenty years or less. Today, marrying for life can mean eighty years! Alternatively, if we continually seek the wrong people we have a long time to get it wrong over and over. Is it then no wonder that there are so many divorces and that a commitment (no matter what) for life is a very big request?

As for the idea of chemistry, witches acknowledge this but with a caveat. We know that we have been designed perfectly biologically to do what is natural, and there is absolutely no shame in this. That amazing feeling of meeting the eyes of a beautiful Being across a room and being flooded with desire is undoubtedly one of the true joys in life. That electric charge of a new lover's lips pressed against yours is real, and a sign that this is no ordinary attraction. However, we also believe that there is a second kind of chemistry, the spark, the force of attraction that allows us to identify that a person is special in some way to our path and purpose. Let's call that spiritual chemistry.

Spiritual chemistry is the feeling that this person has something deeper to offer, an emotional honesty, even that you are on the same path, even that you may feel that you have met before. The easy leap to make here is that you have met your other half, but you have met something far better within the Witches Way. You have recognized and encountered a soul who is here to walk your path beside you (not behind or in front), and who has been sent to teach or show you something, or perhaps to simply give you pleasure. These "somethings" may be so small that they will take only a brief encounter to integrate, or many lessons that will take a lifetime to learn.

Witches have always advised that we need a solid personal foundation and purpose, a clear idea of what kind of relationship and attributes we want in a partner, sexual chemistry and spiritual chemistry for intimate relationships to work, and that we need both to even attract a suitable partner.

Without this combination we continually choose our partners badly. If choosing them just for chemistry you may have a super-hot sexual relationship for a while, but that will wear thin without anything else to hook it to. (This is fine if what you decide you want is a lust relationship.) Choose them just for spiritual chemistry, and you will have a great friend, work partner, or supporter, but you will have no sexual spark to light your life long term. Don't have a good idea about your purpose? You will most probably choose someone to save you, make you whole, or you'll be restless and bored, and will most likely mess up anything great you could have.

So the formula for a Magical Relationship is this:

Purpose + Chemistry +   **/**   Solid personal
Spiritual Chemistry   foundation

If we take anything less, we shortchange ourselves and we just settle for less. We do not get what we want or the magical relationship(s) that we are destined to have. In fact, *born* to have.

And yes, all this may seem like a big request. Yes, it can take time to build your foundation and get your purpose sorted. When you do, though, there will be more eligible partners attracted into your life than ever before. Knowing about the two kinds of chemistries and the difference between them allows you to recognize something special when it comes along and not be tempted to try and force something to happen just for the sake of not being lonely. Plus, you will know sooner and more easily who is right for you, so you won't be wasting your time on those who are not suitable for you. You will not make the same mistake with men or women over and over, and you will experience more satisfaction in the relationships you choose to have. Meanwhile, if you are without the kind of relationship that you seek at this moment, you are not suffering the horrendous abandonment pain that co-dependents do. After all you are never alone: you have your Self (incredible being that you are!), your purpose (which you are living or living toward), and the Goddess.

Ritual for Purpose

Preparation

This spell is ideal to be repeated in a Tri-Lunar pattern. Perform this spell on any night where the moon is full. Ensure the room is warm. Ensure that you will be undisturbed.

Have your intention clearly in mind or written down. Welcome the Goddess and thank Her for being with you here tonight in this beautiful place.

Gather

A candle in your favorite color

Matches

A few pieces of blank paper

A few different colored pens or markers

Charcoal

Herbs / resins: witchbane / frankincense / basil on a heat-proof plate

A comfortable robe that you can slip out of easily for the skyclad elements
    of the ritual

A CD of your favorite music—this should be music that you absolutely
    adore!

Focus

Cast and open a Circle if you wish. Light the candle, dim the lights, and relax. Take several deep breaths.

Put your music on at a level that suits you. Loud or soft is OK as long as you are able to concentrate. Seat yourself comfortably at your altar or simply on the floor. Have your herbs, charcoal, paper, and pens at the ready.

Building Power

Face the moon if you can.

As you light your candle, ask that you receive the Goddess. Ask that you receive guidance and truth tonight. Ask that she who has given you the creative power to know what you need to know will bless you this night.

Look at the candle flame or close your eyes and go within.Listen to the music that you have chosen. Listen to every note, feel the rhythm. This is music that you love. You have chosen this from your very heart. The choice is unique to you. Let the music take you away—move, sway, even dance if you like. Celebrate your own uniqueness.

When you are feeling relaxed and centered, disrobe. Note your thoughts and feelings. If they are negative, note this, but decide you will put this aside until a later time.

Now light your herbs and incense. Breathe in deeply. As you breathe, you are inhaling even more power from the earth, the trees, the moon, and the sky.

The Goddess is still with you on your journey now to find your purpose.

Take in a deep breath of the aroma and with every sweet breath remember times in your life when you felt happy to be you. Recall times when you truly enjoyed what you were doing. Do not judge this process. Let any image come.

In a loud, firm voice, chant:

> *Let me know*
> *What I know!*
> *Let me see*
> *What I don't!*

Repeat the chant faster and faster, at least three times, feeling your purpose, clarity, and energy grow.

Release Your Intention

Now with your dominant hand, the one with which you write, record what you are experiencing. Take as long as you like and feel free to use different colors and draw symbols or pictures.

Ask yourself out loud:

> *What is my purpose?*

With your non-dominant hand, the one with which you do not usually write, allow yourself to answer. Do not try and control what comes out—just write or draw. Limit this to two or three minutes.

You now have a page that will be full of clues to your purpose. Never be discouraged if you feel you have not got much or that you cannot make sense of it yet. These messages will be straight from your unconscious and so may not be immediately clear, although some may be easy to decipher.

Offer Your Gratitude

Know that the Goddess has heard your intention.

Thank the Goddess for allowing you to share in Her power. Be grateful in the knowledge that all is as you have asked it to be, if it be Her will and for the greatest good of all.

Know your mind and body are already responding and sending you toward your purpose.

Complete the Ritual

Close your Circle. Blow out your candle. Extinguish and bury any remaining charcoal or herbs/incense in the garden or yard.

Ground yourself if you need to by dancing to some really upbeat music, by eating or drinking something, or by exercising!

Participation

Examine how you feel about what you have learned about your purpose. Take steps to participate in your purpose, whether newfound or previously known to you.

Consider taking courses, volunteering, or increasing the level of activity at which you are currently participating.

Book of Shadows Entries

Chart your progress by recording your feelings, behaviors, actions, and results, paying close attention to coincidences and details even if they seem insignificant or unrelated at the time.

Remember to date all your entries.

Attraction: The Importance of Knowing What You Want

As you read earlier, the idea of romance and marriage as practiced in Western society is a fairly recent phenomena. As modern people, most of us like to think that we see through society's constraints, or even laugh about them, but they often still filter the way we behave, especially if they seem to contradict our personal purpose. This is not necessarily a conscious set of decisions; it is a powerful set of filters, nevertheless. Sometimes even if we are aware, deep down, of what we want, the pressure to conform to societal or family standards is almost too hard to battle with.

Kathy is a doctor in her mid-thirties who is of Italian-American descent. She is a trauma specialist at a large district hospital. She came to me wanting a love spell after a relationship of two years had broken up, and it had been six months in between anyone else. On the phone, prior to our appointment, she said she wanted to attract a long-term partner. I asked Kathy about her last relationship, and she quickly explained that there was a pattern to all her breakups.

"I was with James for two years. Great guy. Loving, caring, didn't care about my weird hours. After a year together, when he asked me to live with him I almost threw up. I did it anyway. It lasted another six months before I had to cut loose because I just knew he was going to pop the question. And I'm sorry to say the prior three relationships were pretty much identical. There's obviously something wrong with me."

Upon meeting her, I asked Kathy a simple question: *What do you want?*

Like most people who don't really know, her eyes opened wide, she opened her mouth, and nothing much came out. After some more challenging questioning she finally blurted out: "Look, I know I'm supposed to want the big romance, the white dress and the two kids, but I don't. I'm scared to admit this to anyone. My family and friends all have this. I have never envisaged my life this way and yet I've tried over and over to do exactly this. The men I've attracted have been good men, stayers, ones that want the traditional thing, but after I while I get freaked out and smothered, and I run."

I suggested to Kathy that she had answered her own question. Her relationships were so bad because she was attracting what she didn't want, and what her family wanted for her. I also told her that it was OK not to know right now, and that we would work on her own truth and making that a valid place to start her decision-making going forward.

I asked her to write a vision letter so she could get clearer about the life she really desired for herself.

"Writing this vision letter I think is one of the most important things I have ever done for myself. I took a day off work and just sat there and wrote it. It was very cathartic. I cried about all the time I had wasted trying to have these relationships that I didn't want, rather than live the kind of life I have always secretly wanted. It was through this vision letter that I saw that what I wanted for right now, and yes this could change, was not a partner who wanted marriage. In fact, for right now, and until I designated a change was at hand, what I wanted, frankly, was a friend with whom I could also get my needs met sexually."

Although Kathy was fairly shocked at her own revelation, she was relieved also. I asked Kathy then to do the Spell to Attract Your Ideal Partner (page 69). Over the next moon cycle she attracted a man who fit her needs perfectly.

"Right now, this is perfect. I would imagine at some time in the future I may want something different, more long term, but this is what I am more than satisfied with now. This feels comfortable and right for me, and I'm not really caring so much about what my family may think."

Similarly, Graham, a lawyer in his mid-thirties, had also had a string of broken relationships of which he was not proud resulting from misunderstanding what he really wanted. "I had been bought up by my dad, someone who was quite driven and played the field when it came to women after my mother died. When I entered the legal profession I was surrounded by guys who really weren't that interested in settling down; in fact it was quite the game to have a different gorgeous girl for every occasion. Trouble is, I don't think I have wanted to play that game for quite some time."

When Graham was asked what he wanted, he replied very quietly, "Well I want a good, deep, long-term relationship, but you know, I just don't know how to have one, or whether one could fit into my life."

I asked that Graham create a vision letter to clarify his future and his purpose as it stood right now. Confirming his desire for a long-term relationship, he then performed the Spell to Attract Your Ideal Partner (page 69) on a tri-lunar cycle. On the end of the third cycle he met a woman through a friend at a restaurant.

"This woman was someone I wouldn't ever have the guts to approach previously. She was very smart and self-assured, and would not have been interested in just a quick dalliance. I had to lift my game here! I have been learning as I have gone along, but I think the Goddess certainly sent me someone I had to really try hard to match. This is what I asked for in my spell."

Currently, Graham is experiencing the longest relationship he has ever been in, with, according to him, "no end in sight."

So then, what kinds of questions do we need to ask ourselves in order to understand more cleanly and clearly what we really wish to attract in our relationships?

- What has been the nature of our relationships previously, and what have we liked and disliked about these?
- If I am honest with myself, am I aware of any patterns linking my behavior or the kind of people I have attracted in the past, and have these patterns assisted me or hampered me?
- Do I know my vision or purpose at least for the mid-term as a minimum?
- Can I describe easily the attributes of the kind of person I wish to attract?
- Can I describe the nature of the relationship that I wish to attract clearly? For example, I want a lover as opposed to a long-term relationship, or I want a traditional marriage arrangement as opposed to a living-together style partnership.

Once you engage your self-trust and understand what you really want, and can be true to this, attracting this very thing becomes much more easy.

Writing a Vision Letter

The important thing about writing vision letters is that you allow yourself to be fully authentic and truly engaged in the process. This is your life and everything is possible! I have been privileged to read many vision letters and the ones where people have left caution to the wind and written from the heart never fail to move me! It is an incredibly special thing to read a person's deepest wishes, particularly with the knowledge that they are on the way to realizing this vision, often after concealing this even from themselves for most of their lives.

Some Simple Guidelines Before You Start

The process of writing a vision letter should be very fluid and free flowing because we are asking the unconscious mind to take control here and in some ways bypass the filters of the rational mind. Therefore, resist the temptation to edit as you go along, do not reread passages, or correct spelling and grammar. Simply write and continue to write in one session. If you feel a break coming on, make yourself a coffee or eat something, but ensure you get the letter done in one full day.

You may also feel the temptation to edit to fit your current reality. By this I mean the rational mind wishes to denote ideas that may stretch you too much or feel impossible. If you are expressing an idea and you feel the rational mind, try to change this (a common way is for a little voice in your head to interrupt the flow by saying this will never happen, or you can't do this, you don't know how, etc.).

Write the letter in a physical place that you find comfortable, safe, and inspiring. This may be your living room or your favorite spot in nature. Wherever it is for you, it needs to be somewhere that is conducive to the flow of dialogue straight from your unconscious. You can create a feeling of sacred space by lighting a candle, burning incense, or even buying yourself some beautiful nourishing food for breaks—anything that will signal to the unconscious that this is a special time and that it needs to be alert.

Dedicate enough time to write the vision letter. I always suggest to clients that they take a day off work or choose to do nothing else on a weekend but this. If this sounds impossible to you, then you are far too busy!

Vision letters are written in the format of a letter to someone (and it matters not to whom, or if anyone else ever reads it but you), and it is written as if it has already happened. The tense here is very important to the process.

For example, this is the first paragraph of the vision letter written by Graham, the lawyer:

"Dear Mike, I am sitting here on the deck of my boat at dawn and thought I would drop you a line. I am currently anchored offshore from a beautiful island in the Great Barrier Reef. This is the second month of my half-year sabbatical, and boy, I could get used to this! My days are spent island hopping, snorkeling, fishing, and cooking, and I couldn't be happier sharing it all with my new wife."

Graham wrote this in the present tense, although he certainly wasn't taking a six-month sabbatical, didn't have a boat, and hadn't attracted a long-term partner yet, let alone a wife.

Ensure your letter uses lots of descriptive or highly sensate language. Don't just say "I live in a great house with a wonderful partner"—describe it and him or her! Allow your unconscious to have some fun and really go to town on this, but don't get too detailed because it can negate other opportunities. For example, unless you *really* won't settle for a anyone that isn't a blonde, don't specify that specific level of detail. Instead you could say I have a partner who is highly attractive to me physically.

Preparation

Take the phone off the hook, leave your worries elsewhere for the time being, and prepare your space as you feel best.

Gather

Writing materials: paper, pen, or computer
Candle
Matches
Incense

Focus

Open a Power Circle in the usual manner or open a Circle in your preferred way. Be inside your circle when you write.

Say out loud as you light the candle with intent:

Goddess, today I see what is in my heart.
Today allow me to clearly view, not only what I desire,
but what I need, to be at my best.

Today, right here, right now, guide my hand in expressing
what I have always wanted, without limits, without edits.
Allow me to know that nothing is impossible.

Light your incense. Now breathe deeply, and allow any worries or distractions to drop away. This is your time, not anything or anyone else's.

Close your eyes for a moment. Begin to imagine or allow yourself to imagine a life where everything is exactly as you would wish it, a life of contentment, stimulation, and happiness. At the peak of this experience (and you will probably have some images already in your head) begin the letter.

Once you have completed the letter in one sitting, *stop and leave it.* The next day, feel free to correct the grammar or spelling if this is something that is important to you. Now make two copies. Keep one with you and put one away in a sealed envelope.

If you wish to actually read, send, or share this vision letter with anyone do so, but be very selective whom you choose—it should be someone who is supportive and not judgmental of your decisions.

Read the copy that you have kept each night just before sleep for one whole lunar cycle.

At the end of that lunar cycle, make three participatory steps toward your vision, and, if needed, combine with a relationship spell of your choice.

Spell to Attract Your Ideal Partner

This spell is one that I have tried and tested extensively for over a decade,with many hundreds of people, both male and female and of every sexual orientation. Its strength is that it forces you to get very specific about the kind of person you wish to attract at this time, and then leaves some space for the Goddess to co-create with you. There are two important things to remember here.

First, let yourself delve deep into what you really want, just not what you think is possible. Sometimes we edit ourselves when we create our list of attributes, thinking that we are being too fussy or that this will never really happen. Second, be very mindful about participating after the spell. You need to listen with all your senses and be ready to act on instruction! In total, if you ask clearly, you will receive as long as you choose to participate fully.

Allow at least ninety minutes for this spell.

Preparation

Perform this spell on any night where the moon is full or waxing. Ensure the room is comfortable. Ensure that you will be undisturbed. Decide on the location for the spellcraft.

Have your intention clearly in mind or written down. I would also advise you do some pre-thinking about the attributes of your ideal partner.

Welcome the Goddess and thank her for being with you here tonight in this beautiful place.

Gather

Green or white candle

Matches

Charcoal

Herbs to burn on charcoal: sandalwood chips, frankincense resin, bedstraw, or Witches' Grass, snapdragon, dragon's blood

Flame-proof bowl

Symbol of your ideal partner (this can be virtually anything)

Paper and pen

Focus

Cast and open a Circle if you wish. Light the candle with the intent that you wish to attract your ideal partner, dim the lights, and relax.

Take several deep breaths. Imagine breathing in air of your favorite color. As the air travels through your nose and mouth and down into your body, it feels comforting and renewing. It is incredibly pleasant.

There is nowhere more beautiful or sacred than here, right now, in this place, in your body. There is nothing more important than what you are focusing on and what you are intending on doing tonight, for tonight is the beginning of something momentous. Tonight you will be attracting your ideal partner. This person is not your other half, nor will they complete you; they are an individual in their own right, yet they will come freely to you and will recognize that you are someone special and significant.

The Goddess will assist you to co-create this relationship. Welcome her now in your own way.

She now asks what it is about this partner that you so desire? She asks you to describe this person to her clearly, and to speak of them with the lips of your heart.

Take your pen and paper and begin to create a list of attributes that describes your ideal partner. Include as much detail as you can think of, and encompass the areas of personality, relationship type, connection, children, geography, interests, spirituality, physicality, and values. For example:

- I want a male partner for a long-term relationship leading to marriage.
- He will be a confident man, open, loving, and generous with his affection.
- He will be tall, and take care of his body.
- He will be kind-hearted and love animals
- We will travel together and have adventures and share experiences.
- Etc.

Or

- I want a female partner for a loving relationship.
- She will be vivacious, honest, and have a laugh that makes me laugh,
- We will have long, lively, entertaining conversations about everything and nothing.
- We will make love at midnight just because our bodies want to.
- She will be addiction free.
- She will be open to having children with me when the time is right.

This list can be as long as you like. Take your time. Feel free to stop and close your eyes to reconnect with the power of the Universe, and then restart. Remember, make sure you mention positive aspects only, as the unconscious has difficulty discerning negatives—e.g., DO NOT ask for someone who is not mean with their money. Instead ask for someone who is generous.

Building Power

When you have completed your list, read it out loud to the Goddess. Let every word have weight and meaning, and you now should feel confident that this describes the person you wish to attract. Once you have read it, if there is anything else you wish to add to the list, do so now.

Look at the candle flame, or close your eyes and go within. Think about the person you have described. Envision them in whatever way you wish. Hear their voice. Feel their touch, inhale their smell. Imagine yourself doing things with them, from waking up to eating to sleeping to sex. Do this in as much detail as your unconscious provides.

Now be aware of how this makes you feel in your body. This should be very positive!

Now magnify this feeling. Feel it warm you, pulse through you. There is so much anticipation in meeting this person now!

Now light your herbs and incense. Breathe in deeply. As you breathe in, you are inhaling even more attractive power. The Goddess is still with you and validating your choices.

Release Your Intention

Hold your symbol of this person in your hand, and again read out their attributes, prefacing the list by saying:

> *Goddess, great Creatrix, hear my call*
> *This be the person that I desire*
> *This list please take into your hands*
> *And bring him/her to me like a moth to fire*

Read the list out loud with feeling one last time. Then promptly place the list over the candle flame to set it alight and quickly drop into the flame-proof bowl.

As the flames and smoke rise, know that your ideal partner is making their way toward you, Goddess directed. Pass your symbol or object over the smoke. This is now a reminder or talisman of what you have requested. Keep it with you or place it where you will see it many times in one day.

Offer Your Gratitude

Know that the Goddess has heard your intention. Thank the Goddess. Be grateful in the knowledge that all is as you have asked it to be, if it be her will and for the greatest good of all.

Complete the Ritual

Close your Circle. Take the energized symbol or talisman with you. Extinguish and bury any remaining charcoal or herbs/incense in the garden or yard. Ground yourself by eating or drinking something, exercising, or dancing! Celebrate!

Participation

Immediately after you close your Circle ask the Goddess what it is that you need to do to take positive steps toward finding your ideal partner.

Do not try and edit this process. Write down on paper anything that comes to mind, no matter how seemingly insignificant. If nothing comes straight away, sleep on it, and ask that your participatory step is clear to you in the morning. Ensure you follow through on any ideas or messages you get.

Book of Shadows Entries

Chart your progress by recording your feelings, behaviors, actions, and results, paying close attention to coincidences and details, even if they seem insignificant or unrelated at the time.

Remember to date all your entries.

Getting What We Want: Accepting Our Gift

So you're focused and clear about what you really want. You know the style of relationship and the kind of partner you want, and you are aware of the pitfalls and patterns of the past. And you may have even cast your spell for this person.

By sending that strong focus and intention out into the Universe you have started an all-powerful chain reaction that has its ultimate aim in getting you what you have asked for. In short, what you are asked is to step up and move forward into a relationship that is better for you than the ones you've experienced before and one(s) that in its essence is going to give you greater satisfaction, pleasure, and growth. Bottom line, though, you are asking for change—often a *big* change.

And change can be frightening, even if it is exactly as you wanted.

Take the experience of Selene for example. Selene, in her mid-thirties, was in a six-year marriage to Peter. Selene felt most of their problems were caused by an inherent inequality in their relationship, where she felt that she led the relationship in every way, with little connection from Peter. She felt that she had grown over the years but Peter had not, and therefore the gap between them grew ever wider.

"I felt I was at the crossroads of my relationship with my husband and I felt like my next steps were too big a decision for me to make alone. With some consultation from Stacey, I decided to surrender and I asked the Goddess to help me decide what to do. What I needed to do first was get clear about what I wanted moving forward in a relationship. I wrote the list of attributes for the partner I wished to attract, and although it was a fairly simple and straightforward list, I felt it was a deeply honest request. I knew that the Goddess would assist me in attracting a partner with these attributes, and that may well be my husband if he could step forward and meet more of the attributes I knew I needed. I also knew that by creating this list and by working magically around it I had set the course for my own change."

I reminded Selene that by asking for this partner, in her own way she, too, had to step up to meet him equally, wherever and whoever he was. However, at this point she did not realize how much getting what she wanted would affect her.

Stepping up and forward can be a huge point of growth *and* chaos for us.

What happened for Selene was quite rapid.

"My husband did not step up. In fact, he displayed some behavior that convinced me that he did not correlate at all with some of the most important non-negotiable things on my list (and probably never would). I look back now on my entry in my book of shadows and I was bereft. Although it was devastating, I knew, without reservation, that I would have to separate from him. I thought in my weaker moments though that I had asked the Goddess for someone impossible and now I had no one."

Selene was breaking through her old co-dependent bonds with her husband, and although this was extremely healthy for her, it was painful for her to grieve the end of the marriage.

And then something interesting happened. Three months after her decision to break with her husband, the Goddess played out her other side of the bargain. She put David in Selene's path.

"Here was someone who was unmistakably the partner I had been asking for. He embodied almost every attribute on my list! My attraction to him was so deep and strong on so many different levels it was exhilarating, then quickly, totally frightening. I began to get scared that I wouldn't be able to step up and be this man's equal. I felt like I should get out before I was hurt."

So here was this man, everything that Selene had asked for, yet she began to pull away? What gives? Wasn't this like winning the lottery and handing it back? This is a very, very common scenario, and one that we must meet head on or miss the gift that we have asked for.

If we haven't done enough work building our personal foundation,
when we get what we ask for and it involves evolving upwards,
changing for the better big time, we get very nervous about our ability
to sustain that change for any lengthy period of time.

It seems like we have bitten off more than we can chew and, frankly, it feels safer to crawl back to the old safe place from whence we came. Unfortunately, some of us do just that, negating the gift and opportunity to grow that we have asked for and been given.

This is why it is so important to exercise the steps necessary to building that robust personal foundation (including self-knowledge, self-care and self-esteem) and put a firm wedge underneath our new growth so that we can't slip back or at least won't want to for long. Always allow the new gift that you have requested into your life, even if it does completely scare you for a time.

Happily, Selene decided to accept what she had requested.

"I thought one of the best ways to handle my fear about having an equal partner was to communicate in a clear and honest way how I was feeling about it with David. I mean if he was the man I thought he was, he would understand. Over dinner one night I told him how scared I was, how vulnerable I felt, and I have never seen such relief on anyone's face before. He felt exactly the same way! He felt I was this amazing woman who he was very lucky to have and that I would soon tire of him! We both ended up laughing and crying over our spaghetti!"

At the time of this writing, Selene and David have been together for over twelve months and intend to marry this year. They have already collaborated on a business project that has made them over two hundred thousand dollars, and consider each other "equal partners in every sense of the word."

Just imagine what Selene would have missed if she had sent the Goddess' gift back to the refund counter!

Witches' Book of Shadows: Evidence of Growth

When I was a little girl I loved writing diaries—even more so when I was an angst-filled teenager. In fact, the diary from my sixteenth year still survives in my library and it makes interesting reading.

Most of what the sixteen-year-old me had to report I don't actually recall in conscious memory, but my emotional body certainly does. I read about how nervous I felt before my school dance and I know how I no longer would feel that way in a similar situation. I know this on a cellular level through the relief and calm in my body. I read about how excited (and surprised) I was that I won a municipal prize for a painting entered in an exhibition, and I know how similar my feelings would be today if I pulled off the same feat. I study the entry made one July night, wishing with all of my heart to not feel like such an outsider and the me in the here and now sees how different my world is and so grateful that my life is in a place where that is true for me all of the time.

Reading that diary, I am able to see now, by looking back, how the emotional and physical landscape of my life has changed. I have real evidence that things have progressed (or not) through a solid piece of expression.

Witches have been doing the same thing for centuries. We don't call our written record a diary or a journal, but a Book of Shadows.

Witches have always recorded their spells and rituals, their focus and their results, for the benefit of gaining wisdom. Witches believe magic is real and, therefore, reportable. Is it important to see if a certain kind of action you undertake works? Of course!

Witches also create a Book of Shadows to help others as well as themselves. In order to use a successful spell again for the good of someone else, they will record the cause and effect in their personal Book of Shadows. If a spell causes a less than effective result, it is noted through the ongoing information entered over time. If a spell works exceptionally well, this too is noted. The spell can then be offered with confidence when someone else needs a similar solution. Imagine being able to offer tried and tested solutions to others with similar problems. This is the growth of real wisdom, personal power, and confidence. These are the real assets desired in abundance in anyone's life.

Having a Book of Shadows is proof of your participation. There is no use in doing any spell or ritual without taking further action. For whatever reason, many people become fearful to move in the direction they feel they need or want to. They do not listen to the guidance given them, whether it's from their own heart or some oracle message from the Goddess. You must make a move and meet the Goddess halfway. Participation means change.

Starting a Book of Shadows is a sign that you have made a sincere commitment to achieve positive change by using the techniques, spells, and rituals in this book. Documenting your magical journey, and in particular your behaviors and results, is one of the most powerful ways of building success on top of success.

Three Easy Steps to Creating a Book of Shadows

1. Photocopy the following pages as a template, or just download the template for the Book of Shadows that you will find on my website: www.themodernwitch.com.
2. Get something to write with and an intention in mind.
3. Start.

If you have limited access to a computer or if you desire to create a traditional Book of Shadows, get yourself a beautiful blank book or journal. It can be as plain or as elaborate as you like. Make sure you absolutely love the way it looks and then begin to create. Buy some colored pens or a feathered quill if it will make using your Book of Shadows more special. Use my template as a guide if you like. This is your book in which to record what is precious to you—your magical journey of change—so make it as individual as you are.

If you are in a longer-term relationship, you might like to create a BOS together, telling the story of how your relationship grows and changes, and how you have solved problems that have occurred. This can be an incredibly bonding thing to do.

My own book of shadows is a larger size and of a functional design that allows me to add or subtract pages at will. In this way, my book is always growing. I can keep it organized in sections and if I make a messy mistake I can throw a page out with no damage. You could do the same thing inexpensively with a three-ring folder. I enjoy writing my entries by hand, as this seems to further embed them in my mind, but I also often use a computer template, type in what I want, and paste those in with some additional decorations of drawings, photos, or natural objects like feathers and herbs. Whatever the physical format your book of shadows may take, adhere to the outlined headings for maximum benefit.

Creating a Template

The important things to note when completing this template are:

- This is a guide only, but your spells and rituals will be more effective if you follow the five key elements.
- Feel free to get creative with colors, symbols, and drawings. If you are more experienced with constructing spells, cut and paste in your own spell and just fill in the participation sections over time.
- Be extremely honest about your thoughts and feelings as well as your actions. No one sees this BOS but you.
- You may choose to keep your BOS on your computer and create a virtual book of shadows as many modern witches do, or print the template out and create a hard copy BOS.
- Whatever you do, choose the most convenient system for you and one that will enable you to get excited about making regular entries!
- Ensure you are familiar with the sections in this book about moon cycles, consultants, and opening circles before casting.

Book of Shadows Template

Date: _____.

Focus

- What do I want and why, opening circle, collecting tools, planning.
- What do I want?
- Why do I want this?
- When do I want this? What is my time frame?
- Determine if this is important for me.
- A good result for me would look like:
- What magical supplies do I need?
- My shopping/gathering list.
- What phase of the moon would be best for this spell/ritual?
- Timing.
- How do I intend to open the Circle or create sacred space?

Purpose and Intention

- What is the purpose of this spell/ritual and what do I intend to do?
- I need to be specific, concise, and clear.
- The purpose of this spell/ritual is:
- My intention is to:

Raising Power

Generating powerful energy to propel my intention out to the Universe/ Divine. For example: chants, movement, ritual action, recalling past emotions.

Chant

Ritual Actions

Other

Release and Grounding

- How am I going to release the powerful energy I have raised and my intention at its climax point?
- How am I going to get back to my normal space/time/world afterward?
- This spell/ritual calls for me to (smash, pour, exclaim, etc.):

Participation

- What are the first steps toward achieving my purpose and intention?
- I need to think of two or three and be specific.

I will _____ by this date _____.

I will _____ by this date _____.

I will _____ by this date _____.

After completing my spell/ritual I felt:_____

_____.

Results

- Tracking my ongoing participation and success.
- Recording all that is happening in regard to this purpose and intention over time.

Date: _____.

Date: _____.

Date: _____.

Date: _____.

Date: _____.

Date: _____.

Anatomy of a Spell

When I began my first tentative steps into Witchcraft, one thing that bothered me was just how it all worked. How could I trust something to help solve my problems or direct me to something better when I didn't have a firm understanding of what or how it does it? How did this thing called magic direct things so that the world swung my way? I consider myself a creative person, but very rational, so I really needed to sink my intellectual fangs into something other than what seemed at the time lots of mist and smoky curls.

Real magic does have a scientific basis. With quantum physics now putting forward firm theories around some of the ancient principles such as "we are all connected," and "we can influence our own reality," more and more previously disinterested people are going to lean toward discovering more about metaphysical solutions such as the ones featured in this book.

However, I am going to give you a choice. Some people prefer not to know how something like magic works. They just know that things change, and change for the better. They know this happens as they keep records in their Book of Shadows or through the evidence of life changing for the better every day. If you prefer to keep the mystery intact you may choose to skip this next section. Meet me a few pages hence where you will learn some of the traps and obstacles to doing real relationship magic and how to avoid them.

Knowing the miracle of how this works enhances and strengthens the magic and allows me to share its secrets with you. That way, you can learn how to replicate it and weave it for yourself.

The Logic of Magic

Our mind has conscious and unconscious levels—this is a scientific fact. Much of our learning occurs in our unconscious. It is also the place where our dreams, our creativity, our desires, and our motivations develop. Spells and rituals bypass the conscious part of the mind, much like hypnosis and trance do, and send messages to the deeper unconscious. The unconscious then takes these messages and hones in on what you want without your even being aware of it. In other words, what you clearly focus on, especially in your deep unconscious, is what you will work toward and manifest.

The unconscious speaks a language quite different from the conscious. The unconscious loves metaphor, colors, symbols, movement, archetypes, prayer, and storytelling. This is the language of rituals and spells. To get the most out of this language, there are five elements— the grammatical rules, if you like. These elements enable you to reach the power of your unconscious most effectively.

The Five Elements

Strictly speaking, practicing witches observe a variety of different rituals and have a good knowledge of spell craft. What I will present here is the backbone or core elements that make up the anatomy of a spell or ritual. It is important to note they are not specific to a particular tradition. For those of you who are already following a path, feel free to integrate your practices where you see fit.

Most spell craft and rituals are constructed with the same five elements. The ways you express these basic elements is always unique and completely up to your creativeness. These are:

1. FOCUS
2. PURPOSE and INTENTION
3. RAISING POWER
4. RELEASE and GROUNDING
5. PARTICIPATION

Depending upon the purpose of the spell or ritual, energy raising and grounding may or may not be necessary.

Focus

You know that what you put your attention on manifests. Then every action that you take toward making what you want clearer and more focused will bring it closer. In practice, there are certain methods to focus your efforts and intentions. The first step is often to purify your space and yourself. You can create a sacred area by casting a Circle and perhaps arranging an altar in a significant way. Special equipment that is designated only for ritual work can be prepared in traditional ways. An invocation to the Goddess to join the Circle is always offered. However, for those of you new to this work, any preparation for the spell, even if it is making a list of the items necessary and then going shopping for them, helps focus your mind on the purpose and intention of the spell. By focusing, you tell the unconscious that something different is about to occur and to pay attention.

Purpose and Intention

Magic needs direction. Energy also needs direction to be effective and powerful. To do this you need to clearly define and state the reason you wish to perform the magic and what you intend to do with the energy. Similarly, when you begin a relationship of any kind, it would be useful to have an idea about its purpose and your intentions toward the person, whether it is a friendship, a business, a lust, or a love relationship. Without this clarity you are never focused enough to reach your goal or desire.

Feel free to write down your purpose and intention. Do make it short and to the point—no essays here. To be effective, your purpose and intention should be a summary of what you want and why you want it. Although you should be concise and confident, you need not be so detailed that there is little chance for the Goddess to get really creative.

Here is a simple example.

Let's say you want a new house. In a spell, you would not ask for a house that is on a particular street, is white, has a picket fence, green grass, two bedrooms, and a view of apple trees. Instead, what you would ask for is a house that has all the attributes that you are looking for. You would ask for a house that is beautiful, safe, has a garden you love, in a convenient and lovely location, and is spacious enough to accommodate all your needs. You may get your house with the picket fence and green grass—you may not—but what you will get is what you have asked for. This, of course, will be perhaps more than you could have described in detail. You are allowing a cocreation with the Goddess. You will not be disappointed.

Never intend things for others unless you have their permission. This is breaking the Law of Harm None. If you wish to cast a spell on behalf of anyone or include anyone, even if you think it is in their best interests, ask permission first.

These are some of the questions I pose to my clients when they come to me for a spell. As you will see, these questions encourage clients to focus their minds on what it is they really intend.

- What would I like to achieve by performing a spell? Summarize into two or three concise points.
- What would a good result look like to me?
- What do I see as the greatest obstacles to achieving my intention at the moment?
- What is the urgency of this matter to me?

- Am I willing to do my spell outdoors, perhaps in a public place, or would I prefer to keep it completely private?
- Do I have any particular beliefs about spells or rituals that I believe will help or hinder the process?

Raising Power

Even the space shuttle needs a rocket engine to get it into space. Raising natural power is even more powerful than any engineered engine in flinging forth your desire into the Universe. Raising power is the truly magical element of a spell. You will know when you begin to raise power correctly—there is a physical change, and you will always feel it. The physical attributes are different for everyone. You may feel the hairs rise on the back of your neck, you may feel energized, or suddenly feel serene. It is common to feel your hands tingle, your breath pattern change, and to notice your heart beating. The physical attributes are different for everyone, but when raising power you will always feel a surge in emotion.

It has been said that emotions are e-motions: energy in action. This is evident when raising power. Whatever emotional state you were in at the beginning of the spell, that emotional state will change when raising power. It may be amplified or change altogether.

For example, I performed a spell to attract my ideal partner. I had spent quite a lot of time getting clear and working out exactly what I wanted in a love partner and I was really excited and full of anticipation about finally having the opportunity of sending this message out to the Goddess. I created the spell so that it gradually raised the power of this excitement and anticipation to greater levels. My body temperature rose, my heart beat faster, I could feel my body raring to go. I felt beautiful, powerful, and that, with surety, this man would be entering my life sooner rather than later. That sort of increase in energy is physically noticeable and it feels very good. By channeling that energy into the purpose and intention I was working toward, I marked it, set a tattoo of unmistakable focus upon it and my unconscious, and the Goddess took care of the rest.

A witch friend of mine related that she did the same spell, but she ended up feeling very grateful and this caused her to cry tears of joy. This was very powerful for her, and she used this energy to send her intent strongly out into the Universe.

Release and Grounding

You construct spells in such a way that the energy of emotion is raised so that it propels forward the purpose and intention you have. When the energy is at its peak you will feel an irresistible urge to release it—to fling it forth. There will be a moment in raising power when you feel like letting it all out. This is when the unconscious will really sit up and notice that you are serious about this intention. This is usually the point in your spell when you release to the Goddess what it is that you are asking for. It is the climax of the spell. Depending upon the spell or ritual, you may be chanting, blowing out a candle, breaking a bowl, tying a knot, dancing, or burning something. In sex magic, the release is at the point of orgasm. Whatever it is, you will receive a signal that you are releasing your intention to its destination powered by the energy that you have raised.

After you go through the previous three stages and have then released the power you raised, you may feel like you are still carrying excess energy. This can manifest in a feeling of being hyperactive and buzzing. Or, in contrast, you may feel tired and drained. This may develop into a serene, calm feeling or an unpleasant fuzzy feeling. You need to find a way to change the mood and energy flow of the magical plane and return to this reality. This process is referred to as grounding.

Witches traditionally grounded themselves by having something to eat and drink, the "cakes and ale" of the old texts. Witches also chose to ground themselves by uniting with their partner in climactic sex or by masturbation. This enabled them to get back in the body with the bonus of pleasure thrown in. Another traditional grounding technique is to place the hands palms down onto the earth and send the excess energy back to the earth and the Goddess. I love this technique because it improves my garden. Many modern witches choose to ground themselves by having a glass of wine, listening to music on their iPods as they dance round the living room, meditating, running or even gym workouts. I know of one witch who swears that by sucking on a giant gumball she can get back in her body faster than by any other way! Whatever way you choose, the key action here is to rid yourself of that extra raised energy and to stop generating any more by changing your state as quickly as you can.

Participation

Now it's your turn to go out into the world and make things happen. You are cocreating with the Goddess now, so start moving. She doesn't just give that which is magical thinking mentioned earlier. The spell or ritual you have performed contains your focus and intention, and it will be propelled out into the Universe, but very little will happen if you are not traveling along to accept what you have asked for. We need to be reminded to step up in order to receive the better life we have asked for. If you go out into your world and begin to actively participate and move toward your purpose and intention with the confidence that higher forces are working with you, I have no doubt you will experience a higher rate of success. Otherwise it's just smoke and mirrors, isn't it?

Start small if you like—but start. An analogy I like to use is that taking that first step is like tipping over the first domino of a long line. Once that first one falls, there is a knock-on effect of consequences with all the others. You will start a chain reaction of events that will lead you toward what you desire.

Record your progress in your Book of Shadows (learn how, page 79). I cannot emphasize how important this is. You will soon see how what you have focused on is coming to fruition and this only adds to your momentum.

Obstacles to Great Spell Work

The Fear of Getting It Wrong

Most witches remember their first spell or ritual. The first ritual I ever performed was not really a spell, as such.

I decided to celebrate one of the witches' special days, or Sabbaths. I arranged everything well in advance. I made sure I had each and every herb, that I had the right color candles, and that the arrangement of the objects on my altar (a small coffee table) were placed just so. I planned to start when I had the house to myself so that there would be no witnesses, and I took the phone off the hook.

Even after all this preparation, when I began the ritual I could not shake the feeling that I was doing something wrong. It also crossed my mind that if I said something incorrectly that something terrible would happen. I kept imagining that I would conjure up something horrible or get the opposite of what I was asking for—all because I got a couple of words wrong or the candle blew out too early. This feeling is common among first timers and those newer to the Witches Way. In my practice, I ask the client to contact me within a day or so to discuss the spell they have just cast with me. An extremely high proportion mention their fear that they "did not get it right" or "will it still work if this went wrong?"

Allow me to allay your fears.

The Goddess does not care if you remember the exact words. Neither does she care if the herbs do not burn, the flowers get knocked over, or you start to laugh where it says be serious in the spell directions. What does matter is the strength and focus of your intention, the ability to raise power, and your trust in releasing that power. If something goes wrong—like the candle falls over or the herbs blow off, or you forget to bring something—the spell will still work as long as you follow the basic guidelines and speak your words with clarity and intent. Personally, I think the best rituals are the ones where a tiny bit of chaos reigns and often something magical happens that you did not plan for. Just keep those intentions strong as a foundation, trust your own power, and let the Goddess do the rest.

When you read some of the case studies presented in this book, you will learn of a few mistakes that have turned out to be perfect for the results these people were seeking. As for what happened to me that first night, it could have turned me off rituals for life!

I sat down on the floor in front of my altar and lit my candles. I began to read word for word from my ritual notes. I was careful to say everything correctly.

I got a minute or so into the ritual and looked up and realized my notes were on fire! I jumped up and instinctively threw some of the water in the flower vase on them. I was naturally a bit shocked and, in relief, I started to laugh. But this was supposed to be serious! So I slapped my hand over my mouth. The altar (my coffee table) looked totally trashed but I decided to push on. Frankly I had bought all this great stuff for this spell and I was not going to waste it now!

Then the first amazing thing happened. I shut my eyes, focused, and just started talking to the Goddess. I knew what to say even though my prepared notes had literally gone up in smoke. And then the second amazing thing happened.

My dog Indi, who had recently come to live with us, walked quietly over, sighed contentedly, and laid her sizable head on my lap—something she had never done before. So, here I was with no notes, a wet and burnt altar, and a big dog draped over me. Surely I could not have possibly got anything right.

But you know, I did! I received a number of gifts that night that were testimony to how right I did get it. I learned to trust myself. I learned that I had power and it was real. I learned that Indi, like most animals, gets tuned into the energies generated by spells and rituals and can be great company and a useful ally.

I learned that rituals and spells change your life.

Suspending Old Beliefs

There are few of us who know exactly how electricity works, and, unless it is in the explosive shape of a lightning bolt, it is almost always invisible. However, I know it's there as it lights up my home, it's running the laptop I'm using right now, and has just enabled the tea I'm drinking to be boiled. I know there is a law of energy and physics that makes electricity and its harnessing possible, but every day I simply suspend my disbelief that there is nothing there I can see and trust that everything will "just work."

I am asking you to suspend any preconceived ideas or beliefs that you may have around witches and spellcraft that may hamper your flight into magic. Keep an open mind and an open heart. I am requesting that you recognize that there is a law that makes spellcraft work and you must trust that it does.

The most common disbelief that I have encountered is about faith and trust. How can something so simple work in the uber-real world? How do I know that the Goddess exists? Do I have real internal power? I am just asking that you put those kinds of disbelief behind you, one spell at a time.

Fear of What Others Will Say

A number of participants in my case studies have spoken to me about their worry of exposure. "What will my husband/wife/family think of all this?" My answer to that is: They will think what you tell and show them. You may choose to tell them. You may choose to open up to your family and frame your activities in such a way that they are seen just as techniques with which you are trying to better yourself, your business, or to have a bit of fun. You might like to give them a copy of this book to explain what you are trying. Alternatively, you do not need to tell them at all! Witches have hidden their activities from prying eyes for many centuries now, so if you are feeling a bit anxious about what others will think, you can be discreet about your activities for as long as you need to.

Lack of Time

If you tell me, "I do not have time to do a spell" or "I do not have a minute to myself, let alone time to open a Power Circle," I would say your life is too busy and you need to take a good hard look at yourself. Most spells take no more than an hour; opening your first Power Circle takes about forty-five minutes, and then it is recharged in five minutes. If you cannot invest an hour per month to focus on what you want and need in your life, you are wasting time, not saving it.

Let me suggest that you make a diary date with yourself that you do not break for anything. One busy engineer I know, who also happens to be a busy mother of three, actually books her spell time a month ahead in her diary and arranges her work and family life around this. Nothing interrupts this time and she has trained her family to see this as "Mummy's fun time," which is non-negotiable.

Privacy

Yes, if you are casting alone, it is important to situate yourself somewhere where you are unlikely to be disturbed. For some of you, this may be a problem, but humans are ingenious creatures. If you want some privacy you will find it. I have cast in airplane toilets (no candles, of course), in my car (no smoke), cradled in a tree branch (no dancing), and in a friend's garage (roller door down). Again, plan your spells ahead of time and you can plan your privacy.

It is not the end of the world if you are interrupted. It will not take anything away from the end result. Just do what I do: Smile broadly and ask "Can I help you?" If they are not on fire or dying, I tell them I will be with them in thirty minutes or so and make it clear that the conversation is over for now. I have not once had someone press the issue. You can explain what you were doing later to them when you are ready, if you wish.

Going with the Flow

Magic is a wonderfully organic and personal thing. Energy raising is individual and these are suggested guidelines to stick to in a spell, nothing more. Do not feel as though you need to control every element of the ritual. Letting your power mingle with the spell is what makes the magic absolutely yours.

You know now that spells have a clear, proven anatomy that makes them work. If you stick to that strong skeleton, the detailed fleshing out can be as unique as you are, so be in tune with the deeper parts yourself and with the Goddess when you are spell casting. If you instinctively feel like changing a part of the spell as you are performing it, change it. You will *know* when to stop chanting, you will *know* when your power is at its height.

Feel like laughing? Do it.

Like crying? Do it.

Feel like getting up and dancing around? Please do!

Which leads to the subject of *having fun*!

Most people in business and the corporate world can be serious beings indeed. Deadlines, constant pressure, or office politics, just to name a few evils, can get in the way of a peaceful mind and a few good belly laughs. Certainly be mindful of what you are asking for, and be respectful of the all-powerful energies that you are dealing with, but this does not mean you need to be overly heavy and serious all the time. The Witches Way has always been a celebratory way of life, and its joyous nature is certainly a balm to the overworked soul.

Let your mind and body have fun. This is one of the key reasons spellcraft works. You are bypassing your conscious self and targeting your unconscious, which has a sweet love affair with symbols, music, colors, rhyming, trances, intentions, and fun. Whether performing a spell alone or with a group, the fastest way to feel connection is to allow some fun into the proceedings. In fact, it has been my experience that those spells that I have had the most fun creating or the most enjoyment in performing have given me the most prompt results.

Safety Guidelines

Special Safety Guidelines

The following are a few guidelines regarding safety and integrity related to performing spells and being involved in ritual work with others. If you feel safe and know that you are safe, this leaves much more room for great results through clear intent.

As this book is about love, lust, fertility, and relationship, I wish to draw your attention first to some specific guidelines about these subjects.

Free will is the non-negotiable element in spells involving another party. It is a very commonplace request for clients to ask me to cast a spell on someone else so that they will fall in love with my client. It is just as common for a client to also ask that their ex-partner be cursed. Having power means taking responsibility for that power. Real witches will never get involved with specific spells that induce people to fall in love with someone against their will, nor will they curse. There are other very effective alternatives to both, and these are fully explained later in this book. If you are ever tempted, always ask yourself whether you would like someone to cast a spell on you against your will. It may seem an easy decision to just have some fun and cast on someone, but the consequences can be far reaching.

Consensual participation is not only an issue of integrity and intent, but it can be a legal issue. Under no circumstances, unless you have their consent, is it legal to touch anyone in an inappropriate manner. If you are doing a joint ritual with your partner, please explain the ritual in full *prior* to performing it. This way they fully understand what will be happening and why, and it gives them a chance to agree or disagree before commencement. This is particularly important when you decide to undertake Sex Magic or other techniques involving a sexual intent. No always means no.

The issue of being skyclad (unclothed) seems to be a contentious issue wither you are pagan or not. The whole purpose behind being skyclad is to reduce shame, increase trust, and celebrate our humanness. Again, being skyclad is always an optional experience and a choice. If you are doing one of the rituals in this book and it asks for a skyclad experience it is up to you whether you choose to do it this way. In joint rituals, if you or your partner are uncomfortable with the idea of being nude, it is better not to be skyclad until you are ready for it. And a final comment on being skyclad. It does not and will not ever imply sexual promiscuity of any kind. If at any time in your ritual you wish to stop, whether you are skyclad or clothed, do so unreservedly. It is illegal for anyone to touch you in any way, shape, or form without your consent.

If you are casting skyclad, or if those around you may not understand your behavior, do make sure that your privacy is assured. Close the curtains, pull back the blinds, lock the doors. Make sure you don't provide a free show for someone you'd rather not!

As some of you who are interested in conception may well conceive while undertaking some of the rituals, please ensure you use only the herbs and oils I have suggested, and not others that are not safe for pregnancy. I would also ensure that the room is well ventilated should it get smoky and oxygen starved through the burning of incense.

Being skyclad can also mean you have more sensitive areas on which to drip wax or irritating oils. Be extra careful!

General Safety Guidelines

Basic though these may sound, some physical safety guidelines for performing spells are imperative. If you feel safe and confidently know that you are, this leaves you with more energy to send toward your intention.

1. Never leave an open flame unattended. This includes candles. Sometimes it is necessary to leave a candle aflame until it burns down, so put it in the sink, bathtub, or in something completely flameproof. Ensure no children or pets can be exposed to this flame—perhaps by keeping the door locked. It is best to only do these kinds of spells when you can stay attentive.

2. When using charcoal always place it on something heat-and flame-proof like ceramic, glass, or metal. Never leave it on plastic or wood as the charcoal burns at extreme heat and this can damage surfaces.

3. Under no circumstances allow young children or animals access to open flames or matches. You may be in the middle of your spell and completely absorbed while your child may be playing with your matches behind you. Some pets are highly attracted by flames and some of the herbs you may be using. While I love my animals around when I am casting, I only allow them near if the candles are off the floor where they cannot burn themselves. The herbs, when burning on the charcoal, get extremely hot and a few sets of curious whiskers have gotten singed by the heat.

4. Note that some of the herbs and oils used in spellcraft are poisonous if swallowed, so do not allow humans or pets to eat them. Even those that are safe to drink in teas or to eat can be dangerous in high doses or in smoke if you are pregnant. Always err on the safe side and ask a professional herbalist, aromatherapist, or medical doctor if you have questions.

5. Keep some air flowing through your space at all times, even if it is cold outside. Candles and incense do smoke and can disrupt the level of oxygen in the room. You need to be super aware, not red-eyed, sleepy, and smoky.

6. Do not consume alcohol or recreational drugs while performing spells. Witches do not need outside influences to fly! You need to be completely clearheaded and aware of what you are experiencing and what you are asking for. You do not need any substance that may block or alter your natural magic experience.

7. Some of the spells suggested in this book are extremely relaxing and take you deeply into your unconscious. It is tempting to relax that one stage further and fall asleep. Do not do it if you are in the bath or in a public place where it could be unsafe.

One last point. A few spells in this book mention creating a talisman.

A talisman is a little like a charm as it is an object into which we release and store a certain kind of focused energy. Is important that no one else touch your talisman but you. Although a small brush of the fingers will not make much difference, it is important that the energy you have created goes only to you, and that no one else adds their energy to the talisman.

I now invite you to begin your exciting and safe journey into the world of real magic and real results!

Sensual Consultants

No matter how accomplished we are, we can never hope to know everything, and no matter how able we are, a balanced person can identify and ask for support when they need it. In business, it is common practice to use consultants, people who have a particular set of expert skills that we require, but may lack to get a job done. In our private lives we can call upon experts to assist us with particular obstacles—anyone from relationship counselors to sex therapists and even a great lingerie designer!

Similarly, in the Witches Way, when you want to increase the strength of your spells, need some expert advice, or need to draw upon energies or attributes you may not have at the time, you can call on your consultants. These are powerful aids and helpers that instruct you and enable you to achieve your intention more fully. Within the context of love, lust, relationships, and fertility I like to call these sensual consultants.

Herbs, Woods, Oils, and Flowers

The huge amount of information available about herbal lore surrounding love, lust, and fertility is mind-boggling, but also interesting and fun. Since herbs, woods, oils, and flowers were often the first and only line of defense against disease and other maladies in the past, most cultures have some kind of herbal history. Although some of those remedies seem so light-hearted, many are now proven scientifically to have some effect. From culinary purposes (don't worry about garlic breath as it's a powerful aphrodisiac and blood heater) to plants that have a direct healing effect on the body and even particular organs, many of us could not get through a month without being exposed to some benefit from these kinds of consultants. Examples of this are many: St. John's wort is a popular remedy found in almost every health food store and praised in clinical trials as a contemporary treatment for depression and melancholy. For those wishing a healthy pregnancy, squaw vine as a hormone regulator and raspberry leaves as a uterine tonic are also well known. Mandrake (*mandragora officinalis*), an extremely powerful and popular plant used in Witchcraft over the centuries, is particularly interesting.

Mandrake is a highly poisonous plant if used incorrectly and is a close relative of the nightshade family. Incorrect use could result in sickness, delirium, and death. Its key active ingredient is a muscle relaxant and so the combination of a muscle relaxant and the ability to raise the body temperature in the right low dose would obviously be a good start for an aphrodisiac. The root of the plant is the part that is used most as it resembles a naked human body and Witches often chose them for their shape for particular workings. The mandrake root is shaped like a male body, while woman drakes are shaped more like a woman's body. Female witches would often chose to work with the "woman drakes" if they were casting a spell for a woman. Male witches would do the opposite. Fertility and lust were said to increase under the magical enchantment of mandrake. It was used in a variety of ways, from placing a root in the bed to secure a fertile night, to dissolving a tiny particle of powdered mandrake in a cup of wine to secure a lengthy, wild session of love making. Although mandrake was much maligned over time, with the plant being banned during the Inquisition as something that only witches cultivated, it was modern medicine that explored its usefulness again. If we look at the American Association of Anesthetists' coat of arms, we will see two plants, the opium poppy and the mandrake. Mandrake was used in some of the earliest modern anesthesia, although replaced today by far less dangerous and more predictable compounds.

Being a witch a thousand years ago meant that you would need a fine knowledge of herbal medicine. There was great respect for these particular plants—wisdom on how best to plant and propagate them was vital to a witch. Herbs and other magical plants were so precious that only a boleen (a special knife used only for harvesting the herbs), was used. Laws in most countries today ensure that only trained herbalists, naturopaths, and medical practitioners can prescribe botanical remedies for internal use. I am not a medical practitioner, and cannot legally advise you to take any herbal, wood, or flower derivatives internally or topically for health reasons. However, I want to introduce herbs to you in the context of how they can work for you within magical rituals and spells for proven results when it comes to love, sex, and fertility.

Modern witches use oils, herbs, woods, and flowers as sensual consultants to help them focus on increasing personal energy, and empowering themselves and their spells. Witches believe that each plant has an inherent signature energy that can be used in synergy with the personal energy you are raising. Many herbs, flowers, and oils are used for healing, and some are used for specific purposes such as to relax or connect, but all evoke some response. The method with these consultants is to call upon the right one to assist in solving a particular problem. For example, I may suggest the combination of rose petals, jasmine essential oil, and cinnamon bark as a blend for the bath. The rose petals are a traditional symbol of love and the fragrance is both stimulating and relaxing, the jasmine is a powerful aphrodisiac and relaxant (and also a real treat for the skin), and the cinnamon bark wakes up the mind and heats the body. This combination of relaxants, powerful aphrodisiacs, and clarifiers for the mind makes for a powerful result just before bedtime! Or, as I often prefer, I may suggest burning on a charcoal a selection such as frankincense resin, angelica, and catnip to evoke the energies of these substances and stimulate the unconscious with an unforgettable and anchoring scent.

As modern witches, we can really use our imaginations to capture the wisdom and energies of these consultants. I know a witch who slips little sachets of aphrodisiac and peace-inducing herbs into the pillowcases on her bed so that she can help to ensure either a great night in bed or a great night's sleep—or both! You may choose to sprinkle them under your bed or over your doorway if you wish to entice that new date to take it one step further. You may carry a potion made of the oils and flowers that attract love or lust in your handbag when you hit the town. You could dip a ring or earrings in aphrodisiac oil, transforming them into talismans, and waft that energy around with you. All are new ways steeped in the old ways!

Herbal Consultant Table

Herbal Consultant Legend:			
Code: Part	**Code: Part**	**Code: Part**	**Code: Part**
F: Flower	N: Nut	R: Root	W: Wood
H: Herb	O: Oil	S: Stem	V: Various

Name	Part	Wisdom
Acacia	H	Money, love, protection, psychic powers
Agrimony	H	Protection, peaceful sleep
Angelica	H	Banishes hostility from others, protection, healing, warming
Ash	W	Expansion of horizons, healing, strength, prosperity
Azalea	F	Hidden emotions, secrets
Basil	H	Love, exorcism, wealth; conquers fears of stepping up
Bay Leaf	H	Protection, psychic powers, healing, purification, strength, and endurance
Birch	W	Cleansing, health, wisdom, new beginnings, lunar workings, protection of the young
Bladderwrack (Seaweed)	H	Protection against accidents or illness, especially at sea, sea rituals, wind rituals, action, money, psychic powers
Borage	H	Aids the expression of sorrow, grief, and strength
Cactus	F	Protection, purity
Calamus	W	Healing, protection, helps bind long-distance lovers
Caraway	S	Protection, passion, health, wisdom, mental powers
Catnip	I I	Love, beauty, happiness in the home, fertility, appeal, cat magic
Chicory	H	Invisibility in hostile situations, removing obstacles, receiving favors, melts frigidity both mentally and physically
Chili	F	Heats up waning relationships, brings problems to a head
Cinnamon	O	Spirituality, success, healing powers, psychic powers, money, passion, and love
Clover	L	Luck in love, happiness
Devil's Shoestring	G	Wealth and protection
Dragon's Blood	H	Love, magic, protection, dispels negativity, increases male potency
Eucalyptus	WO	Clarity, strength
Fenugreek	S	Attraction, seduction

Name	Part	Wisdom
Fig	FRW	Wisdom, creativity and creation, fertility, harmony, and balance
Frankincense	RO	Worth, psychic powers, prosperity
Garlic	H	Aphrodisiac, protection, and healing, banishing negativity, passion, warming, and toning
Guinea Pepper	H	Dispels negativity
Hempseed	S	Marriage divination
Honeysuckle	F	Money, psychic powers, protection
Jasmine	F	Fertility, lust, seduction
Juniper	HW	Protection against negative forces, love, banishing negativity, health, increases male potency, purification
Lady's Mantle	H	Conception, restoration of natural menstrual cycle, protection
Lavender	H	Love, protection (especially of children), quiet sleep, long life, purification, happiness, peace
Lemon Balm	H	Calming, purification
Licorice	R	Good luck, cleansing, attraction
Lotus/Water Lily	FR	Protection, reveals secrets
Lucky Hand Root	R	Employment, luck, protection, money, safe travel
Mandrake	R	Aphrodisiac, protection, love, money, fertility, health
Marigold	F	Protection, prophetic dreams, legal matters, increases psychic powers
Mint	H	Money, love, increasing sexual desire, healing, banishing
Mugwort	H	Fertility, female sexual organ tonic, healing
Oak	W	King of the waxing year and sacred tree of the Druids, supreme tree of knowledge, power and independence, confidence, prosperity, and potency
Olive	WO	Peace and reconciliation, forgiveness, healing, fertility
Orange	FOW	Love, abundance
Passionflower	F	Sacrifice, peace, quiet sleep, friendship
Pennyroyal	H	Female stimulant
Pine	OW	Healing, fertility, purification
Poppy	F	Fertility, rest, money, luck, invisibility
Raspberry Leaf	FL	Fertility, uterine tonic, flexibility
Rose	FO	Aphrodisiac, beauty, connection, long-lasting love

Name	Part	Wisdom
Rosemary	H	Love, passion, increases mental powers, banishes negativity and depression, beauty.
Rowan	W	A tree of the White Goddess of the Celts, domestic protection
Rue	H	Female lust
Saffron	FS	Lust, fertility, "higher love," money.
Sage	H	Long life, wisdom, protection, purifies, fertility
Sandalwood	W	Protection, healing, banishes negativity, masculine strength
Sarsaparilla	H	Love, attraction
Snake Root	H	Luck, money
Snapdragon	F	Keeping secrets, finding what is lost
Southern Wood	W	Masculine energy, lust, love
Squaw Vine	H	Feminine, balance, hormonal healer, solidness
St. John's Wort	H	Health, power, protection, strength, love and fertility, divination, happiness
Sunflower	FS	Developing potential, fertility, confidence, self-esteem
Tansy	H	Spring equinox herb, health, long life, conception/pregnancy
Tiger Lily	F	Purity of spirit, wildness
Valerian	H	Love, love divination, quiet sleep, purification, protection against outer hostility, inner fears and despair
Vervain	L	Lust, seduction
Violet	F	Modesty, secrecy, uncovering hidden talents
Walnut	WN	Intelligence
Willow	W	Traditional Goddess tree, a moon tree, intuition, moon magic, healing, making wishes come true, increasing psychic energies, empathy
Witch Hazel	H	Mends broken hearts and relationships, finds buried treasure and underground streams, protection
Witchbane	WH	Protective, transformational, attracts good energy where there was a void of negativity
Witches Grass	H	Attraction, intensity, happiness, unhexing
Yarrow	H	Courage, love, psychic powers, divination, assures long-term love, banishes negativity
Yucca	H	Transformation, change, protection, purification

The handy table on the previous pages lists the various properties of some of the most effective herbal consultants that specialize in love/lust relationships and fertility. Feel free to combine as you will, but take care with the essential oils and the respective dosages—usually a few drops each in a tablespoon of carrier oil is enough, and always check the contraindications—especially if you are pregnant or taking medication. Herbs can be obtained through witchcraft supply stores, fresh from most produce shops, or better still by planting a garden of your own. By using these green energies you can be connected to the millions of women and men who have come before you, each respecting and utilizing the benefits of these amazing consultants.

The Moon

The moon has always been one of the strongest symbols of the Goddess and of witches. The way the moon travels over the sky each night is a keen reminder of the power of change and of cycles. For me, even the simple action of looking up and connecting with the moon each night, even if it is cloudy, links me directly with my own power as a woman and certainly with my powers of creation. Each full moon I often choose to celebrate by performing one of the oldest Goddess-based rituals, that of Drawing Down the Moon. This is a simple ritual typically involving a reflective bowl and athame, where the moon is reflected in the water of the bowl and the reflection drawn down to either be used to anoint one's body or to be drunk. This ritual is also very special to me as I always feel that I am connected to every woman or man throughout time who has done just the same thing: looked up at the moon in wonder and gratitude and allowed her to unite us.

The Witches Way sees the moon in three main aspects traditionally, and these stages describe stages in the natural life of any goddess. The three stages are that of maiden, mother, and crone. Each of these three stages is different energetically and symbolically.

The maiden aspect of the Goddess is waxing, growing in size and power in the sky after the dark moon. The mother aspect is when the moon is at its creative peak, at full moon. As she diminishes and grows darker, we see the face of the wise elderly crone. These three stages reflect our own life cycle closely. We are born and grow, we mature and create (not necessarily children), and we will eventually grow older and die.

The idea of working with the moon as your consultant is to go with the flow of these cycles, not against them. As you track yourself against the changing face of the moon, you will begin to know when you feel high or low energy, when you feel introverted or extraverted, when you wish to create or lie fallow to refill your well. Knowing which moon and which aspect to use to further strengthen particular intentions is useful wisdom.

Waxing Moon

This is when the moon is growing in size toward the full moon from the half moon. It is in the maiden stage, growing toward fullness and full power.

Waxing moons are perfect sensual consultants:

- When you want to grow a relationship or new attraction
- For all attraction desires
- For first date hopes
- For the beginning of joint projects
- When you need your personal energy or health to grow stronger
- For protective spells

Full Moon

When the moon is completely full in the sky, large and round with no edge shadows, it is considered full. Being at the peak creatively it represents her at her most powerful.

Full moons are the traditional time to do many magical workings and are particularly good for:

- Deciding to change your current level of relationship, e.g.: from single to being partnered
- Asking for assistance for fertility
- Asking for specific money and prosperity goals
- To boost your faith at any point of your endeavors
- Using sex magic

- Dedicating yourself to a relationship or both of you dedicating your-selves
- Legal wins

Waning Moon

This is when the moon is diminishing from full moon to half moon. It looks smaller in the sky. The energy is changing from full and creative to a more introverted, self-examining feel and this is considered the Crone aspect.

Waning Moons are perfect consultants:

- For when you wish to rid yourself of a behavior, belief, or experience that no longer serves you in particular, or fear of any kind
- For gradually going within to discover more about yourself
- When you wish to improve your self-care by getting rid of a bad habit: smoking, overeating, too much TV
- For invisibility and cloaking
- Removing obstacles

Dark Moon

This is when you cannot see the moon in the sky or where you see her circular shape but covered by the earth's shadow. Dark moon is an extremely powerful consultant, just as powerful as her more extraverted sister, the full moon. There are some stories about the dangers of casting when there is no moon in the sky, these beliefs reflecting the darker nature of this part of the cycle and certainly a belief around more uncontrollable forces being evident. Personally, whatever the phase of the moon, it is a natural part of a whole cycle. There is no good or bad about this cycle, just degrees of usefulness. I may be biased, as I was born on a dark moon, but I have always found dark moon a very restful, unchaste time where I can use the energy to spring clean my life.

It is also important to note that dark moon is the bridge between death and rebirth and, as such, can be an extremely powerful consultant for:

- Cutting the cords (getting rid of relationships that no longer serve you
- Letting an old life stage die and moving onto the next; moving from one relationship to another, divorce

- Uncovering your vulnerabilities and moving forward to transform them into strengths
- Turning your awareness inward to discover more about yourself and your behaviors
- Looking at and accepting your shadow side
- Personal purpose work—moving from the darkness of the unknown to the light of the revelation of being on purpose

Tri-Lunar Spells

In *Witch in the Boardroom* I discussed the effectiveness of what I call Tri-Lunar Spells. This is a progressive pattern of three Witchcraft techniques over three moon cycles. I normally ask the client to work a spell each moon cycle for three moon cycles during the time of the moon cycle that best suits achieving their intention. This way, the client has time to see how the results are playing out for them and they can then boost, change, or enhance the energy with another spell during the next lunar cycle if needed. This is particularly important in the areas of love/lust relationships and fertility, as things do change quite rapidly at times. For example, if we were running some spells to achieve conception, and the couple achieved this on the second tri-lunar cycle, we would definitely be changing cycle three to a Welcoming Baby spell!

The client then tracks their results in their Book of Shadows, which makes it easy to decide what they need for the next spell. Within three moon cycles there is always a clearly read result. This pattern also takes away a lot of the temptation of inappropriate magical thinking and brings us into thinking magically and participating fully.

Tides

The tides are linked closely to the movement of the moon and, therefore, we can also use them as powerful consultants. Just as the moon's various phases direct energy, so does the pull and flow of the sea.

High Tide or Tide Coming In

- When you are asking that something increase for you
- Asking for natural flow

- Building partnerships
- Asking to move forward with something or something to move toward you—attracting a new relationship
- Increasing intimacy
- Attracting fertility and a child

Low Tide or Tide Receding

- When you wish to diminish something that is a barrier
- Cutting cords
- When you wish to reduce the power of problem people—negativity, resentment
- Great for saying good-bye to bad habits or old patterns
- Shame reduction
- Asking for the natural flow of rest, relaxation, and pause
- Avoiding conception

Animal Consultants

Animals, in particular cats, hares, and stags, have been linked with witches and the Craft over the centuries. This linking, like other misconceptions propagated against the old religion, is often negative. These creatures were called familiars. Within the craft of the wise, animals are used to lend their particular energies to magic. They give us a deeper connection to the powers of the natural world.

Familiars are animals with which you have a particularly close relationship, similar to the way in which Native American tribes use animal totems. These familiars guide, teach, warn, and protect.

Part of the core of Native American beliefs and those of the Australian Aborigine are the borrowing of attributes of animals to help achieve goals. Both these great indigenous cultures utilize shapeshifting. Shapeshifting is the taking on of the body and characteristics of another animal or being. Native Americans believe that each animal has a power, a particular medicine or essence, to help heal. It is common practice in earth-based spirituality, from the Amazon Indians to the Inuit, to have a special animal akin to a familiar.

Most modern witches do not normally believe that they actually become the animal cell by cell, but believe instead that they can incorporate the attributes needed to achieve a particular task. They believe that animals are natural teachers and their inherent qualities can assist in carrying out intentions and raising power in spells.

Just as the ancestor witches used the animals' energies from the forests or land in which they lived, modern witches in the comfort of their bedrooms can still do the same today. For example, you may be feeling tired and listless, but truly wanting to feel more energetic to connect with your partner. It is very easy to let intimacy slide with the consistent and persistent wearing down of our energies by the day to day assault of life. You need energy, sensuality with a good dash of playtime, to help you break out of your tired state. Why not call upon an animal to help who embodies those qualities? The cat naturally embodies the attributes that you lack in this situation. What if you and your partner have had a fight and you are finding it hard to work through or forgive what has been said. You could try frog energy (cleansing and rebirth) or even dog energy, which promotes a loyalty and solidness.

One of my favorite personal totems for love and relationships is the hare or rabbit. When I was a little girl, my grandmother took me on a magical journey to discover my totem animal. I didn't know what she was doing. I just thought it was a bedtime story where she was asking me to imagine a little more than usual! I discovered something that night that I have never forgotten. I discovered that my totem animal was a hare. At the time I thought, boy how boring! I want a cool animal like a lion or a big bear. But no, the hare was what I saw—his pelt shiny in the sunlight and his great whiskers twitching in the breeze. I remember answering my grandmother when she asked me who was there. I said "Oh, Gran, it's only a rabbit." My grandmother laughed out loud and said, "Oh, darling, it's ONLY a rabbit!"

You see the basis of my grandmother's amusement was that rabbits or hares are found in many cultures, the animal that all others are born from. Rabbits have also been associated as witches' animals or familiars, due to their alignment with fertility and creativity. I use rabbit energy when I wish to create a different situation, and when I want to come up with a new solution to a difficult problem. Rabbit energy is also wonderful for increasing personal fertility or resetting a *wonky* menstrual or androgynous cycle. I often combine rabbit energy with goddesses that favor them, such as Artemis and Eostre, further strengthening and focusing my intentions and connecting me with the power of both worlds. Frankly, there is nothing wrong with adding a little rabbit energy to any bedtime activity!

You can incorporate an animal consultant into some of your spells and rituals to increase the power and personal potency of your magic. Instructions on how to call the individual essence of the animal into your spells and rituals are outlined as well as a special visualization on how to find your own familiar.

Below is a table listing some of the animals and their attributes that you may find useful in business situations. There are real animals and mythical animals from which to choose, including those with which you have an instant connection. One small proviso, though—do be mindful in combining animal consultants. I wouldn't imagine that snake and rat energy or cat and dog energy at the same time would bring much but distraction and chaos!

Animal Consultant Table

Animal	Wisdom
Ant	Patience and forethought
Bandicoot	Decision-making, honesty
Bear	Being prepared, invulnerability, strength
Beaver	Home building, industriousness, vigilance, and peacefulness
Butterfly	Transformation, new beginnings
Cat	Energy, sensuality, play, protector, independence
Chameleon	Mastering change, transformation, sexual games of transformation
Cougar	Fury, remorselessness, cunning, hunting and seeking, freedom, power
Chicken	New beginnings, home, fertility, friendship
Dog	Loyalty, companionship, willingness to follow through, solidness
Dragon	Conscious awareness of past patterns

Animal	Wisdom
Elephant	Remover of obstacles and barriers, fertility, mothering
Elk	Stamina, strength, speed, sensual passion
Fox	Fun, cunning, slyness, stealth, and wisdom
Frog	Cleansing, initiation, transformation, and rebirth
Goat	Sacrifice, mischief, fertility
Gorilla	Communication through action
Hare	Fertility, transformation, quick thinking, strengthening and intuition, traditional witch's animal
Horse	Power, surrender, feminine freedom
Kangaroo	Birth, abundance, leaps of faith
Kookaburra	Happiness, optimism, protecting the true self
Lion	Pride, relaxation, strength, courage, and energy
Owl	Discernment, swift and silent, wisdom, our shadow side, freedom
Parrot	Developing skill, imitation, mockery, thinking carefully before you speak, and guidance
Peacock	Visualization, dignity, warning, self-confidence
Phoenix	Rebirth and spiritual growth, strength, and renewed energy
Polar Bear	Clarity, intuition, self-trust
Porcupine/Echidna	Innocence, trust, mind your own business
Raven	Magic, wisdom, eloquence, and divination
Red Panda	Unexpected fierceness, versatility, agility
Reindeer	Male potency, male power, and stamina
Seahorse	Balance of the sexes, transformation
Skink	Lust, forward motion
Skunk	Interconnectedness, dreams
Snail	Reputation, courage, willpower, self-respect
Stag	Taking it easy, stress-free, masculine power, hunter
Sugar Glider	Trust, surrender, yes!
Tamarin	Preciousness, cherishing what you have, curiosity
Tiger	Keen scent, grace, swiftness, gentleness
Unicorn	Unexpected lessons, power, energy, no procrastination
Vulture	Unconditional love, goodwill, fame, prosperity, gentleness, and purity
Wolf	Natural cycle of death and rebirth

Find Your Animal Consultant Meditation

This meditation has been passed down through my family. It is special to me. This is a great meditation to record on tape for yourself or for your children. It includes a shapeshifting element.

Begin

Lay on the floor or bed. Ensure that you are warm and comfortable. Close your eyes and center yourself.

Breathe deeply and slowly. Feel yourself breathing into the floor. Beginning with your big toe, flex and relax each and every part of your body slowly, one by one. Allow yourself to feel the muscles and bones stretch as you relax. Visualize all the stress and tension running out of them. Even imagine your hair stretching and relaxing. You may notice that some places of tension or that some worries that you have keep popping up. Notice them and set them aside to come back to later.

Now, imagine you are lying on a bed of the softest grass. Every breath relaxes you deeper and deeper onto the grass. It is unbelievably soft. Like ribbons of satin. You are so, so relaxed and comfortable. You can feel the warm sun on your face and body. Mmmm. You can hear the sound of a small creek or river. The soft babbling is making you even more relaxed. You can see the creek. You stand and walk down to the bank. You are barefoot and the grass is soft against the bottoms of your feet. The water you have now reached is cool and sparkling. Bend down and drink from it if you wish. It is so fresh and clean. How delicious!

Now, it is time to leave behind those tensions and worries that you noticed before. You are going to put them in the river. It is safe to do so. Watch as the pure energy of the water washes your problems and your stress away. Watch them being carried far away from you by the current.

Now, you are ready to meet your guide. Notice that to one side is a path that you did not see before. Follow it. As you walk, notice that there are many sounds and smells around you. Take in the whole vista of the earth, of the water, and of the sky. Take your time and enjoy this as these are your kindred, your sisters and your brothers. Continue to walk along the path.

The path is now starting to enter a forest. As you walk the canopy is getting thicker and thicker, blocking the sunlight. There are eyes of all shapes and sizes watching you from the shadows. Some are large. Some small. It is much quieter now. You can hear the sound the wind makes as it rustles through the trees.

Notice how you are feeling. Are you afraid? Are you calm? Are you excited? What are you feeling?

Continue walking, the path is still clear for you. There is nothing here that can do you harm. You are safe.

Ahead, you see some light. You are coming out of the forest now into a clearing. You are in a circular area surrounded by trees, rocks, and water. The sun is shining here and when you look up the sky is boundlessly blue.

Sit at the edge of this Circle. You are here to meet someone.

Ask: Come.

Will you come?

Now wait. Look around, above and below, for signs of your guide.

Ask again if necessary.

I am here. I am waiting. Will you come?

Take your time, there is no hurry.

You will see your guide or guides. They will enter the Circle.

Notice its appearance, its special strengths, and its markings. How does it move? Is it making any noise? Staying seated, will it approach you? Will it allow you to touch it? How close can you get?

If your guide welcomes you to touch it, then gently stroke it, talk to it, and play with it. Take your time. This is an important time.

Does your guide have a message for you at this time? Listen. If so, thank your guide. If not, know there may be one at a later time.

If your guide seems willing, ask if you could become one with it, if you can shapeshift with your guide. If the answer is no, accept this.

If you feel shapeshifting is allowed, look into the eyes of your guide, and begin to see what it would see, from its height, from its viewpoint.

Listen now for your guide's heartbeat. Breathe deeply and hear yours. The two rhythms are different at first, but now slowly they are moving to one rhythm. Your bodies now are moving toward each other, closer and closer, until suddenly you are inside the skin of your guide. Feel the power of the muscles inside that body. Stretch! Move! Experience how different it is from yours.

Begin to hear what it may hear. Perhaps it hears more than you and you can hear the tiniest whisper of leaves brushing together.

Smell what it can smell.

If you feel it is allowed, move around, run, fly, and jump as your new shape. How does it feel? What possibilities are there in this body?

When you are ready, choose to venture back to the Circle. It is now time to take back your human form. Say your name and begin to visualize your guide outside of your body.

Thank your guide. Say your good-byes. Again take your time. Now is the time to leave a small gift. This could be a piece of food, shelter, anything you think your guide will appreciate.

Always know you can come back to this place whenever you wish and meet with the guide you have met, or any other, who has a message for you.

Leave the Circle by the path and walk back the way you have come. If you wish to pick up any of your stress and problems at the river, do so, but you are probably feeling so relaxed and secure that they can stay there.

When you are ready, lay down again on your bed of soft grass. Begin to wake up every part of your body one part at a time until you have surfaced in this world again. Say your name three times out loud and ground yourself further should you need to.

Feel blessed if you met your consultant and/or guide today! Take heed of their message and their medicine.

If you did not meet your guide this time, know that you have established the path to the place where you can meet them another day. Guides will appear when they are ready.

Gods and Goddesses

The Goddess has many faces and takes many forms. Just as each of us on this earth is different, it seems there is a god and/or goddess for everyone. The Goddess has always appeared in a form to which we can relate. An African goddess is dark-skinned, a Greek goddess is dressed in a traditional column dress of the ancient time, and a Native American god may be half animal and half man. For mothers, she is a mother. For warriors, she is a warrior.

Eons ago, these different aspects began to become individualized and what we call pantheistic. Most of us studied the Greek or Roman myths in school or at least saw movies that featured the Pantheon, or family of gods and goddesses such as Athena and Zeus, Apollo and Hera, Aphrodite and Venus, and their infamous children such as Hercules. Equivalents are found geographically and historically worldwide: Isis and Osiris, Vishnu and Kali, and Jesus and the Virgin Mary. As we all have complex personalities and resonate to different paths, so too, does the Goddess.

Witches believe that the Goddess/God lives in us. We may choose a particular face of the Goddess to deepen our connection with her, to strengthen our faith and to overcome obstacles blocking our way. When I feel clear about the nature of a problem I can really relate it to a particular face of the Goddess rather than to the all-encompassing power of the Goddess. I will call upon the specific wisdom and aspects that I know that Goddess has for me.

Every day I see the power that results in calling upon these consultants. I have one friend who uses the wildly sexual Freya when she wishes to get in the mood with her partner after a hard day's work has drained her libido. I have another friend who uses the creative Brigid to help her pick out the perfect outfit to wear when she is going on a date.

You may find you already have a favorite god or goddess. You may have loved a mythical story as a child. Or you may have seen one of those classic 1950s films like *Hercules* or even television shows such as *Xena, Warrior Princess*, where the gods and goddesses are featured. However they have come to your notice, there is something about them that struck a cord in you.

Jung referred to this phenomenon as archetypes. Jung suggested that there is a collective wisdom of all mankind that is stored in each of our unconscious. This deep wisdom has been passed down through all geographical places and ages. Modern witches should be aware of the gods and goddesses that strike deep connections within them. These are often signposts from the Goddess to the forward path you should take or as a model for how you can more successfully and fully live your life.

In *Witch in the Boardroom* I wrote about how as child I was transfixed by a perfume bottle featuring Artemis, the goddess of selfhood. Today Artemis has been a huge influence on my choosing to find and continually honoring my own Self and its purpose. The ability to not give myself away and to know myself for the best chance of success has been a strong theme in my adult life.

I thought that perhaps Artemis would be my only patron goddess, but as an adult witch I have found two others. One, the goddess Sekhmet who has many faces but who I understand and invoke as the goddess of healthy anger and purification, seemed to just be everywhere once I set an intention for what I needed to overcome some obstacles in my life. She was in a book someone gave me, she was on a card that I pulled, she was featured in a lovely poem I read on a site I just chanced to skim. She seemed everywhere, and this is what true oracles are if we have the eyes to see them. I decided to create a ritual to invoke her, using fire, which she loves (lots and lots of candles), and for my own safety I tried all this from a warm fragrant bath with the waters colored her favorite hue, red.

Sekhmet represents the ability to express somewhat unfashionable emotions like anger and rage in a safe way. Her mythology delves into destruction, fury, and the flip side of this, purification. Her alliance with red and fire means that sometimes we need to walk through the fire to get what we want, even if we lack the courage to do so. Sometimes we need to express what seems incredibly uncomfortable or even spiritually painful to allow our old crusty skin to be burned away and our tenderness, openness, and love of life to return. My first invocation of Sekhmet allowed me to see that walking through the fire to get to a better place seemed scarier than it actually was when I did it. By having the courage to walk through a wall of flame that she created in my mind, only to be embraced lovingly in her arms on the other side, meant that my fears really were only illusions and that I would be protected. I know this fierce Cat-Headed Goddess is there to purify me and allow me my full range of healthy emotion whenever I feel encumbered by unexpressed anger or fear. This expression enables me to move forward in my relationships rather than hold grudges and unconfirmed fears.

God Consultant Table

Legend for the God and Goddess Tables:			
Code: Origin	**Code: Origin**	**Code: Origin**	**Code: Origin**
A: African	E: Egyptian	Ir: Irish	Pe: Persian
Ba: Babylonian	G/R: Greek/Roman	J-C: Judeo-Christian	P: Phoenician
Bu: Buddhist	Ha: Hawaiian	M: Mayan	S: Sumerian
Ce: Celtic	H: Hindu	N: Norse	SL: Slavic
Ch: Chinese	I: Inca	NA: North American	Y: Yoruba

God	Origin	Wisdom
Apollo/Apollo	G/R	Wise strength, leadership, legal matters, inquiry, curiosity
Ares/Mars	G/R	Confrontation, fertility, ideas
Balarama	H	Strength, fertility, ideas
Coyote	NA	Transformation, growth from one stage into another, to be fool and wise man at the same time
Cronus/Saturn	G/R	Fertility, patience, using size to one's advantage
Dionysus	G/R	Play, wine, finer things, pleasure, sexual abandonment
Hades/Hephaistos	G/R	Death of old, shadow side
Hermes/Mercury	G/R	Speed in communicating, clarity, god of SMS!
Krishna	H	Love, goodness, leadership
Lao Tzu	Ch	Passion
Loki	N	Trickster, play, versatility, emotional blackmail/ dishonesty
Osiris	E	Rebirth, birth, sperm quality, and masculine fertility
Poseidon/Neptune	G/R	Making waves, breaking through obstacles, healthy fierceness, anger
Ptah	E	Creativity, skills,
Raven	NA	Communication, intuition
Set/Seth	E	Destruction, war, power through fierceness, baptism by fire, difficult travel
Thor	N	Freedom, negotiation, creativity, healthy fierceness, and physical action, useful when you are feeling stuck
Thoth	E	Wisdom, magic, health, music
Thunderbird	NA	Beginnings, fertility, ideas
Vishnu	H	Protection, faith while risk taking
Zeus/Jupiter, Jove	G/R	Game playing and strategy, taking the lead, removing yourself from co-dependence

Goddess Consultant Table

Legend for the God and Goddess Tables:			
Code: Origin	**Code: Origin**	**Code: Origin**	**Code: Origin**
A: African	E: Egyptian	Ir: Irish	Pe: Persian
Ba: Babylonian	G/R: Greek/Roman	J-C: Judeo-Christian	P: Phoenician
Bu: Buddhist	Ha: Hawaiian	M: Mayan	S: Sumerian
Ce: Celtic	H: Hindu	N: Norse	SL: Slavic
Ch: Chinese	I: Inca	NA: North American	Y: Yoruba

Goddess	Origin	Wisdom
Aphrodite/Venus	G/R	Love of one's self as well as romantic love, beauty, desire, passion
Artemis/Diana	G/R	Walking one's own path, courage, independence, self-trust, helps break co-dependence
Astarte	P	Guidance, good directorship of your life and your child's
Athena/Minerva	G/R	Wisdom, good counsel, justice, decisiveness
Baba Yaga	SL	Allowing your wildness to rule, breaking free of the mold, getting in touch with your core freedoms
Bast	E	Cat goddess, pleasure, joy, finding the lighter side of things, laughter, play to stimulate creativity
Brigit/Brigid	Ce	Creativity, fertility, ideas, conception
Ceres/Demeter	G/R	Prosperity, consciousness, knowing there's always enough, reaping the harvest, growth, participation, plenty
Cerridwen	Ce	Protection, tolerance, integration, recycling, and rebirth
Eostre	Ce	Growth, new beginnings, fertility, conception
Eurynome		Sexual abandonment, surrender, ecstasy
Freya	N	Sexual power, joy in one's body, birth, fertility, feeling irresistible
Gaia/Tellus	G/R	Mother Earth, abundance, creativity, growth, connection
Hathor	E	Pleasure, contentment
Hecate/Trivia	G/R	Births and deaths, beginnings and endings
Hera	R	Protective, power with confidence, tradition
Hestia/Vesta	G/R	Misrule and order in the home
Inanna	S	The mother, birth, also exploring your shadow side and honoring this
Ishtar	Ba	Goddess of war, strategy, female victory, death, rebirth, healthy fierceness
Isis	E	The mother, birth, strategy

Goddess	Origin	Wisdom
Ixchel	M	Creativity, healing through creativity, magic as a solution, connectedness, resilience, purpose
Kali	H	The destroyer as a catalyst for change, healthy fierceness, defending one's purpose
Kwan Yin	Ch	Compassion, needs rather than wants
Lakshmi	H	Abundance and creative energy as the other half of male energy
Lillith	S	Female strength, independence, power being taken back, equality
Maat	H	Justice, fair order, law, letting go of grudges and resentments
Mary	J-C	Unconditional love, mercy under difficult conditions
Morgan le Faye	Ce	Dancing to your own drum, finding your own way and pace in order to get something done, not fighting against your natural style
Ops	G/R	Abundance
Oshun	Y	Sensuality, power through the senses, artistic endeavors
Oya	Y	Welcoming change, change management, protective, and persuasive
Pachamama	I	Healing and becoming whole, completion
Pele	Ha	Success and creation through fire and passion, enthusiasm, ensures healthy expression
Persephone/Kore	G/R	Planning for growth, research, death of one thing so something else can begin, taking an unknown path, the Void
Rhiannon	Ce	Speaking up, fear, speaking for those who cannot speak for themselves, doubt
Saraswati	H	Listening, learning, beginner's mind, breakthroughs
Sekhmet	E	Purification, cord cutting, expression of healthy anger rather than rage, boundaries
Shakti	H	Sexual energy, connection, letting go
Spider Woman/ Thinking Woman	NA	Wisdom, creation throughout, new ideas, patience
Tara	Bu	Compassion, protection, relief for perfectionism, liberation, empathy
Vila	SL	Flexibility, open to change, seeing something from another's point of view
Yemaya	A	Surrendering so that the Goddess handles your problems, faith, risk-taking

Invoking any god or a goddess is easier if you know something about them. It helps you visualize easier and raise the necessary power when there is a link established between you and them, even if it is as simple as knowing their story or where they originated. I would also recommend knowing some of the key descriptors of the Deity you are working with so that you can further use these elements in attracting them For example; Artemis is a huntress and loves dogs. I often have dog fur on my altar and an arrowhead, which she would like. Freya loves amber and white feathers, Loki a joke or two. Eostre loves fresh flowers or rabbits. I have listed some of the gods and goddesses that are wonderful to work with particularly for bedroom witches. Their origin and some of the aspects they bring forth are included. I have also included a favorite invocation for Artemis/Diana for you to experience.

Invocation for Artemis/Diana

This invocation has the added advantage of creating a special talisman you can take with you everywhere as a reminder of your encounter with the Goddess.

Tonight you will be calling the Goddess Artemis (or Diana) into your Circle. Artemis is one of the virgin goddesses. A virgin goddess can be called upon whenever a woman (or man) is pursuing her desires and ideas for herself. The development of selfhood is one of Artemis' special skills. In relationships it's deceptively easy to be swallowed up in each other. It is hard not to start to live your loved one's life or to get distracted by them so that your needs and wants seem to come off second best. You matter most and Artemis teaches you to balance this fact with the connection and intimacy that you desire with your significant other. She is the ideal consultant to assist with the reduction of all kinds of co-dependency.

Preparation

Perform this spell on any night when the moon is full if possible. Ensure the room is warm. Ensure that you will be undisturbed. Have your intention clearly in mind or written down. Welcome the Goddess and thank her for being with you here tonight in this beautiful place.

Gather

Candle

Matches

Herbs for the bath: 2 drops of rosemary, bay, orange oil

A handful of sea salt

Herbs for the charcoal: rosemary, myrrh resin

A small piece of Oak; a twig will do

A comforting robe that you can slip out of easily for the skyclad elements of
the ritual

Red cotton

Focus

Cast and open a Circle if you wish. Light the candle, dim the lights, and relax.
Take several deep breaths.

Have a bath using the herbs gathered: bay, rosemary, sea salt, and orange
oil. Soak and relax for at least fifteen minutes. Visualize how good each part
of your body feels in that soft warmth. As you come out of the bath, gently
towel off and slip into your robe.

Building Power

Face the moon if you can. Have your herbs and your oak branch and cotton
at the ready.

Ask that you receive Artemis, goddess of the hunt and the moon, in your
Circle and within you tonight. Ask that she who embodies purpose and connection and is generous yet discerning with it, bless you this night.

Look at the candle or close your eyes and go within.

Visualize the Goddess before you. She can look as you wish—there is no
wrong image. Imagine the Goddess of the Moon and Hunt as you see her—
vital, glowing, all woman, all powerful. She is perhaps with her bow and
arrow, her hunting dogs, or her hunting cat. She stands as a warrior woman,
yet she is soft and compassionate.

She is reaching out to you. She is telling you that you too are a Goddess.

Disrobe. Notice how you feel and what thoughts enter your mind as she
affirms this. If your thoughts or feelings are negative, note this, but decide
you will put this aside until a later time.

Now light your herbs and incense. Breathe in deeply. As you breathe, you are inhaling even more power from the earth, the trees, the moon, and the sky.

The Goddess is still with you and sharing with you her attributes of focus, purpose, strength. She is also sharing her attributes of vitality and sensuality of internal power when it comes to your work. Accept these gifts in your own body. Allow these energies to begin to mingle, yours and those of Artemis, Goddess of the Moon and the Hunt.

Take the oak branch and picture in your mind the strength and deep serenity of the massive oak tree. Imagine its roots going deep down into the earth so it is immovable and solid. Imagine the web of branches and leaves that are flexible and sway peacefully in the wind. The oak is a combination of strength, solid foundation, and flexibility.

Begin to wind the red cotton around the oak. As you wind it around imagine you are winding the Goddess' attributes into it, binding them there.

As you wind the thread, say in a loud, firm voice:

I allow my light to shine
Confidence and power are mine
I live my Strength and Beauty
Blessed Be the Goddess within Me!

Repeat the chant faster and faster at least three times, feeling your power, focus, and energy grow.

Release Your Intention

When you feel your power is at its peak, state your intention loudly and blow out the flame in the candle.

Concentrate on your oak with the red cotton. Pass it through any remaining smoke and say:

This is my talisman of Artemis' strength and power. I will be empowered
to remember the Goddess within me whenever I carry this.

You now have a highly energized talisman. Take this with you everywhere during the next moon cycle. This is a reminder of the Goddess' power. It will help you build your internal power and banish fear when you need it. Carry it in your hand when you feel the need.

Let no one else touch it.

Offer Your Gratitude

Know that the Goddess has heard your intention. Thank the Goddess Artemis for allowing you to share in her power. Be grateful in the knowledge that all is as you have asked it to be, if it be her will and for the greatest good of all.

Know your mind and body is already responding.

Complete the Ritual

Close your Circle. Take the talisman with you. Extinguish and bury any remaining charcoal or herbs / incense in the garden or yard. Ground yourself by eating or drinking something, exercising, dancing!

Participation

Keep your talisman close at hand or even on your desk ready for use. When you find yourself in a situation where you feel your power waning, touch, hold, or view the talisman.

Book of Shadows Entries

Record your feelings, behaviors, actions, and results, paying close attention to coincidences and details, even if they seem insignificant or unrelated at the time. Remember to date all your entries.

Casting Circles

As a witch, one of the first and simplest lessons in magic you learn is how to cast a Circle. The creation of a Circle is the creation of a sacred space within which you will perform processes that are markedly different from anything else you do in your "normal" world.

The idea of casting a Circle is to ready and focus the mind on the magic that you are going to perform. Its protective nature gives the mind and body notice that you are safe and will not be disturbed. By marking this new space, it signals to the mind that you are traveling to another realm where everything and anything is possible. *It is a signal to the subconscious to pay attention.* Stepping into your Circle is stepping into another world and another state of mind.

Traditionally, Circles are opened by "cutting" the fabric of time with a special double-bladed knife called an Athame. Athames are only used ceremonially and are never used to cut anything else. Athames are sacred tools and each Athame is used only by its owner. However, if I find myself somewhere where the use of an Athame is inappropriate, like a public place, there are many other ways to create your sacred sensual space.

There is no one way to cast a Circle, although most traditions open and close their Circles in a particular way. Circles are usually opened clockwise and closed counterclockwise. At the beginning of many spells, there is a call to cast your Circle. At the end, there will be a directive to close your Circle. Here are some preferred ways of casting Circles:

- Use the Athame and cut the fabric of time to create a sacred Circle.
- Throw rose petals on your bed in the shape of a circle
- Stand in the middle of the Circle and trace it in the air or ground with a pointed finger.
- Sprinkle sea salt around the edge of your Circle to mark the boundaries.
- Place small votive candles around the circumference of the Circle.
- Trace a Circle into the soil or sand around where you are standing.
- Mark the Circle with a sweep of a wand, feather, or special crystal.

A simple prayer or invocation is usually spoken as you trace the Circle, such as:

> *I open this Circle. I ask that only good enter and that I am protected.*
> *As above, so below.*

And when you close the Circle:

> *I close this Circle. I leave it blessed and protected. As above, so below.*

You are free to use these simple invocations or to create your own, but what you say is really up to you.

Power Circles: Your Key to Power Building

As modern witches, we often need to be able to call upon our own Goddess-given power at a moment's notice, whether we are in a bedroom or in the boardroom. Wouldn't it be handy to be able to call up real power when you most need it? Instead of feeling nervous or unconfident or fearful, to be able to extract our natural qualities of charisma, confidence, and fearlessness instantly? Allow me to present to you another way of using the traditional Circle—a way that you can use whether or not you are performing a ritual or spell.

Welcome to Power Circles. This is the technique that has perhaps stuck in peoples' minds most after reading my first book, and the technique that I am always asked to present at workshops. It is one of the most effective ways to instantly invoke self-esteem, self-trust, and the benefits of self-care. These Circles contain the raised power and energy that you have deposited into them at earlier times, and you can now simply step forward into them for a boost of that same power when you need it.

First, you will need to create and charge your Circle. The more power and/or positive energy raised, the stronger the hit of power will be when you step into it at a later time. Like batteries, your Power Circle will need to be charged or layered regularly with power. The more power you can layer into your Circle, the greater the impact of feelings of self-esteem, self-trust, and self-care.

I use my Power Circle at least once or twice a week, sometimes more. I find it really useful in both personal and business contexts. In a business context I use it to handle stage fright before I am about to make a presentation. I also love it as it builds my confidence and puts me in a strong position when negotiating. On a personal level, I use it to balance any energy that I know is unnecessary or if I need to bring up something scary for me with a friend or partner.

I definitely would advise using your Circle before first dates. I have a number of case study participants who step into their Circles before entering the place where their date will be meeting them. Not only do they feel more confident, but they look fantastic too! Another participant opened her Power Circle just prior to going into labor with her second child. She reported back that she felt stronger and more in touch with her inner resources and felt she was in a more empowered place than she was with her first child.

Of course, no one needs to know what you are doing. From the outside, all you are doing is stepping forward, but you know better! You are stepping forward into your internal power, your true, authentic, powerful Self!

Creating Your Own Power Circle

Preparation

Stand somewhere quiet where you will be undisturbed.

Gather

All you need to build your Power Circle is your hand or other tool with which to open and close your Circle.

Focus

Imagine that there is a Circle at your feet, a step away. You may want to imagine that it is your favorite color or you might even like to open it by stepping forward and tracing a Circle on the ground with your finger. Then step back.

Once you imagine your Circle in front of you, shut your eyes and take three deep breaths. Inhale the energy of the earth, exhale any anxiety or worries you may have at that moment. Take your time.

Call the Goddess and God to participate with you in building your personal Power Circle by saying: I call upon the power of the Goddess and the God. Help me see that I have power and that it is real!

Now, relax and remember a time when you felt powerful. A time when you felt your self-esteem at its peak. Perhaps when you looked particularly good on a special occasion, perhaps when you won an award, did well on a test, received a pay raise, or achieved a long-forgotten wish.

Recreate this event in your mind in detail.

See it. Hear it. Smell it. Taste it. *Feel it!*

What does it feel like in your body?

Begin to re-create that feeling in your body—is it excitement? Pride? Happiness? These emotions raise power and energy.

Now intensify these feelings. You will feel the power growing stronger and it will be pulsing through your body.

At the peak of this experience, step forward into your Circle. Stay there and feel the power emanate from your body, filling the Circle.

Say your name confidently three times out loud.

Now step out.

This time, remember a time in your life when you really trusted yourself. This occasion of self-trust perhaps resulted in a great outcome such as a win, a fantastic job performance, or an achievement of a long-held goal. Maybe it was a hunch that proved correct or when you accomplished something physically difficult. Maybe it was just a great decision! Perhaps it was a time when everyone else lost faith in your vision but you. Self-trust—what a magnificent feeling!

See it. Hear it. Smell it. Taste it. *Feel it!*

What does it feel like in your body?

Now, begin to recreate that feeling in your body. Is it anticipation? Satisfaction? Joy? Confidence? Again feel your power begin to rise. Stronger and stronger.

When the feeling is at its peak, again step forward confidently into your Power Circle. Stay there and radiate the power toward the barrier of the Circle. You will notice that you feel the power stronger than before because you are layering this energy over the previous power. Move around if you wish, mixing the two together!

Say your name confidently three times out loud.

Now step out.

Think of a time when your body and mind felt good. Really good. Your body and mind felt this good because you were actively looking after it, consciously making decisions that cared for your body and mind.

Remember back now to a massage that seemed to take away all your pain and leave you floating, or perhaps to that afternoon you just curled up on the couch reading a book you could not put down. Was it the time that you chose to do what you really wanted over what everyone else wanted? Perhaps it is the rush of letting your body function at its peak in sport or choosing to eat delicious healthy food rather than junk. Self-care—putting yourself first!

See it. Hear it. Smell it. Taste it. *Feel it!*

What does it feel like in your body?

Now, begin to recreate that feeling in your body. Is it Contentment? Vitality? Purpose? Again, feel your power beginning to rise. Stronger and stronger.

When the feeling is at its peak, step forward confidently into your Power Circle. Stay there and radiate the power toward the barrier of the Circle. You will notice that you feel the power even stronger than before because you are layering this energy over the previous two layers of power raising. Move around if you wish, mixing the three together!

Say your name confidently three times out loud.

Release Your Intention

This exhilarating feeling is your personal power. Know that you have power and it is real.

Now step out of your Circle.

Offer Your Gratitude

Thank the Goddess and the God for their help in creating your Circle and imagine the Circle closing inward or retreating back into your body.

Complete the Ritual

Close your Circle.

Participation

Begin to live what you have experienced!

After performing the Creating Your Own Power Circle Ritual, why not test your Circle now? Imagine your Circle. Step forward into it and repeat your name three times in your mind. You should be feeling that same rush of positive power and confidence that you had when creating the Circle.

For the Circle to remain powered up, you must recharge it regularly. This can be done in one of two ways. First, by recalling previous experiences such as the ones you had in the exercise above. The second way is by using real time energy. Every time something really great happens, such as winning a piece of business, receiving a compliment, achieving a goal, or doing what you love, invoke your Circle and place that experience within it at that very moment. This literally takes fifteen seconds to do and the benefits are enormous!

Book of Shadows Entries

Chart your progress by recording your feelings, behaviors, actions, and results, paying close attention to coincidences and details, even if they seem insignificant or unrelated at the time. Remember to date all your entries.

You have now created a personal Power Circle that is available at all times to you. No matter where you are, you can simply imagine your Circle in front of you and step into it. The power of self-trust, self-esteem, and self-care that you have raised previously can be instantly accessed, wherever you are.

Section Three

Witches in the Bedroom

Welcome to the pumping heart of the book, where you can discover how everything comes together with real-life examples. Every section features a number of detailed, real-life case studies where people just like you and me have tried and tested each ritual or spell, with real-life, rational, and proven results. There are rituals and spells for you to explore, all tried and tested with powerful results. I would encourage you to not just read these techniques, but try them, if you want change in your life. Remember, participation is the only way we escape the trap of Magical Thinking. Enjoy. . . .

Equality

I was never one of those little girls who dreamed of a handsome prince rescuing her from a dark and dreadful castle. Most of my friends played princesses, but not me. I liked the idea of being the one astride the bright white stallion, the one doing the rescuing. This was the role I played over and over again as I grew up.

One man after another. Save after save after save.

I consciously chose men that I thought had potential. Nothing seems wrong with that. The trouble was that, *unconsciously*, this ensured I didn't choose men who were already *living* their potential. I chose men who were behind me in many attributes, but whom I thought I could *fix*. Although this may sound arrogant, this is no superiority complex but a pattern of unconscious choice to choose a partner who could not match me in a whole raft of ways such as energy, motivation, intelligence, ability, ethics, and awareness.

Why on earth would I choose to do this? Don't we all want someone as an equal, at least as better if not more brilliant than us? Choosing men this way was a kind of control for me; a safety blanket that meant I could mold and shape this person into something that would not harm me. Maybe even support me! I believed I had a right to do this, and of course I could ensure the deep love and loyalty from this man by what I could do for him.

Better to bend and shape someone that I actually had than wait for someone who was what I desired, but who might never come!

This behavior cost me dearly. It cost me my precious time, my energy, and sometimes money. It broke my heart and built in me a wall of resentment. Relationship after relationship, I craved an equal partner's presence in my life, yet thought, like Frankenstein and his monster, that I could create one.

While I was doing that, some of my friends were fulfilling the role of princesses. Some were waiting, literally putting their lives on hold, for a man to come and save them from the lives (or non-lives) that they had created for themselves. Why go out and become successful when it's best to marry someone who already is? When a prince came a'calling they would simply take on his interests, hobbies, opinions, and lifestyle so that they could capture him and allow him to create their life for them. So much easier! Even if things didn't quite go according to plan, everything would be OK, because as they negated responsibility for their own decisions, it was never their fault if something went wrong.

It wasn't just the girls doing this. My male friends were also caught up in the same patterns, being rescued or being rescuers, many getting tangled up in this weird, unwired fairyland where the power struggle ruled and love was almost always lost.

Thankfully, I woke up to my pattern. I won't kid you; I would love to tell you about an ethereal, dreamlike awakening. Unfortunately I'm a stubborn learner at times and it was the excruciating pain of yet another failed relationship, for the very same reasons, that smashed my illusion. I just couldn't miss the lesson—again. At the same time I was becoming aware of the Witches Way in relationships. A way that encouraged the development and love of self as key to successful relationships. A way that made it easier to wake up to my patterns, lift my illusions, and gain the support I needed to make the changes I needed to make.

One of the most amazing feelings in the world is that of being in love, and it is easy to be intoxicated by another person. It is easy to forget yourself, your needs, your wants, your problems, when you have someone who seems perfectly capable of making you happy and your life better.

The difficulty with this is that we forget our own Selves and rely upon external forces to give us our spark, our happiness, our direction. Put simply, someone else, no matter how loving or wonderful, is in charge of our life. If and when something should go wrong, or this person does not live up to expectation, we have little left of our Selves with which to be resourceful and resilient.

The Witches Way asks that we build our core strengths and unravel our purpose so that we are growing and excited about our own lives. It is easier then to take risks and stretch ourselves so that we attract an equal, an equal who does connect with us on a spiritual and physical level, an equal who will not be afraid of or smother our purpose but one who will support it.

Equality is not dragging someone kicking and screaming to where you are, or climbing over someone to get where you wish to go. It is not marrying for economic or status reasons. It is not saving or attempting to fix another. It is not a relationship where one of you has the upper hand or power over another. It is not adversarial or competitive, although it will be frequently challenging.

Equality isn't walking in front of someone. It is not walking behind. It is walking side by side, collaborating, but separate.

Experiencing an equal relationship is knowing when to support and when to allow space for self-discovery. It is knowing when to work together and when to experience and relish solitude. It is when the expression of love comes first and not the ego.

Shadow Side of Equality

It is my belief that there is no shadow side to equality, but there are consequences of bringing it into your life. These may not be pleasant consequences in the short term. For example, if you are already in a relationship that is inherently unequal, this relationship may dissolve once the dynamics are evened up. If both partners don't want to change the paradigm this is commonly the case.

Earlier in the book I spoke about the fear/delight in "getting what we want." For those new to a true relationship of equals, it may initially seem too open, too free, too challenging. It seems easier to slip back to saving or serving. If our self-esteem isn't solid enough we may also find our partner, this amazing person who we have dreamed of, "too good for us," and we become unsure and anxious. I invite you to follow the Witches Way in this and concentrate on building your personal power from the inside out. This is a sure cure for the jitters that sometimes plague the beginner.

Witches in the Bedroom

Diana is a personal assistant in her mid-thirties. She asked for a consultation to "get over a long-term bad relationship." Diana had just broken up with Simon, a boyfriend of three years. Diana and Simon experienced an extremely bitter break up, characterized by a lot of emotion and yelling, which she found horrendous. She totally disagreed with much of what Simon had thrown at her in their last meeting, but a few things rang true to her, which disturbed her most of all.

"I'm ashamed to say it, but I think he was right about a few things. He told me that I was a drain on him because I didn't have my own life. He told me that he felt smothered. He also told me that he felt I was calculated in the way that I became different from the woman he was initially attracted to. I was very angry and denied all this, but he got specific and gave a few examples. I wouldn't admit it to him then, but he was pretty much spot on.

"I did have quite an active life prior to meeting him. I was busy; I had a job I liked (but not loved), I played sports twice a week, I painted, I went out with my girlfriends. I actually met Simon on one of those nights out. But somehow when I met him, I got swept up in that initial big attraction, and one by one my own things began to drop away."

Diana also related that as the relationship got more serious and they began to discuss living together, she began to fantasize about giving up her job. After all, his wage was higher and she was "just a PA." After further questioning, Diana admitted that after a year of living together she had encouraged him to take the lead in just about every major decision that concerned them both. Meanwhile, this behavior became increasingly disturbing to Simon, who began to feel the pressure of Diana's laser-like attention. He had asked her why she wasn't playing sports or having the odd night out with her friends. Why did he have to make every decision? Where was the stimulating, unique, interesting woman he had met?

I advised Diana to create a Power Circle to build her self-esteem and self-trust to a level that she could build from again. Additionally, the Invocation to Artemis would also assist her to begin to walk her own path. During the following three moon cycles she performed the Ritual for Equality.

As a result, Diana is enjoying her own life more than ever before.

"I realized that I did not feel my life was worth living compared to the men I chose. I decided I could live through them. This was a serious blind spot for me and a belief I possibly inherited from my mother. I also realized through the ritual that I was valuable and it was not necessary to sacrifice my own life, pleasures, and beliefs in order to have and keep a relationship with a good man. I know the next relationship I'm in, I will be vigilant in continuing to grow my Self."

Tom is a professor in his mid-fifties. Obviously someone who prides himself on his knowledge and scholarly pursuits, he was known around campus as a notorious womanizer. Tom dated only specific kinds of women, students much younger than him. This pattern might have gone on indefinitely, until he realized these women were becoming younger and younger, and even he began to think this was, in his own words, "unseemly."

Tom and I began an email exchange. He explained his situation: "I have always found it easy to attract younger women. They are really into the wisdom and I guess the power of a man in my position. They know what they are getting, though. I tell the ones that I think have stars in their eyes straight out that I can't guarantee anything other than something light. As soon as they begin to get a little demanding, I normally cut them loose.

"This has been fine all these years, but I have to admit it's a bit lonely. The game is getting boring and stale. I realized this as I seduced yet another student, and I discovered she was only eighteen. I had this flash that I would be trying to do this at seventy-plus with much less success, and, frankly, it made me feel disgusting. Maybe it's all catching up with me."

I asked Tom what it was that he now wanted.

"I want to be able to have a proper relationship with someone who challenges me."

It was obvious to me that Tom had rejected an equal partnership throughout his life out of fear and lack of self-esteem. I spoke to Tom at length about the reasons why he was afraid of this outcome he had set for himself, and in order to get clearer, I asked him to perform the Ritual for Equality.

After performing the ritual, Tom sent me the following email.

"Well, that wasn't fun! I saw just how I have avoided having equal partners by choosing control over the challenge of real love. It's so much easier to do what I have done, but really short-term gratification."

Tom and I also discussed the consequences of his actions, both to himself and some of the more vulnerable young women he had dated. Tom then performed the rituals surrounding fear (pages 145–146). As one of his participatory points, Tom was directed to make amends to some of the women he had hurt in the past, and to begin to turn his attention to women whom he felt challenged by.

After a year of practice runs, at the time of this writing, Tom is in a six-month-long relationship with a "scarily smart barrister named Katrina, who challenges me daily with both her vulnerability and her immense strength. This is like no other relationship I have had in that I cannot, and don't want to, have power over her. It is very stimulating and frightening at the same time. I am just regretful I didn't have the insight and the courage to drop my schoolboy prowess earlier."

Ritual for Equality

You may wish to invite to the ritual some relevant goddesses: Artemis (selfhood), Maat (justice and balance), or even Aphrodite (self-love). This is also a good spell for a couple to perform together if you have identified any level of inequality within your relationship.

Preparation

Perform this spell on any night where the moon is full or dark. Ensure the room is warm. Ensure that you will be undisturbed. Decide on the location for the spell craft. Have your intention clearly in mind or written down.

Welcome the Goddess and thank her for being with you here tonight in this beautiful place.

Gather

White, gray, and black candles

Matches

Charcoal and herbs: a pinch each of Mugwort, Life Everlasting, and Sandal-wood

A comfortable robe that you can slip out of easily for the skyclad elements of the ritual

If you are calling in Maat, have a white feather or scales handy

Paper and pen or BOS

Focus

Cast and open a Circle if you wish. Slip off your robe or dress.

Building Power

Bring your candles and all the other equipment into the room or outside if it is warm enough. Set up the candles: white, gray, and black, all in a row.

Face the moon if you can. Light the white candle, dim the lights, and relax. Take several deep breaths. You can do this spell standing or sitting.

Open your Power Circle. Feel your own self-knowledge, self-trust, self-esteem, and self-care flood every cell. Breathe in your power.

Ask that you receive the Goddess, she who embodies love and courage, to bless you this night. If there is a special patron or protective goddess that you wish to invoke, do it now.

You might like to try the following invocation for Maat, while holding the feather in your right hand and the scales in your left:

> *Great Maat, mother of balance and justice, I ask that you be with me*
> *here to enable me to see what is balanced and equal and what is not.*
> *I wish to walk beside a partner. I wish to find equality in my actions*
> *and behaviors. I call on you to assist me in my endeavors.*

Look at the white candle you have lit.

This candle signifies you. The black candle (yet unlit) signifies your partner or previous relationships. The gray is in the place of equality.

Look back in your mind now. Ask that you be taken back to the different situations that most show you the inequality in your relationships. Allow this to happen in the order that it does. Your subconscious will send forth the situations, times, and dates. Look to these times in detail. Take your time.

Choose one scenario (you may choose others later). If you are performing this ritual with a partner, take turns in doing this and speak out loud what you are experiencing. It is important that you do not speak to the partner who is expressing at the time, nor judge their experience in any way. You are merely there to witness. See this and *feel* this time clearly in your mind and body. Notice how this inequality actually manifests. Is it a feeling? A color? Where do you feel it or see it first? Feel this inequality and its consequences. Allow it to show these real-life consequences to you. If you feel the need, write these consequences down.

You may now choose to go to the next scenario. Repeat this. You should be feeling the effects of this experience. You may feel sad, regretful, frightened, disappointed, relieved, or something completely different. Just allow this and notice it.

Ask yourself now: what has this dealing on an unequal basis cost me? What has it stopped me from doing, enjoying, or discovering? Notice how you feel and what thoughts enter your mind. Write these down if you wish.

Now light your herbs and incense. Breathe in deeply. As you breathe in, you are inhaling even more power from the earth, the trees, the moon, and the sky.

The Goddess is still with you and sharing with you. She is with you, standing beside you, assisting you to explore and weave equality into your life. You are all powerful. You are Goddess/God.

Now light your gray candle, saying out loud:

> *There is a middle way. I choose to step up, or step down,*
> *to meet and walk side by side. I choose to be strong and separate,*
> *yet connected and loved. I can be who I am fully and completely*
> *and attract/be loved by an equal."*

Ask now out loud:

> *What is it that I need to do to be blessed with equality?*

Close your eyes and breathe deeply. You will have some answers to this question. Write this down.

Accept these gifts in your own body. Allow these energies to begin to mingle: yours and those of the Goddess. Feel your own strength and that of the Goddess course through you.

Offer Your Gratitude

Know that the Goddess has assisted you and that she is already helping you incorporate equality in your beliefs and your relationships now and into the future. Thank your patron Goddess or any Goddess you have invoked. Be grateful in the knowledge that all is as you have asked it to be. Know your mind and body are already responding.

Complete the Ritual

Close your Circle, and your Power Circle. Clarify at least 1–3 participatory steps. Extinguish and bury any remaining charcoal or herbs/incense in the garden or yard. Ground yourself by eating or drinking something, exercising, or dancing!

Participation

At the end of the ritual, ask yourself what three steps you can take immediately to create greater equality in your life. What changes need to happen? If you have done this ritual as a couple, discuss strategies together. Act on your steps as soon as possible.

Book of Shadows Entries

Chart your progress by recording your feelings, behaviors, actions, and results, paying close attention to coincidences and details even if they seem insignificant or unrelated at the time. Remember to date all your entries. Watch how your life transforms!

Fear

They don't call Africa the darkest continent for nothing. Night, in the middle of the African bush, was very, very dark—so dark that even a grown woman like me would get the spooks sometimes when the room where I lived was an absolute vacuum of blackness. It was so dark you couldn't even see the shadow of your hand in front of your face, and so everything seemed to go bump. Even outside the house, no stars punctuated the night sky on some nights, and mother moon hid.

It was Africa, so anything or everything could be lurking and what's more, you couldn't see it coming.

On those nights, I often decided to sit and listen to the wise women of the village tell their children bedtime stories as they gathered together in the one room of their home. I was often lulled by their gentle voices speaking the softest Swahili, and as I only understood a little, the effect was almost hypnotic in its loving restfulness. That is, until the stories about the tokaloshie.

Tokaloshies are the demons that hide under your bed at night. Yes, really. Many African people are so afraid of tokaloshies that they often traditionally put their bed legs up on rocks or tin cans so that the tokaloshies will have a harder time of climbing up in bed with them. And what is so bad about these little demons climbing into bed with you? Well the thing is, tokaloshies strangle you in your sleep. Unless of course you know how to conquer them.

Tokaloshies are very special in their wickedness. They know exactly how to extract the maximum amount of fear in each and every person because they are the embodiment of your worst fear. Just imagine, your own personal demon that knows exactly how to scare you into inaction, into absolute terror, and knows the exact combination of moves to strangle any joy, rest, and life that you may have. The mothers told their children that if you have more than one worst fear, the tokaloshie will be a combination of all of them!

I sat wide-eyed and sweating just like every other kid in the bedroom when I heard my friend animatedly relate the horrors of the tokaloshie. I would certainly be making a detour to the kitchen to get some cans for my bed legs on the way to sleep that night.

Not exactly the subject for great bedtime stories you may think. However, there was an upside.

They could be defeated.

The only way to beat the power of the tokaloshie is to shine a light on it—full on and square. To be able do this was, of course, very brave, because first you had to search for this demon of fear, and second, because who knows how ugly and terrifying the tokaloshie actually was. But if we did have the courage to search and find the tokaloshie, if we did shine the light on it to see what it really was, it always lost its power and ceased to strangle the life from us.

I wonder how many of us have been to afraid to shine the light on our own tokaloshies? I wonder how long we have feared what is hiding under our own beds, how long we have endured the agony of terror and the torture of no peace of mind?

How long will we allow our fears to strangle the life out of us?

Like the myth of the tokaloshie, Witches have been the object of fear and have been used to conquer fear paradoxically throughout millennia. As such, fear has always been a constant companion to us and this has bred a fine arsenal of weapons to be used against its power, if need be.

In the bedroom, fear is, more often than not, something that disrupts or blocks the flow of love, lust, and pleasure. Having an unhealthy level of fear, I also believe, can be a block to a regular fertile cycle and successful conception.

There is always a healthy level of fear, the kind that warns us to keep out of a dangerous situation or stay clear of someone by whom we are instinctively repelled. However, it would be a rare person who does not have at least one fear that does not serve them—a fear that is unrealistic, untrue, perhaps based on an outmoded experience or something that is buried so deeply that we only see the symptoms rather than the fear itself.

Some common symptoms of buried fear include:

- Self-sabotage and other self-destructive behavior.
- Continual patterns of addiction.
- Co-dependence.
- Lack of purpose.
- Feelings of unworthiness, lack of self-esteem.
- Feelings of disconnection.
- Fear disguised as jealousy.

Fears that typically manifest this way need a powerful light shined upon them, first to reveal them, then to see them in enough detail to begin to form a strategy to battle them. Only then can we reduce their power or totally conquer them and restore flow and life to our Selves so that our relationships cease to be strangled.

Some powerful fears are linked to actual trauma in our past. These traumas, such as sexual abuse or violence, may do huge damage if we do not take steps to deal with them and shine light on them. It is fiercely damaging emotions such as toxic shame and repressed anger that keep the tokaloshies formed by such traumas active and focused in their terror. I would urge the many men and women who have experienced such traumas to take firm steps to seek professional counseling involving supportive and emotionally safe full debriefing of their abuse. I would also suggest that they get further support by deciding to perform some of the suitable rituals in this book. A good start is the regular use of power circles to boost feelings of self-esteem, self-knowledge and self-trust. The Exposing and Conquering Fear rituals in this section are also useful, and of course, with the right support and expertise, Cutting the Cords with both the experience itself and perpetrator, would be the most powerful healing tool.

Fears, however, do not need to be linked to obvious trauma. Many fears are much more covert than that, and because they fly low, they miss our conscious radar. Most fears have been formed with a positive intent of protection. We need to separate that intention out and deal with it in a more resourceful and less destructive way if we are to create ease and flow in our lives.

Witches in the Bedroom

Belinda, a twenty-nine-year-old trader in London, was, in her own words, "ready to give up men forever." Time and time again, Belinda would attract men who she felt were unsuitable, but they didn't seem that way at first.

"It never starts out that way. They all seem so okay at the beginning, and then over time everything becomes a disaster."

I asked Belinda what she meant by "okay" and by "disaster."

"Well, 'okay' means that they seem okay to go out with, you know, nice enough. I don't have to have this huge attraction really, but that they are okay. And the word 'disaster'? That always means I lose out because they end up leaving me or I am forced to leave them due to really bad behavior. My last boyfriend ended up cheating on me after an eighteen-month relationship. He did it on a ski trip when I wasn't with him. I hated skiing."

I asked Belinda two questions. One: why did she agree to date someone who was just okay, rather than someone who truly excited her on all kinds of levels, including sexually and emotionally? And two: did she normally have a bit in common with the guys she dated, or did she tend to just date, go along with it, perhaps even work hard at it to make it work and then things tended to go awry?

"I'm not sure why I agree to just date someone who really doesn't make me feel that excited. It just seems more important to have a date full stop."

I suspected that Belinda had a fear of being alone and that she would rather date someone unsuitable than no one at all.

Belinda performed the spell for Exposing Fears on a dark moon. Her email the next day read, "I realized, time and time again, that I had chosen badly for me. All the signs were there but I ignored them rather than be on my own any longer. My fear could be summed up as 'I am afraid to be alone.'"

Belinda then performed the ritual for conquering fear on a waxing moon. "This was a humbling experience. I realized my fear of being alone was really unrealistic. I'm still not sure where it started, but I know for sure I have more choices now. I have the resources to have a great life, even if I am alone. I can afford to be choosier and I know this will assist me in having a better strike rate! I am alone right now, and I am taking the steps to enjoy this time rather than just run out and find someone to fill the hole."

One of Belinda's participatory steps involved catching up with old friends she had let fall away due to her last unsuitable relationship. Another step was to cast the Spell to Attract Your Ideal Partner. The final step was to go on a holiday alone.

"These three participatory steps were the best three things I had done in years. Catching up made me realize how much support and love I had through friends and that I didn't really need to grasp at this with boyfriends who I had little in common with anyway.

"The Ideal Partner spell showed me what and who it is I really want. Some of it was a surprise to me and boy, have I been way off the mark! Now I have this list, I know what I'm looking for! And going on holiday alone, this was a big scary step. I was so self-conscious. I went to a resort in Spain and I thought everyone would think that there was something wrong with me because I was alone, but I had the best holiday I have ever had. I did what I wanted, when I wanted, how I wanted, and I met some wonderful other single travelers who I saw certainly were not having a bad time traveling alone. I can tell you, I will not feel being alone is as frightening as I thought it would be."

At the time of this writing, eight months down the track, Belinda is now involved with a man she calls "as close to my shopping list as humanly possible." She is, however, continuing to have a solo holiday once a year just as a reminder of the fear she has conquered.

Julie is a bright and voluptuous woman in her forties, who came to me wanting a love spell to "brighten up her marriage" of twenty years. After speaking with Julie about the nature of the sexual relationship with her husband, it was clear that Julie had a number of fears that were interfering with her experiencing greater freedom and satisfaction with her husband in the bedroom.

"He wants us to be much more adventurous. I don't mean anything too out there. Just a bit of role playing, or more explicit positions. But I'm uncomfortable about this because of the way I look. I would prefer that we do it in the dark or maybe with some very soft candlelight. I really just cannot think about what I would look like in full view with all my dimples and jiggles. I mean, when we got married I was big breasted, but now I'm big all over!"

I asked Julie what she was most afraid of.

"That someone I love will be turned off by me if they really see me. I would rather not go there."

I then asked her whether, if she did not have this fear about her body and her husband, she might find what he was suggesting pleasurable. "Well sure! If I liked what I saw in the mirror, well, it would be great fun. Actually a great turn on, too!"

Julie performed the Health and Vitality Ritual once a week for a tri-lunar cycle. At the same time, she did the Ritual for Conquering Fear over the same tri-lunar cycle at full moon.

Julie related: "I really resisted the Health and Vitality Ritual. I just didn't believe anything I was saying. But slowly I could see the beauty of the Goddess in me. It was the Conquering Fear spell that really affected me more overtly. I got that it was wholeness, not my body alone that my husband found attractive. It was my fear that he wouldn't love me for what I looked like that made me so insecure. And insecure is really unsexy! I trust him. I know now that he wouldn't be asking for more of me if he didn't fancy more of me!"

Julie decided to surprise her husband with a very special dinner. Served by her in a gorgeous, totally diaphanous gown, she created a number of aphrodisiac dishes which she would feed him by candlelight (but lots of candles!) on cushions on the floor. She ran a perfumed bath and did the Ritual for Health and Vitality prior to the dinner, and opened her power circle just prior to him coming home, so she was confident and ready.

"I was nervous, but as soon as I opened the power circle I felt calm and confident. I was so excited. He walked through the door and I can tell you, he couldn't believe his eyes. We ended up having sex like it was when we first met. Now he can't get enough of me. He calls me his new woman!"

Lee is an accomplished man in his early forties who recently married Ella, an artist in her early thirties. Both very physically attractive and successful people, they seemed well matched to any outsider, but Lee found himself behaving more like a stranger to himself as time went on.

He explains: "When I met Ella I couldn't believe how equal I felt with her. This was perhaps the first woman I had dated that I saw could give me a run for my money and was confident enough to do her own thing. Many of my previous relationships were with women who got 'lost' in relationships. I always ended up taking the lead in everything after a while.

"Ella's abilities, confidence, and beauty just blew me away. She does attract quite a bit of attention sometimes and at first I enjoyed this. After all, I wasn't a bad catch either. But since I turned forty, I guess something must have changed, because I find myself feeling really jealous of the attention she gets. This escalates into thinking that she is going to find someone better.

Recently, I found myself doing things like not wanting to go out with her and withholding affection. When I found myself cajoling her into staying at home with me rather than her doing a course she wanted I realized I was eaten up with jealousy. This is such awful behavior and I want it to stop."

I felt congratulations were in order. Lee was self-aware and awake enough to see that his jealousy was present, useless, and destructive, and that it had to cease. I explained to Lee that jealousy was fear, deeply disguised.

We explored and revealed what his real fears were through the Meditation for Exposing Fears. This took some time and a huge dose of courage.

"I'm afraid I'm getting older and unattractive. I'm afraid that she won't love me anymore because I'm not good looking or talented enough. I'm afraid I compare badly to other men. I guess, in summary, I am afraid I'm not good enough in comparison to others."

Once we could shine the light on Lee's fears, we could attack them one by one. Rationally, Lee admitted they were a good match, but it was his self esteem and a deep-seated fear that he wasn't good enough that was threatening seeing himself as the powerful, desirable man that he was. Lee practiced power circles every day, and performed the Ritual for Conquering Fear. He also began to practice some of the bonding techniques in the Sex section of this book.

Over a three-moon cycle period, Lee could see how his fear was diminishing.

"I've had some interesting insights. I know and accept that I will be getting older, but my attractiveness really isn't in my physical beauty. I know now the more I get to know myself the more there is to be happy with. What's the use of comparing me? With who? For what? Yes, my wife could leave me for someone else, or have an affair or whatever. I have no control over this other than to offer her my love and support as a husband. My fear was trying to control her and me, and by surrendering this control, I can be free to love myself and her—and I think that makes me happy, empowered—and yes, attractive! Besides, she is very happy with some of my new tricks in bed!"

Meditation for Exposing Fears

This meditation can be done at any time on any phase of the moon. I do find however that the dark moon is particularly powerful in exposing fear.

Find yourself a comfortable place to sit or lay down. Take the phone off the hook to ensure you won't be disturbed for the next thirty minutes or so.

Close your eyes. Say the word "Relax."

First, be aware of your breath entering and leaving your body. Bring all your awareness inward to your breath and your breath alone. Use every sense to experience your breathing. Feel it, taste it, see it, hear it.

With every breath you are becoming more, and more relaxed. With every breath you are returning deeper and deeper into yourself to the place where your wisdom lives, the place where your dreams are known, the place where *you* are. When you feel you have your awareness in this place, we will now ask for you to see your fear(s). Replay in detail, using all your senses, the last time you felt fear.

Say out loud: "Show me, show me my fear."

Allow yourself to be taken to that fear. If you aren't being shown anything, recall the situation that has triggered the desire to perform this mediation (Lee recalled cajoling his wife to not do her course).

Once you feel the fear, no matter what form it takes, ask to be shown any fear that lies under that fear. Ask for the real fear to be exposed—the fear at the root of it all.

This may feel very frightening, or even overwhelming. If it does, trigger your power circle to envelop you. You will feel your strength and self-trust return. You might also like to call in a protective deity such as Artemis, Maeve, or Mars to assist. If you feel it necessary, write down what comes up for you right there and then.

When you feel that you have a good indication of the fear, return your attention to your breath.

When you feel ready to return to the room, place your attention there.

As soon as possible write down in a succinct manner what your fear(s) are—particularly the root cause. This is the nasty one that needs to have the most light shined on it.

If for some reason you do not have your fears revealed on the first occasion, try again on the next night.

***

Ritual for Conquering Fear

Before attempting this ritual, you *must* have created a power circle and know that it is effective. This is a necessary step because it will give you the foundation, strength, and knowingness to be able to battle and conquer your fear. You must also know clearly what your fear is. You should be able to state it in a short sharp statement, or even one word. If you are not clear, do the Meditation for Exposing Fears.

Preparation

Perform this spell on any night where the moon is full or waxing. Ensure the room is warm. Ensure that you will be undisturbed. This spell must be done solo or with an experienced practitioner. Decide on the location for the spell craft. Have your intention clearly in mind or written down.

Welcome the Goddess and thank her for being with you here tonight in this beautiful place.

Gather

Red or black candle

Matches

A symbol of your courage

Your athame or blunt knife, or something else that you feel you can use as a weapon against your fear

Moon-charged water

A comfortable robe that you can slip out of easily for the skyclad elements of the ritual

Sea salt—a handful for the bath, a handful for use in the ritual

Paper and pen or BOS

Focus

Cast and open a Circle if you wish. Light the candle, dim the lights, and relax. Take several deep breaths.

Run a bath. Add a handful of sea salt. This is very purifying. Soak and relax for at least fifteen minutes. Visualize how good each part of your body feels in that soft warmth. As you come out of the bath, gently towel off.

Slip into your robe or dress comfortably and go somewhere right away to do your spell.

Building Power

Bring your candle and all the other equipment into another room or outside if it is warm enough. Face the moon if you can.

You can do this spell standing or sitting.

Open your Power Circle. Feel your own self-knowledge, self-trust, self-esteem, and self-care flood every cell. Breathe in your power.

Ask that you receive the Goddess, she who embodies love and courage, to bless you this night. If there is a special patron or protective goddess you wish to invoke, do it now.

Look at the candle or close your eyes and go within.

State your intention and fear:

> *Tonight I wish to face and conquer my fear. Goddess,*
> *my fear is/I am afraid of (insert your fear statement).*
> *I now call forth my fear. Come! Let me see you!*
> *Let me see all that you are! From beginning to end!*

Look back in your mind now. Ask that you be taken back to the different manifestations of this fear. Allow this to happen in the order that it does. Your subconscious will send forth the situations, times, and dates. Look to these times in detail.

Choose one scenario. See this and *feel* this time clearly in your mind and body. Notice how this fear actually manifests. Is it a feeling? A color? Where do you feel it or see it first? Feel this fear and its consequences. Allow it to show itself to you. You may now choose to go to the next scenario. Repeat this. You should be feeling the effects of this fear.

Ask yourself now: What has this fear cost me? What has it stopped me from doing, enjoying, discovering? Notice how you feel and what thoughts enter your mind. Write these down, if you wish.

Now light your herbs and incense.

Breathe in deeply. As you breathe in, you are inhaling even more power from the earth, the trees, the moon, and the sky.

The Goddess is still with you and sharing with you. She is with you, standing beside you, assisting you to conquer your fear. You are all powerful. You are Goddess/God.

Pick up your athame or weapon. Once more ask:

I call you, fear of XXXX. Show me what you are. Meet me here. Now.

Now imagine your fear manifesting into a shape, a color, a symbol, creature. This is your fear. You may feel very frightened now, or you may feel relieved. Perhaps your fear isn't as nasty as you may have first thought now you can see it clearly. No matter, you are ready now to be rid of its influence.

Ask it first: What is the positive reason that you are here? Allow the fear to answer. There will always be a positive intent for a fear, no matter what it is. (Normally this is a misguided protectiveness.)

Thank this fear for its positive intent. Tell your fear that you now have the abilities and the knowledge to be able to _____ in a better, healthier way. Tell it that you have no need for the part of it that induces consequences and behaviors like (insert some of the costs and consequences of having this fear). Tell it that you already know how to do this.

Now watch for any changes in the fear. It may accept defeat or it may keep coming. Ask the Goddess and your patron goddess to be with you and now state loudly while holding your weapon:

I am warrior. I am Goddess. I know who I am and this fear
no longer serves me. I let it drop away, die if it be for the good of all
and in its place be reborn a better life. The lesson has been learned.
I choose another way. Be gone, you are defeated!

Be prepared for your fear to disappear, melt, turn, and walk away. Or it may attack you. Use your weapon now, being careful to not injure yourself or anything else near by. You may even use it as a warning. The Goddess will assist you in the battle if need be. You feel her power, or the special gifts of your patron Goddess.

Accept these gifts in your own body. Allow these energies to begin to mingle—yours and those of the Goddess. Feel your own strength and that of the Goddess course through you.

Release Your Intention

You both conquer the fear. In a loud, firm voice: *"Be gone, you are defeated."*

As your fear disappears (if it already hasn't), look and feel ahead at what your life will be like now that this fear is no longer part of your life.

Now pick up your symbol of courage, and chant:

> *I am here again*
> *Change is real*
> *I am free to grow*
> *This is my seal.*

Repeat the chant faster and faster, at least three times, feeling your strength, confidence, and energy grow. Look to the symbol. This is now your talisman of courage. Keep it as a reminder of how you have conquered this fear.

Offer Your Gratitude

Know that the Goddess has assisted you and that she is already helping you find better ways to protect yourself now and into the future.

Thank your patron goddess.

Be grateful in the knowledge that all is as you have asked it to be, and that your fear has transformed.

Know your mind and body are already responding.

Complete the Ritual

Close your Circle, and your Power Circle. Take your talisman with you. Write your three participatory steps. Extinguish and bury any remaining charcoal or herbs/incense in the garden or yard. Ground yourself by eating or drinking something, exercising, or dancing!

Participation

At the end of the ritual, ask yourself what three steps you can take immediately to create in the space where your fear was. What else is there that you can do that has the same protective effect as the old fear? If you can't think of three things, ask that you wake up with three steps in the morning.

Book of Shadows Entries

Chart your progress by recording your feelings, behaviors, actions, and results, paying close attention to coincidences and details, even if they seem insignificant or unrelated at the time. Remember to date all your entries. Watch how your life transforms!

Pleasure

Earlier in this book we discovered how the Goddess has been venerated in her role as creatrix since time began. From prehistory to postmodernism we have witnessed the magic of creation, whether it be the growth of a plant to nourish us from a tiny seed, to the miracle of the birth of a baby.

The Goddess is said to have celebrated and rejoiced in her creations, whether they be plant, animal, wind, rain, sight, sound, human, or animal. Creation always brings with it a spark of joy and of pleasure. The Goddess especially took pleasure in the fertility and growth of her creations. Sensual pleasure and sexual pleasure in particular, with growth and fertility, were something to be rejoiced in and from where ecstasy came.

Witches, therefore, believe that pleasure is sacred and sacred is pleasure. Every time I experience the fullness of joy, happiness, and pleasure for the sake of it, as long as I do no harm, this is a prayer to the Goddess.

This may seem a strange way to look at pleasure, especially if we look at this through a traditional Western Christian point of view. Witches view pleasure as holy rather than something to be controlled by guilt, regret, or total uncontrolled hedonism. We see that without allowing ourselves to experience pleasure—whether it take the form of laughter, of play, of sensuality, or sex—that we remain less than whole and wanting. We are less than effective in our lives in every way, whether it be career or relationships.

Without refilling the well with the sacrament of pleasure we cannot continue to give out of ourselves and be who we wish to be.

In regard to the allowance of pleasure in your life you may want to ask yourself:

- What is it that stands in the way of your daily pleasure prayer?
- Witches have been burned for their right to take joy in their own bodies, minds, and creations. What is it that is non-negotiable for you when it comes to pleasure?
- What is it that gives you pleasure?
- What is it that makes you laugh?
- What do you do for pure fun?
- Do you take the time to take pleasure in the small things each day rather than in planned blocks (holidays, for example)?
- Would your friends or partners consider you a balanced person when it comes to pleasure?

As well as those above, take these and look at them as a couple if you are choosing to be in a relationship at present:

- What is it that you have in common as pleasure points?
- What is it that you would like to try together that perhaps you haven't before?
- Can you schedule minimum pleasure points that are non-negotiable, even if you are busy?
- Is sex pleasurable? If so, what is so pleasurable about it? If not what can you do individually and as a couple to improve this? (See the section on sex, page 159.)

Obstacles to Pleasure
- Shame
- Guilt
- Disconnection

Let's talk about the last point in detail. It is my experience that when we allow ourselves to become unconnected with our bodies (and live the majority of time in our minds) that we begin a drought of sensation and of pleasure. Life is hugely overwhelming at times and our rational mind seems to need every available minute of our time to be able to cope with the demands of the everyday. Even those of us who have more naturally physical natures, such as those who participate in sports on a regular basis, are able to turn this activity into primarily a mind game by the mind processes of competition.

Getting Back in the Body

I can tell you that most of us have become incredibly cerebral creatures. We live mostly in our minds and heads in order to get around and navigate in this increasingly complex world. There's nothing wrong with that some of the time, but the problem is that we forget our bodies also need to be fully inhabited for us to experience a rounded life. We often forget the body's amazing ability to connect us to what is divine and good through pleasure.

I know intimately how it feels to be unconnected this way. If I become overly busy in my corporate work or even when I begin to increase my output of books, one of the first things to go are some of the pleasures associated with my body. Exercise declines because I prioritize other activities over it. With a deadline looming, I may also stay firmly rooted in my mind and let other pleasurable activities fall away, forgetting to schedule a massage or eat foods that have textures and flavors that excite me. Everything begins to become quite mechanical if I don't release the iron hold my mind has on me. Happily, because of the work I have done over time with the Witches Way, this state of mind does not last for very long and it's rare that it extends into disrupting regular pleasures that my partner and I share.

Here is what some of my case-study participants have said about forgetting pleasure:

- "I work, I look after my kids, and I do what I need to do in the house. If my husband initiates sex it's almost a hassle. I need to change gears to get back into my body, and it's hard." —Julie, Sydney

- "When I was diagnosed with a gall bladder problem, my doctor asked me whether I had felt any pain prior to seeing him. To tell you the truth, I probably did, but didn't become aware of it until it became really bad." —Anna Louise, London

- "I exercise, and most of the time that's the only regular body-type experience I have. Having sex is pretty mechanical. I don't particularly feel connected with her, just with my climax, I guess. I feel relieved from my stress, just as I do when I exercise." —Robbie, Perth

- "Since my break up, I haven't had anyone. That's almost a year. My body feels asleep." —Dawn, Detroit

The following are a number of rituals and techniques that will help you to connect or reconnect with your body and that of your partner.

The first is a ritual for connecting without filters to Gaia, the Earth as Goddess, and it is a way of gently opening all your senses again—a way of experiencing your body without too much interference from your mind.

The second is a ritual for reconnection with your partner that is a gentle introduction perhaps to some of the more advanced techniques in the Sex section.

Ritual to Gaia: Connection to the Senses

Go into a favorite place in nature, one that speaks to you of Gaia. Light a candle with intention.

Begin to breathe slowly and deeply, slowly becoming aware of the relationship to the environment around you. As a woman, you may want to begin to take your breathing down through the belly into the womb. Imagine breathing in and out through this sacred place of creation. Now begin to open all your senses to Gaia—extending yourself and reaching out to her as roots would search through the soil. First use your vision: look around you, open your peripheral vision, also look at the detail of her—from the tiniest insect to the expanse of the sky. Soak in what you see and give thanks to Gaia.

Next go to your aural sense. Close your eyes and concentrate on the sounds around you. Listen closely to the layers of life. Be very still and listen to your heartbeat and the way it melts into her soundtrack. Again, give thanks to Gaia for her connection with you.

Continue this through the other senses: taste, touch, smell.

When you have connected completely this way, stay in this very open state and allow any messages that Gaia has for you to be integrated into your body and mind. Feel the unfiltered pleasure that exists in your body when you open to your senses.

Thank Gaia, and slowly now close your senses back to their usual level (or a little more open than usual if you like), and close your circle.

Practice this ritual at least once a week.

Meditation for Pleasure with a Partner

You will need nothing but each other for this meditation.

Sit side by side or face to face on the floor, touching each other in some way. Some couples choose to sit cross-legged, face-to-face, holding extended hands; some lay side by side, holding hands, some back-to-back. It's your choice.

Breathe deeply and begin to relax. One of you may take the lead in this part of the meditation, guiding both into deeper relaxation:

Take three deep breaths. On the inhale, imagine that you are breathing in clean clear air and the energy of the universe. On the exhaled breath you are breathing out any worries or anything that no longer serves you at this point in time. Be very aware of your body. Feel the pressure of it when it touches something, even the floor. Be aware of its temperature, its texture, its moisture, if there is any ease or pain within it. If there are any feelings of pain or uncomfortableness, let this go by breathing it out.

Concentrate now on the area of your body that touches your partner. Feel its warmth and the energy of your partner. Does this energy or force have a color or a texture? If so, experience this to the full now. How does it differ from your own energy? Enjoy the differences by experiencing them.

Now, out loud, speak to each other of the most recent pleasurable experiences you had as individuals. Use detail.

- Yesterday I had a long, hot bath. I added all kinds of beautiful oils so it smelled so good and it was this beautiful turquoise color. It made my skin so soft and I just floated there, all relaxed and warm!

Then, open your eyes and face each other. Now tell each other about the most recent pleasurable experience you have had with each other. Use detail and do not edit or judge your first gut response.

- Last week when you massaged my head it felt so great. I was so tense from work and it melted away my stress. It felt like I could just drift off to sleep.

- On Wednesday when we made love, I loved the way you ran your hands up my back and held me tightly against you. I looked into your eyes and felt so connected that I could have just stayed there. It gave me shivers it felt so pleasurable.

- A month ago, when we went to the movies together and we laughed and laughed at the film, I remember looking at you and your eyes were watering and you just looked so happy, and I felt exactly that same way.

State out loud what your next pleasurable experience will be as an individual, and ask the other to help you keep to this.

Now together plan what your next pleasurable experience will be together. This must occur within the next twenty-four hours.

Resume your original position, breathe deeply, and return your awareness back into the room.

Your participation will be to ensure you experience your individual and joint pleasure prayers.

Ritual for Reconnection with Body and Partner

Preparation

Perform this spell on any night, but especially on your Lunar Return (see fertility section) or full moon. Ensure the room is warm. Ensure that you will be undisturbed. Decide on the location for the ritual. Have your intention clearly in mind or written down.

Welcome the Goddess and thank her for being with you here tonight in this beautiful place.

Gather

Red, silver, or white candle

Matches

A comfortable robe that is easily removed for the skyclad elements of the
ritual

Notepad and pen or book of shadows

Mirror

Focus

Take a shower or bath, towel dry, stay skyclad under your your robe or comfortable clothing, and go somewhere right away to do your spell.

Cast and open a Circle if you wish. Light the candle, dim the lights, and
relax. Take several deep breaths. Ask that the Goddess or your choice of one
of the goddesses of love be with you:

> *Great Goddess! You who teach us that pleasure and love are your rituals,*
> *assist me to again receive your sacrament. I have been living in my*
> *mind my Moon Sister, and I feel so out of touch with my body,*
> *with my partner, and the magic therein. I ask that you come now,*
> *and facilitate a journey back to love and my beloved.*

Now sit or lay back and feel the presence of the Goddess fill the room,
your body, and heart. Now go back in time to the specific time just before
you met your current partner. (Or the positive, pleasant encounter of your
choice if you do not have a partner right now.)

Breathe deeply and evenly. Look back in your mind now. Imagine clearly
and in as much detail as possible the events and situation you were in just
prior to meeting your partner or just prior to your first date. Just ensure the
situation is a memorable one and one charged with emotion.

- What are you seeing through your eyes?
- What are you hearing? Is there music, are there many voices, what is
  the nature of the conversation, is it quiet?
- Is there a scent in the room or are you wearing perfume?
- Is there a taste in your mouth? Are you drinking or at dinner?

- Feel what your skin is feeling—what is the temperature, is there a breeze, what is the texture of your clothing?
- What emotions are you feeling? Identify where these emotions now sit in your body. Is there anticipation, nervousness, excitement, sadness, boredom? Are you laughing? Are you totally engrossed in someone or something else?
- Remove your robe and become skyclad.

Replay this situation and allow your partner to enter the picture just as you remember them doing.

How is this different? How do your senses change? How do your feelings change?

Where in your body are you feeling the effects of your partner? Feel it, touch it, taste it, see it, hear it.

Building Power

Allow your body to become fully engaged in this experience. Take pleasure in this! Stay in this experience by following the situation through until its natural close. Take your time. Feel fully everything you felt back then. You may even choose to magnify and replay the really wonderful bits!

Now ask yourself: What was it that attracted you initially? What were the elements of this person in front of you that caused this reaction to happen in your body?

Take your notepad or BOS and write down the details of what it was that attracted you back then. This is easy to describe as you are living it again right now! Note in particular how and where your body is reacting—for example: "I felt my pupils dilate. When he spoke to me, I felt a heat in my throat. I caught my breath. I couldn't stop smiling. I blushed."

After making notes, close your eyes again for a time to reconnect with the experience.

Release Your Intention

When you are again experiencing the peak of this connection, hold the mirror up to your face and open your eyes. Look!

Witness how you look fully flushed with the power of love, pleasure, and that essence that first connected you with your partner (or to yourself). See the evidence of how pleasure changes your body. Note how you feel: laugh, smile, do whatever it is that your body now wishes.

Then say out loud:

> *I feel what it is to be connected*
> *To pleasure, to body, to you*
> *I remember my own greatness*
> *This connection, so strong, so true.*

Offer Your Gratitude

Know that the Goddess has heard your intention for the reconnection of pleasure to your body and to your partner.

Thank the Goddess. Be grateful in the knowledge that all is as you have asked it to be, if it be her will and for the greatest good of all. Know your mind and body are already responding to this.

Complete the Ritual

Close your Circle. Ground yourself by eating or drinking something, exercising, or dancing! Or if she or he is available, grab hold of your partner and initiate something delicious!

Participation

Know that all you need do to reconnect to your body and to your partner is to look in that mirror and recall how you looked and felt during the ritual. Take your notepad or BOS and ensure you are aware of the elements that attracted you to your partner in the first place. Are these elements still there or just buried under layers of everyday life or history? Have you forgotten why you felt so attracted to your partner or to the experience of this in your own body?

Reminding each other or yourself of the power and pleasure of attraction is in itself a very connecting, intimate exercise. You may wish to share your experience with your partner as a bonding exercise or for healing.

Book of Shadows Entries

Chart your progress by recording your feelings, behaviors, actions, and results, paying close attention to coincidences and details, even if they seem insignificant or unrelated at the time.

Remember to date all your entries.

Sex

I thought long and hard about the form this section would take; after all it would be discussing possibly one of the most popular subjects in the world. What hasn't already been said, seen, or written? There are so many books on the shelves on sex, so many films, so much information, misinformation, tools, toys, science, and, of course, porn. The way forward was made crystal clear one morning when I sat with two friends of mine, one male and one female, over coffee.

Both of these friends were single, but in the early parts of a new coupling. The subject of sex was raised, I guess, as a natural consequence of the freshness of both their relationships. My girlfriend, who had not had sex with someone in almost a year, said, "I didn't realize how much I missed it, although it's that feeling of being desired that I really missed most. It's such a turn on to be desired, to see that light flash up in his eyes when he sees me."

My male friend, someone who has had lots of sexual encounters in between this new relationship, answered.

"Interesting. I never thought about it that way. Yes, I like being desirable and desired, but it's really the act in itself that stimulates me. It's the actual bump and grind. I must admit I have a pretty good inner fantasy life though. When I'm feeling horny, I can just turn that little TV on in my head and boom, I'm having a great time and I don't need anyone else!"

Listening to these two completely different but equally valid points of view, I realized that sex, and our attitudes, bodily responses, and beliefs toward it, were so uniquely personal that it could only be the Goddess' work in its diversity and richness in action. Recognizing this, it was all the more important to find through tolerance and understanding the common threads that make sexual connection and intimacy all the more possible. One such commonality is that sex contains a pure creative energy.

The Witches Way tells us that there is an undercurrent of creative force in each of us that hums away in every cell of our bodies and flows through our spirits like quicksilver. This is the Goddess' gift to us. When we choose to open ourselves fully to that creative force, in this case through sex, we continue that creativity, magnify it, and send it back as a gift to her. Whether that creativity takes the form of pleasure,or as an additional expression of love, we have an equally precious gift. Should that sex lead to the creation of a child, then we have a physical manifestation of that multiplication.

Witches' Beliefs About Sex

There has been so much misinformation about how pagans, and specifically witches, view sex. Everything from virgin sacrifices, public sex, and having sex only with Satan has been popularly raised over many centuries, so to clear things up, here is my attempt to summarize the basic beliefs of witches about Sex.

Sex is a Natural, Healthy Act: Witches see nothing shameful, unnatural, or unhealthy about consensual sex, nor with a healthy amount of self-pleasuring. This does not mean in any way that we could be considered promiscuous; it's just that we tend to have less hang-ups about it. Sex is something that we see as an active prayer to the Goddess and praise for her innate creativity and love.

It is important to note that we also see sex as a synergistic act, which celebrates an equality and balance between the sexes. Sex is a direct expression of our inner creativity and our synergy with another's creativity. There is no room for power games in the witches' view of sex. We only acknowledge a combining of two equal (but different) energies creating something new, unique, and far greater than the sum of its parts.

Its Expression is Highly Individual and Should Be Honored as Such: Here again, the honoring of and respect of the individual and the individual's needs is paramount. We ask that moralistic judgments be left to one side and differences celebrated. As long as the rede of Harm None is being adhered to, the Witches Way accepts all sexual orientations and preferences. This is one reason why Paganism and the Witches Way is attracting more and more gay and lesbian people and those who do not typically fit cultural norms sexually.

As the Harm None rede is our guide, any sexual act that harms another—for example, deliberate violence or any activity such as sexual addiction or pedophilia—is totally abhorrent and unacceptable. The Witches Way is highly beneficial and greatly aids healing for those touched by sexual crimes, and I have personally witnessed many survivors of sexual assaults who have experienced breakthroughs in their recoveries through spiritual practices such as Cutting the Cords.

Sex Should Never Be Used as a Weapon in Any Way: Sex is considered a source of natural, divine-given pleasure and thus is a prayer to the Goddess. To use sex as a weapon in any way intentionally is to misuse a great gift and cause harm to our Selves or others. We normally have an idea if the sex is a celebration of life or love, or something else.

Typical methods of using sex as a weapon could include:

- Repeated one-night stands with intentions not made clear to the other person, causing hurt and misplaced desire.
- Unprotected sex.
- Intentional dissociative sex.
- Withholding sex.
- Choosing porn over partner.
- Any kind of manipulative or unconsensual sex.

Witches see it as important to acknowledge our misuse of sexual energies and transform it into something beneficial. Coming to terms with the fact that you use sex as a weapon either toward yourself or others is the first step in ridding yourself of the destructive beliefs underpinning this action and moving into wholeness and balance. Developing a solid personal foundation is key to winning the battle against this kind of sexual dysfunction and into paving the way for better relationships.

Sex Is Not Shameful Unless It Is Bound to Something Shameful: Sexual repression became one weapon used in the fight against the old ways, and, in particular, over the power of women. Even today, in many extreme codes of religion, sex is considered deeply shameful, or sometimes even a criminal act should sex happen outside these religious norms. We live in a world where the pleasure of this natural act is denied by some societies under the label of religious tradition. For example, in many parts of the world, female circumcision is still widely practiced.

Having lived in the Swahili regions of Kenya for a period, I was privy to a female circumcision and the celebration around the ritual by the village. I can share with you that being exposed to this was probably one of the single most powerful turning points in my life. I had the rude awakening to the real consequences of the control of pleasure by religion/tradition, and the power over feminine rights to pleasure. The force of tradition at this event was so powerful that it was trance-like in its ability to take an incredibly violent and painful mutilation and almost (but not quite) make it acceptable to everyone, including the recipient. I say "almost" because up until shortly before the actual circumcision the girl and her family were looking very excited and made to feel special by the other villages. Feasts were prepared, special clothes and jewelry made, and there was much anticipation.

Then I watched as the women, who were all singing traditional songs, led the young woman into the special hut. Among those voices, the girl's mother suddenly broke down sobbing and had to be restrained by the other women. This panicked her daughter, and in this moment the truth of the situation broke through the veils of the ritual activity. The young woman screamed, but was quickly subdued and carried inside the tent. There was much clucking in disapproval by the other women at the weakness of the mother who sat on her haunches outside the hut, head down, grieving for not only her daughter's lost joy, but her own.

Shocked and angry, I found myself crying too, knowing that something had changed for me having borne witness to this. I was completely devastated at the injustice and my own powerlessness to do anything. Later, these feelings wove themselves into a vow that I would always stand for the honoring of the power of women and their birthright to shame-free, equal expression.

Even if we do not buy into the religious controls of sex, we often have individuals sanctioned by society that have passed judgment on the act in order to *protect* us. Sometimes, our parents, teachers, and other authority figures shame us into thinking sex is a dirty or naughty thing. This extends to our attitudes to our bodies, and our genitalia in particular. For example, I was at the beach last week and a little boy was on the beach playing close to me. He was building sandcastles and having a brilliant time. Unfortunately, he was sitting right where the shore met the waves and sand was getting washed into his little Speedos! So he did what any three-year-old would do—he whipped them off, laughing! He then gave his penis a good shake to get the rest of the sand off it. His mother saw him do this and rushed over saying: "David! Don't do that! That's very naughty! Put your swimmers back on NOW." And she promptly pulled his wet, sandy swimmers back on him. He then again did what a three-year-old would do after being shamed: He cried.

I wonder how being shamed for just doing what came naturally would affect him in the future?

Shame in its positive intent can be a protector, a canary in the coal mine if it is bound to something truly inappropriate. The pendulum can swing the other way, with inappropriate displays of nudity within the home or with sexual abuse.

One client of mine, let's call her Gina, spoke of the way her father would walk around the house naked. She never really noticed it much until one day he had what she later understood to be an erection. This, of course, is inappropriate and not so innocent. Many experts on child sexual abuse agree that generally the rule is, if it feels inappropriate (or shameful) it probably is.

If you are feeling shame about the sexual act, your own sexual body, or even the thought of sex, I would invite you to explore why. Are these thoughts your thoughts? Or are they cultural norms, your parents' view, or someone else's view? Do you need to update your points of reference or clean out your old belief system? Perhaps you need to uncouple the shackles that link normal healthy sexual experiences with toxic shame?

Sex Raises Power and Can Therefore Be Used to Project Intention: There are many ways to raise power to send out our intentions in ritual and spell craft. Any powerful emotion (e-motion) or physical action can set energy moving, growing, and rising, and can be used to direct intent, whether you raise energy as a solitary practitioner or are raising energy as a coven to be directed and funneled by a priestess or priest.

I want to set the record straight when it comes to the way witches use sex to raise power. As mentioned earlier in the Mythology vs. Truth section, witches do not engage in orgies or any other mass practice as per popular media reports. In covens, if the particular ritual calls for it, the priest and priestess may practice what is termed the Great Rite. This is a ritual joining of the male and female energies. The "sex" is extremely ritualized and rarely involves actual penetration, or if it does, rarely ejaculation. The Great Rite is something that is only practiced in closed covens where the members have complete trust in one another and strict rules about what is appropriate are strictly upheld.

Solitary practitioners or those in partnerships may choose to use the peak experience of orgasm to send intentions out into the Universe. You may wish to refer to the basic framework below, should you be interested in trying this. Again, if you are performing this kind of power raising with a partner, it is important that it is consensual and that you have an intention that you both want or with which you agree. One person may assist with another's intention but must fully support it.

Basic Framework for Raising Power Through Sex

- Set your intention prior to your ritual/spell. Be very clear about what it is that you require and you should be able to state this in one simple sentence, phrase, or word.

- Decide where you will be: bedroom, bed, or outdoors, and prepare accordingly. If your partner is involved, discuss the outline of the ritual.

- Light a candle with intent and begin to burn your preferred herbs.

- If you are Wiccan, you may wish to use the athame and chalice as a symbol of your creative union and the joining of the masculine and feminine energies. You may also wish to call in patron deities if relevant.

- After stating your intention, begin to raise power in the way that you planned. This is a highly creative process, as previously mentioned in the Anatomy of a Spell section. The key things in raising power sexually are that you first connect with your partner, then build power in a consistent yet gradual fashion, and that you attempt to climax together to power and release a shared intention. Knowing your partner's body and knowing your own is essential to great power raising. Know what he or she likes, working with this in its infinite variety. Use sound, smell, and sight, as well as touch.

Some tips:

- Maintain eye contact as much as possible.
- Utilize some of the bonding exercises in this book.
- Use each other's names.
- Avoid being distracted by other parts of the ritual (herbs, candles, etc.).
- Communicate.

When you are both near or at the point of orgasm, begin to verbalize your intention. At the point of orgasm, yell out your intention loudly, projecting it out into the Universe. Imagine the power of the release of sexual energy propelling your intention toward the Goddess.

For example: Should you wish for more freedom in your lives, you might exclaim at the point of orgasm: "Free me! Free me! Free me!" Or simply, "FREEDOM!"

Then, as usual, offer gratitude and ground yourselves after you have had some time to relax and recover.

Witches Are Present and Fully In Their Bodies for Sex: For many reasons we sometimes find it difficult to be fully present during sex. This may be either a chronic problem or a short-term one.

People who have learned to disassociate themselves from sex normally have done so as a defense mechanism. This defense may have been created to cope with trauma, rejection (real or imagined), or toxic shame. Being the partner of someone who is not present during sex is a rather uncomfortable experience.

Leandra, a filmmaker from England, discusses her husband Jacob's behavior: "Jacob is really there one minute and completely gone the next. It's almost like turning off a light. I can't really describe it other than that he just isn't paying attention. I understand Jacob learned to disassociate due to his experience of sexual abuse as a child, but it is heart-breaking to look into his eyes and see no one there for me." Along with a program of sexual therapy and psychotherapy, Leandra and Jacob also began some of the Getting Back into the Body exercises, and Jacob later Cut the Cords with his attacker, bringing a new level of intimacy to their relationship.

Abbey, a woman in her thirties, only realized she was disassociating when her husband was apparently talking to her during sex, but she had absolutely no awareness of this.

"Eric was asking me sweet little questions and whispering things to me and I was just off with the fairies. I was vaguely aware of what was happening but I really wasn't even in my body."

Eric comments: "Frankly, I thought she must have been really bored or that she didn't find me attractive anymore. You know, maybe she was just going through the motions."

Abbey's problem proved to be only a short-term one brought on by extreme tiredness during a period of intense work. She began to incorporate the Eye-to-Eye Technique into their lovemaking (see below) and asked Eric to ground her with his eyes and by calling the magical word. They had quick and positive results.

Eye-to-Eye Technique: Try this simple exercise to assist you to be present and associated during sex:

At some stage in the exploration (or foreplay) part of your sexual practice, ensure you have deep eye contact with your partner. Really look at the person behind those eyes. Connect with that being. (This may feel very confrontational at first, especially if you find being seen difficult.)

The first time you both do this, allow a magical word to float to the surface of your unconscious, a word that will signify a connection or grounding to that person. This can be a talismanic word, if you like. This word can be uttered safely by your partner to you if they feel you are disassociating, or by you, if you wish to bring yourself back to the here and now. Agree on and share a word for each of you. Only use this word in this context.

Discovering Your Beliefs About Sex

Each of us has a set of beliefs about sex that have been built over time. We each have a set of dos, don'ts, buttons, taboos, and they are extremely powerful and deep rooted when about sex. It is useful to examine and if necessary challenge our beliefs around sex in order to get clear about what our needs, wants, and desires are, and what may be the obstacles in our achieving them. As part of the process of building a powerful Self, gaining self-knowledge about sex and our attitudes toward it is vitally important.

For example, I invite you to examine how you feel/believe about:

- Self-pleasuring: masturbation. Is this a healthy, shameful, or habitual act?

- Same sex relationships.

- Sex outside marriage.

- Sex after childbirth.

- Experimentation. Are you open to trying new experiences in a safe environment?

- Expectation of romance as an essential part of the sexual process.

- Sex as a weapon or bargaining tool. Do you withhold sex to get what you want? Do you use sex or sexual advances to manipulate others?

- Rules around sex. Do you have a set of rules or values around sex that haven't changed since you were a teenager? Do you think sex is a naughty or secretive thing? Do you only approve of sex sanctioned by marriage? Do you think that by giving yourself in sex, love should automatically follow?

- Sex as a painkiller: Do you have sex to just cover the pain of loneliness, shame, fear, or low self-esteem?

- A pre-determined level of desire. The idea that you do or do not have a large or small sex drive. The idea that libido will automatically wane as time marches on.

Let us look at some of these points in greater detail.

Self-Pleasuring: As my male friend said over coffee, having a healthy sexual life, whether or not you have a partner to share it with is nothing to be ashamed of, for exploring your own fantasies is part of exploring your Self. Many of us do not have the healthy, shame-free attitude of my friend, and feel that masturbation is somewhat dirty.

The Witches Way facilitates an honoring of one's unique sexual self and encourages the exploration of fulfilling the potential of this. It guides us to gently see that our bodies are beautiful, our nakedness is precious, and our Selves are too magnificent to be offered to sex that is empty or unpleasurable. If we do not have a partner to share the sexual dance with we are shown that we should not hold back waiting. The Goddess does not ask us to suffer by relying on the permission or presence of another.

Familiarizing Yourself with Your Own Body: Many clients tell me that they are unsatisfied with their sexual lives because they rarely, if at all, experience orgasm. When we begin to explore the reasons it is common to find that many women feel uncomfortable with their own bodies, and are not actually exploring physically what does push their desire buttons. Her own body image may be so poor that the woman cannot let herself go and enjoy sex. If you are experiencing any sexual dysfunction, it is important to have this examined by your health provider. There may well be a medical reason for your problem. Either way, the Witches Way can support you in building both your self-esteem and allowing you to freely explore you own body.

I would suggest performing the Health and Vitality Ritual (paying particular attention to the genital region) and performing Power Circles on a regular basis as starters. I would also recommend calling in some suitable Goddess/God consultants such as Freya, Yemaya, or Oya to assist you in your endeavors, in particular if you decide to eventually try to raise power sexually.

Loneliness: Feeling lonely is a natural part of life for all of us at one time or another. Unfortunately, in this world of increasing speed we are becoming more isolated from each other and less inclined to connect with others in a real or deep way.

Witches tackle the problem of loneliness by reminding themselves that we are never truly alone. We grow the faith that enables us to know completely that we are connected to the Goddess and everything and everyone else. This is not a uniquely Wiccan view, but one that permeates many Pagan and traditional belief systems.

The American Indians, Inuit, and Australian Aborigines have spiritual practices and mythology that support and understand the fact that we are part of the same web of life, connected in ways overt and covert. When we believe that we belong to and are an important member of a wider web, it is difficult to feel as isolated and ignored.

We make the distinction between loneliness and being alone. Having enough solitary time where we can reach inside and reconnect with our Selves should be a primary need for all of us. Finding a balance between being alone and being with someone is often a challenge for many of us, and is only exacerbated when it comes to our sexual partners.

The witches' view on achieving this balance is an interesting one. By building our power from the inside out and acknowledging that we are inherently connected to all things, we can choose more freely whom we give our intimate time to. We do not feel that we must be with someone in order to not feel the pain of abandonment and loneliness. Instead, we can choose more carefully and with more intent, resulting in more suitable and satisfying partnerships.

Theo came to see me with his wife Denise. He felt that Denise wanted to spend every minute with him and he found this draining. Denise, on the other hand, believed that Theo was ignoring her and that couples should spend as much time together as possible. A cycle had developed where the more desperate Denise became for her husband's time, the more time Theo needed to be apart. Clearly, both had a different expectation of what being alone meant.

"I simply am someone who needs some down time, some me time on a regular basis. This is the time that I use to just recharge my batteries. I do this by either running on my own a couple of times a week, or tinkering in the garage with my car. I reckon this would take up, oh, maybe four hours a week. I don't think I'm asking for much!" explained Theo.

Denise commented: "We are both busy at work and I want to be able to spend as much time with him as possible when we are home. It's not just four hours. It's four hours at the end of the day, and by the time he gets home and showers or whatever, he is too tired to talk to me. I put him first and he doesn't do the same."

We explored this theme, discussed their expectations, and delved deeper into belief systems.

"I thought being a good partner meant we did everything together. I can see that this isn't really true. I can see that perhaps we can come to some compromise situation that involves me doing some things on my own that I may enjoy," said Denise.

Theo agreed. "I can see that I have a lifestyle that isn't conducive to building a good relationship and that perhaps I can rearrange things to spend more time together. However, I'm most happy about Denise realizing she has few interests without me. This will be great for her and for us."

Six months down the track, after Denise practiced Power Circles consistently, she and Theo are much happier. Denise comments, "I think by building my own interests and self-esteem, my life seems fuller and our relationship is much closer. Who would have thought that by letting go, I got more time with Theo after all?"

Understanding that we need to grow independently of each other, clear and strong, yet remain connected, is perhaps one of the key teachings of the Witches Way as it applies to relationships. Being alone does not equate to being lonely.

Desire

One of the most truthful sayings I have ever heard about the nature of desire is that the biggest aphrodisiac for many women is having their husbands help around the home!

We are busy. We do have countless things to do, and strangely, being desired is one of the last things on our list. Some of us just don't do desire or pleasure much anymore. If we were really rational about it, we would engage in more sexually related activity, even if it was purely just for the chemical and physical benefits it gives us, including increasing our feelings of happiness and reducing stress levels.

Take some of these comments about desire and sex from some of my case study participants:

- "I love sex when I do it, but getting around to it, choosing it, is the problem." —Allan, 32, UK
- "I really fancy my husband, but the idea of sex just doesn't appeal to me most of the time." —Julie, 40, UK

- "My husband doesn't make me feel desired. We just go through the motions. There's no excitement." —Greta, 50, USA

- "I love feeling desired and I love to desire someone. I'm really into it when it happens but I just don't seem to have the stamina to keep it all going after a while." —Tate, 27, Australia

- "Our holiday sex is fantastic. It's just a shame those holidays last only four weeks!" —Calle, 33, Australia

A recurrent theme is that life gets in the way and that we just do not choose to connect with sex—even though when we do, we enjoy it!

The Witches Way guides us to see that pleasure and sexual connection is as important to schedule into our lives as work or eating. It asks us to take time to safely open our channels of creativity in this way and connect with ourselves more deeply through ecstasy, rather than hard work.

As far back as we know, witches have been involved in increasing desire and in the reestablishment of soul priorities such as better relationships and greater connections. Through spell craft, building a stronger personal foundation and making pleasure and play a balanced part of life is more than possible. Additionally, witches have always had their vast herbal and food knowledge to give a gentle (or not so gentle) push to flagging or lagging desire.

Aphrodisiacs

For literally thousands of years pagan peoples, including witches, have been prescribing herbs or food to boost desire and sexual performance. These days, many herbs have been through stringent processes of independent clinical trials to assess their effectiveness, and such is their effectiveness that some combinations are available only by prescription in some countries.

Although herbs are completely natural substances, never take any herb internally without professional advice from your herbalist or healthcare practitioner. While I cannot personally prescribe any herbs to you as each of your situations are unique, I would especially recommend the following herbs to you as aphrodisiacs:

- Damiana (antidepressant, relaxant, testostermimetic)
- Ginkgo (boosts peripheral circulation, mind tonic)

- Ginseng (stamina inducing, stimulant/relaxant)

- Horny Goat Weed (boosts peripheral circulation, antidepressant)

- Yerba Maté or Yerba (Gentle stimulant, increases overall energy levels, induces stamina)

- Sarsaparilla (aids movement, anti-inflammatory, and latest clinical studies are proving that it is useful in the treatment of sexual dysfunction with psychological causes.)

- Saw palmetto (For men only: assists penile function, balances hormones, sperm production)

Foods that have high levels of aphrodisiac substances include: oysters, fresh green vegetables, blueberries, wheat grass, seaweed, chocolate, and chili.

Aphrodisiacs generally act by affecting the mental and/or physical aspects related to sexual function in the body to correct imbalances.

Mentally: Certain herbs and foods have a direct stimulating effect on the brain, triggering a cascade of responses linked to desire. In simple terms, in some of the recent clinical trials of herbal aphrodisiacs, those taking the herbs registered increased feelings of overall well being, and actually took the initiative to instigate sex more often. We also know that a vast majority of couples in a committed relationship actually love sex when they have it, but don't initiate it often enough, so this kind of herbal assistance should be just what the witches ordered!

Physically: Herbs and foods that we call aphrodisiacs perform a variety of different functions on the body. Some are stimulants that increase blood flow, which in turn can increase sensitivity to the genitalia, which of course can lead to more satisfying orgasms. Some offer the body a relaxant effect that enables one to turn off stress more easily and to relax into the experience. Combined in specific quantities, there is a proven synergistic effect that often creates a more powerful effect than using the herbs singly.

If you have never tried an aphrodisiac, why not give it a try? Cooking an aphrodisiac dinner for your lover or deciding to take some herbal aphrodisiacs (again only with professional advice) may well be that extra encouragement that will allow you to have more fun, more often. Combining an aphrodisiac with some of the suggestions in the next section once in a while should give you a night (or day) that you won't forget!

Sex by the Seasons

One of the attitudes that sets Paganism and Wicca apart from other spiritual practices is its veneration of and reflection of the natural cycles of nature. As you have read, Witches pay special attention to many natural rhythms of the earth, including the phases of the moon, the ebb and flow of the tide, the gradual change of day into night (and back again), and the balance of light and darkness over time.

Witches also mark the seasons and see them as times reminding us to weave ourselves into the innate and unique meaning that each season brings.

Let's look at some meanings that we consistently place on the different seasons within Witchcraft Traditions:

- Summer: Extroversion, pleasure, freedom, plenty, abundance.
- Autumn: Planning, preparation, consolidation, beauty in change, harvest.
- Winter: Introversion, rest, hibernation, incubation.
- Spring: New birth, new growth, a time for cleansing and the release of stagnant energy.

Whether or not you call yourself Wiccan or Pagan, there appear to be some links between fertility and sexual behavior that are connected to these seasonal changes. Even today, most births happen in the early spring months. Most conceptions therefore are the fruits of summer pleasures. A higher number of weddings in Western cultures occur in the spring or autumn (new growth/consolidation) than at any other time of the year. These are not coincidences, but perhaps, accidents of nature.

Considering the natural flow of nature seems to increase our satisfaction when it comes to sex. Why not create some suggestions that would reflect the attitudes of the seasons rather than go against the grain?

Summer Sex

Summer is a time when everything is at its peak, when the earth stretches out fully after its period of growth and awakening in spring. It is when people are more likely to be outside, relishing the warm weather—traditionally the time for parties, for socializing, and celebration. In Australia, we are blessed in most areas with a fairly temperate to hot climate (with some notable exceptions) and our culture is one that has grown up around the external. Like the TV commercials, we do tend to have lots of barbeques in our backyards or enjoy our meals alfresco in beautiful surroundings. Most of our population lives on or close to the coast, so enjoying life by the sea is desirable for many of us. Most of our major festivals are summer ones and there would be few Australians who would prefer the middle of winter to our glorious summertime.

Summer sex, therefore, should reflect the qualities of summer itself. Consider it to be extroverted, daring, open, and the culmination of your experience and technique, having at its heart a healthy sense of fun and much laughter. For those of you planning a pregnancy, summer is your ideal time to conceive at the peak of the earth's energies.

Summer Sex Suggestions

Outdoors: While some traditional pagan rituals such as Beltaine involve sexual activity outdoors in nature, many of us are uncomfortable with the idea. Perhaps this is something you may have tried as a teenager but not since then. Summer is the ideal time to reconnect with the fertile powers of the earth by making love on it and within it. It is warm enough and the smells and sounds of a summer night are certainly aphrodisiacs if we choose to involve ourselves. You don't have to go too public if you are a little shy—your deck, verandah, or backyard are viable choices! Remember, this is not an exercise in exhibitionism, and do ensure your own safety. One regular outdoors man I know goes on reconnaissance trips prior to bringing his partner along to a chosen place in nature. He checks for privacy, safety, even insects!

Experiment: Summer is the time to open up our minds and bodies to the fullest and experiment. Be mindful that everyone is different and be respectful in discussing this with your partner if you wish to try something very new. Summer is the time to extend our current techniques and open ourselves to new kinds and intensities of pleasure. If experimentation makes you feel nervous or anxious, now is the time to ask yourself why this is so, especially if you do have a partner you can trust. This may well be the time to look at your fears (see chapters on fear and pleasure respectively) and overcome this.

Timing: If you are in the habit of having sex in the morning or evening, summer is the time to try sex by solar! Plan a sweaty session in the middle of the day when Father Sun is at his zenith. The often-unexpected thrill of connecting with this very masculine energy can produce some hot results!

Planning a pregnancy? Summer is the best time to do it! Often when we are deciding to have a child together, sex becomes often all about conception rather than the combination of pleasure and love that ignites the creative spark.

Faking summer: For those of you living in parts of the world where summer isn't a true season (i.e., it's still very cold) you might consider upping the ante a little. Why not turn up your heat very high or even have a quickie in the sauna (please ensure your health is up to this). Instead of giving a massage with massage oil at room temperature, why not heat it gently so that your partner experiences a heated "summer" massage. Be sure to use essential oils of tropical flowers such as frangipani or orchid for extra effect.

Summer Sex Ritual

Preparation

Planning Ahead: Decide which room or where outdoors you will have your ritual. Ensure it's a comfortable temperature. Make this Summer Ritual one celebrated during the day in full sunlight. Ensure you will be undisturbed. Have your intention clearly in mind.

Gather

Candle, preferably red or green
Charcoal with herbs: damiana, life everlasting, basil, sandalwood, and myrrh
Glass of your favorite champagne or wine, or tropical fruit juice

Welcome the Goddess and thank her for being with you here tonight in this beautiful place.

Focus

Cast and open a Circle if you wish. Light the candle and sit within or near the sunshine.

Now invoke the Goddess and God:

> *I call you, great Goddess of Summer and heat.*
> *You who delights in the full bloom and full fruition of all things*
> *green and growing. Today I/we call upon you to help us celebrate*
> *summer's glory and (insert intention). I call you Great God of Summer and solar.*
> *You who encourages us to celebrate the heat and energy of summer.*
> *Today I/we call upon you to assist us with (insert intention).*
> *Great Goddess and God, I/we ask that you be here tonight*
> *to bless the union that will soon take place.*

Light your herbs or incense. Breathe in the energies.

Now relax and connect with each other. Share a sip or two of champagne or juice. Slip out of your robes and begin the eye-to-eye technique. Take several deep breaths, breathing out all stress and tension.

Building Power

First, connect your bodies with the sunshine. Feel how it generates vitality and heat within you and outside you. Touch your partner and feel the heat on their skin.

Begin to talk to each other about why you love summer and what you find "hot" about each other. Use detail and touch. This will soon lead to more physical connection.

Feel how desired you are, how much the feminine or masculine draws you. Take your time and enjoy this. Allow yourself to feel the absolute pleasure of making love/having sex. There is so much power in each one and they belong to you.

Feel how good each part of your body feels in the soft warmth now being generated from your genitals. You feel fully alive!

Feel how this sexual power is now racing through your body and that of your partner.

Accept these gifts in your own body. Feel your own strength and that of the Goddess course through you. Now focus on the feeling of that power coursing through you.

In a loud, firm voice begin a chant around your intention if you have prepared one or are an advanced practitioner.

Release Your Intention

When you are both near or at the point of orgasm begin to verbalize your intention if you haven't already. At the point of orgasm, yell out your intention loudly, projecting it out into the Universe. You may wish to release your intention by shouting: "Yes!" or a word or two that expresses your intention. Imagine the power of the release of sexual energy propelling your intention toward the Goddess and God.

You should feel a huge surge of energy and of heat. Allow yourself to express with abandon: shout, laugh, or whatever else you may feel.

Offer Your Gratitude

Know that the Goddess and God of Summer have heard your intention, and are speeding your intention through your body and mind.

Thank the Goddess and God in your own way. Be grateful in the knowledge that all is as you have asked it to be, if it be her/his will and for the greatest good of all.

Know your mind and body is already responding.

Complete the Ritual

Enjoy some quiet breathing time together and enjoy the remainder of your champagne or juice.

Put on your robes if you wish.

Extinguish and bury any remaining charcoal and herbs/incense in the garden or yard.

Ground yourself by eating or drinking something, or perhaps sharing with your partner what happened during the ritual.

You may wish to light the candle during some quiet time over the next few nights to remind you of your intention.

Participation

Sit down together and agree on three participatory points toward achieving your intention. Act on at least one of these within the next forty-eight hours.

Book of Shadows Entries

If you wish, record your feelings, behaviors, actions, and results. Share these with your partner if you wish.

Autumn Sex

Fall is one of the times of year where we can witness the changing of the seasons most vividly. We watch as the leaves change from green to rich reds and oranges and then, in time, fall to the earth, to be reassimilated with the soil.

It is a time of relief from the burning hot heat of the summer and a time for preparation for the scarcity of the winter ahead. Traditionally autumn was the time for the last harvest before the cold snap, and as such was a very busy time of year for the folk of the land. They would preserve the last of the summer and early fall fruits, begin to store grains, salt meat, and plant seeds to be ready for spring.

Allow autumn sex to reflect the nature of the season by incorporating the themes of planning, preparation, consolidation, and change. I love the idea of extending your repertoire and building on your existing techniques.

Autumn Sex Suggestions

This is a time for vision building, consolidation, extending your new tricks, and trying something new.

Reading Each Other Sexy Stories or Writing Them: You don't have to be a best-selling writer to pen a special fantasy just for your loved one! Take a risk and write a bedtime story that she or he will never forget. If you are not sure what your partner might find stimulating, why not ask? You may get some hints that will liven up your practice. If writing really isn't your thing, go to a bookstore and buy some quality erotica. Snuggle up between the sheets and take turns reading. You may not even get to the end!

Taking Turns: As change is one of the keys of autumn, why not make a special effort to take turns in a sexual theme. This could be as simple as each of you taking turns to choose a location, or something more elaborate. For example: why not allow one partner total control one night, encouraging them to create an ideal setting. Of course, get clear consent from your partner, especially if this is a new activity for him or her. Remember "no" always means "no." This is a particularly challenging exercise if the same person always initiates sex or generally directs the act. The idea of taking turns to control the setting or activity exposes any mistrust in the relationship, and accordingly builds trust between you.

Harvest time: As the harvest and preparation of food happens in autumn why not incorporate food into your sexual life. Perhaps you haven't been out as a couple to a wonderful restaurant in a while (and especially without the kids!), so make a reservation, dress up in your sexiest gear, and have the dessert in bed at home! If you have never played with food, this may well be the time to experiment! Honey, mango, whipped cream, and champagne are all delicious, decadent things to lick, sip, and suck from your partner's body.

Autumn Sex Ritual

Preparation

Planning ahead: Decide which room or where outdoors you will have your ritual, and ensure that it is a comfortable temperature. Make this autumn ritual a nighttime ritual. Also ensure you will be undisturbed. Have your intention clearly in mind.

Gather

Candle, preferably orange or yellow
Charcoal with herbs: dill, lotus root, orris root, and frankincense
The biggest, yummiest apple you can find

Some suitably fun foods to play with: cream, honey, chocolate—whatever takes your fancy!

Welcome the Goddess and thank her for being with you here tonight in this beautiful place.

Focus

Cast and open a Circle if you wish. Light the candle and sit within the light or near the sunshine.

Now invoke the Goddess and God:

> *I call you, great Goddess of Autumn. You who delights in the growth,*
> *change, and the celebration of the harvest of all things.*
> *Today I/we call upon you to help us celebrate autumn's glory*
> *and (insert intention). I call you Great God of Autumn and plenty.*
> *You who co-creates in our strength and potential.*
> *Today I/we call upon you to assist us with (insert intention).*
> *Great Goddess and God, I/we ask that you be here tonight*
> *to bless the union that will soon occur.*

Light your herbs or incense. Breathe in the energies.

Now relax and connect with each other. Slip out of your robes and begin the eye-to-eye technique. Take several deep breaths, breathing out all stress and tension.

Building Power

First, one of you take the apple. The apple signifies the harvest of your lives together (or singly) up to this point. Everything you are is harvested today, right here, right now.

Think about what you have achieved as a couple or singly in relation to each other. Think about positive aspects only.

Now take a bite: Tell your partner about one of these aspects and how it has changed or benefited your life. Talk about this harvest in a detailed and honest way. Then kiss your partner, and pass the apple to him or her. They should take a bite and do the same. Continue passing the apple, telling harvest stories, and kissing until the apple is consumed.

Now, begin to play with some of the delicious ingredients you have gathered. You might like to paint each other with cream, suck honey from the places that your partner finds most sensitive, and don't just concentrate on the genitals—get creative! Above all, have fun!

Feel how desired you are, how much the feminine or masculine draws you. Take your time and enjoy this.

Allow yourself to feel the absolute pleasure of making love/having sex. There is so much power in this harvest and this power can be directed toward what you desire. Feel how this sexual power is now racing through your body and that of your partner.

Accept these gifts in your own body. Feel your own strength and that of the Goddess/God course through you. Now focus on the feeling of that power coursing through you.

In a loud, firm voice begin a chant about your intention if you have prepared one or are an advanced practitioner.

Release Your Intention

When you are both near or at the point of orgasm, begin to verbalize your intention if you haven't already. At the point of orgasm, yell out your intention loudly, projecting it out into the Universe. You may wish to release your intention by shouting: "Yes!" or a word or two that expresses your intention. Imagine the power of the release of sexual energy propelling your intention toward the Goddess and God. You should feel a huge surge of energy and of heat.

Allow yourself to express with abandon: shout, laugh, or whatever else you may feel.

Offer Your Gratitude

Know that the Goddess and God of Summer have heard your intention, and are speeding your intention through your body and mind.

Thank the Goddess and God in your own way. Be grateful in the knowledge that all is as you have asked it to be, if it be her/his will and for the greatest good of all.

Know your mind and body is already responding.

Complete the Ritual

Enjoy some quiet breathing time together. Put on your robes if you wish.

Extinguish and bury any remaining charcoal and herbs/incense in the garden or yard. You may also wish to have a quick bath or shower to get rid of residual food!

Ground yourself by eating or drinking something else, or perhaps sharing what happened during the ritual with your partner.

You might like to light the candle during some quiet time over the next few nights to remind you of your intention.

Participation

Sit down together and agree on three participatory points toward achieving your intention. Act on at least one of these within the next forty-eight hours.

Book of Shadows Entries

Record your feelings, behaviors, actions, and results. Share these with your partner if you wish.

Winter Sex

Winter is traditionally a time for rest as well as braving out the leaner, more difficult times. Within the circle of the witches' year, winter is a time for introspection, of deeper thought, and of the examination of the Shadow side of our selves. It can be the time where we allow to wither away and die what does not serve us or our relationship.

Winter Sex Suggestions

Integrate the energies of winter into your sexual relationship by weaving the themes of rest, hibernation, and cleansing.

The Best Kind of Hibernation: Weekends in bed! Why not do what bears do and snuggle down in your own cave. This one though is a lot more comfortable and built for two! This may take some preparation, but it is so worth it. Arrange it so that you actually don't need to leave the house the whole weekend. Buy all your favorite foods in advance, and choose some good wine. If you don't have a bed tray for food, invest in one. Buy some luxury bath products for a decadent bath for two. If you are lucky enough to have a fireplace, have enough wood handy to keep it burning the whole forty-eight hours. Do not, under any circumstances, answer the phone (you can check it once a day in case of emergencies) or allow the outside world in. Talk, plan, and, most of all, reacquaint yourselves and your bodies with each other.

Hot Ice: Incorporate the extremes of temperature into your lovemaking by using ice. Why not try holding an ice cube in your mouth while you kiss or perform oral sex.

Removing Obstacles: Setting an intention to remove obstacles you may have as a couple is a spell perfectly suited to winter sex. Discuss what it is in your relationship that no longer serves you, and raise power together to banish the behaviors or obstacles you have identified.

Winter Sex Ritual

Preparation

Planning Ahead: Decide in which room that you will have your ritual. Ensure it's a comfortable temperature. Make this winter ritual a nighttime ritual and if possible on a waning or dark moon.

Ensure you will be undisturbed.

Have your intention clearly in mind. However, this spell is geared toward letting go of the parts of your relationship that do not serve you. You must have discussed and agreed on this *before* beginning this ritual.

Gather

Candle, preferably silver, white, or black
Charcoal with herbs: Five finger grass, lotus root, mistletoe, and frank-incense
Robe for before and after the skyclad parts of the ritual
A few ice cubes in a decorative bowl
A few small towels so that the melted water does not wet your bed or floor
    too much

Welcome the Goddess and God and thank them for being with you here tonight in this beautiful place.

Focus

Cast and open a Circle if you wish. Light the candle.

Now invoke the Goddess and God:

> *I call you, great Goddess of the Winter season.*
> *You who takes joy in the rest, refinement, and regeneration of all things.*
> *Today I/we call upon you to help us celebrate winter's glory*
> *and (insert intention). I call you Great God of Winter and death.*
> *You who encourages us to bravely let go of shadows that do not serve us.*
> *Today I/we call upon you to assist us with (insert intention).*
> *Great Goddess and God, I/we ask that you be here tonight*
> *to bless the union that will soon take part.*

Light your herbs or incense. Breathe in the energies.

Now relax and connect with each other. Slip out of your robes and begin the eye-to-eye technique. Take several deep breaths, breathing out all stress and tension.

Building Power

First, hand each other an ice cube or two. Place it in your palms. Allow it to cool your hands as much as possible on the edge of it being painful. Tell each other about the aspect that you want to get rid of. Tell each other how much this thing has cooled your relationship or frozen your positive emotions.

Now petition the Goddess/God:

> *Great Ones, transform these icy shadows and let these things that no longer serve us die. Allow them to be transformed into* (state what you want instead).

Then pop the rest of the ice cube into your partner's warm mouth, and as you do this, say: "The cold shadows are transformed."

Now concentrate on the positive aspects of not having this aspect(s) in your life. Tell your partner about one of these aspects and how it will change or benefit your life together. Talk about this in a detailed and honest way.

Begin to play with some of the remaining ice cubes. This is the time to celebrate the fallow field of your relationship. You might like to try kissing each other with the ice cubes in your mouth or running the ice along the sensitive parts of your partner's body. Have fun!

Feel how desired you are, how much the feminine or masculine draws you. Take your time and enjoy this.

Allow yourself to feel the absolute pleasure of making love / having sex. There is so much power in wiping the slate clean, and this power can be directed toward what you desire. Feel how this sexual power is now racing through your body and that of your partner.

Accept these gifts in your own body. Feel your own strength and that of the Goddess / God course through you. Now focus on the feeling of that power coursing through you.

In a loud, firm voice begin a chant about your intention if you have prepared one, or are an advanced practitioner.

Release Your Intention

When you are both near or at the point of orgasm, begin to verbalize your intention if you haven't already. At the point of orgasm, yell out your intention loudly, projecting it out into the Universe. You may wish to express the release of your intention by shouting: "Yes!" or a word or two that expresses your intention. Imagine the power of the release of sexual energy propelling your intention toward the Goddess and God.

You should feel a huge surge of energy and of heat.

Allow yourself to express with abandon: shout, laugh, or whatever else you may feel.

Offer Your Gratitude

Know that the Goddess and God of winter have heard your intention, and are speeding your intention through your body and mind.

Thank the Goddess and God in your own way. Be grateful in the knowledge that all is as you have asked it to be, if it be their will and for the greatest good of all. Know your mind and body is already responding.

Complete the Ritual

Enjoy some quiet breathing time together.

Put on your robes if you wish.

Extinguish and bury any remaining charcoal and herbs/incense in the garden or yard. Wash the towels. Ground yourself by eating or drinking something else, or perhaps sharing what happened during the ritual with your partner.

Blow your candle out.

You might like to relight the candle during some quiet time over the next few nights to remind you of your intention.

Participation

Sit down together and agree on three participatory points toward achieving your intention. Act on at least one of these within the next forty-eight hours.

Book of Shadows Entries

Record your feelings, behaviors, actions, and results. Share these with your partner if you wish.

Spring Sex

There are few people who don't enjoy spring. The sun returns after its long hiatus, and it certainly seems the whole world wakes up, stretching and smiling. Witches see the spring as a key marker in the year, heralding the return of creative power and the rebirth of light and hope. In the Northern Hemisphere Easter is normally at the beginning of spring and the celebration harks from the celebrations for the spring and fertility goddess Eostre. It was not until later, when the Christian religion was overlaid on the Pagan that it became the time marking the death and rebirth of Jesus.

Instill the creative energies of spring into your sexual relationship by allowing the seeds of your love to grow, to renew what is valued, or begin something afresh. This is the time for births, so if you are due to give birth in spring, rejoice in your bounty and celebrate the birth of your own child of hope and light. You might check the Fertility section for some ideas.

Spring Sex Suggestions

Write a Sexy Letter to Your Partner: Be your own Cyrano de Bergerac and write your way into your lover's bed! You don't need to be a best-selling author to be able to write from the heart or from the body! As a starter, why not write your letter in advance and then read it to your lover in bed. If you are feeling really confident you might even like to begin to act it out. One couple I know takes turns each month doing this, each time thinking of something new and fresh to say and do.

Have Sex Somewhere New: Spring is the time to come out in the world and let your fertility back into the world. If you are not ready to have sex outdoors Beltaine style, why not just try somewhere new. Examine your fantasy life and see whether there is somewhere you have always wanted to try. Discuss this with your partner (or surprise him or her).

Flowers: Yes, it may be corny, but flowers can be the language of love. Surprise your partner, male or female, with a bunch of flowers at work, accompanied by a suitably saucy invitation, or prepare a petal-strewn bed or bath for two.

Renew your vows/relive your first date.

Spring Sex Ritual

Preparation

Planning ahead: Try to do this ritual outdoors if at all possible. For those of you lucky enough to own or have access to a bit of land, use it to its full advantage and run free, privacy and safety permitting.

Make this spring ritual a nighttime or dawn ritual, and if possible on a waxing moon. Ensure you will be undisturbed.

Have your intention clearly in mind, however this spell is geared toward creating new things for your relationship. You must have discussed this and be in agreement *before* this ritual.

Gather

Candle, preferably silver or light green

Charcoal with herbs: jasmine or rose petals, ladies mantle, sarsaparilla, sandalwood

Robe or clothes for before and after the skyclad parts of the ritual

Seeds with a small pot pre-filled with soil

A rug if you are going to lie down outdoors

Welcome the Goddess and God, and thank them for being with you here tonight in this beautiful place.

Focus

Cast and open a Circle if you wish. Light the candle.

Now invoke the Goddess and God:

> *I call you, great Goddess of the Spring. You who are all creative and all loving.*
> *I call upon you great Goddess of rebirth and refreshment.*
> *Today I/we call upon you to help us celebrate the awakening of Spring*
> *and (insert intention). I call you Great God of Spring and Hope.*
> *You who encourages us to break through our apathy and be reborn.*
> *Today I/we call upon you to assist us with (insert intention).*
> *Great Goddess and God, I/we ask that you be here tonight*
> *to bless the union that will soon take part.*

Light your herbs or incense. Breathe in the energies.

Now relax and connect with each other. Slip out of your robes and begin the eye-to-eye technique. Take several deep breaths, breathing out all stress and tension.

Building Power

If you do have plenty of space and privacy you may want to have some fun playing a variation on the traditional Beltaine run. The woman should hide and allow her partner to find her with the expectation that they will join together. However, the longer this takes the more fun it actually is! The female partner should feel free to change her hiding spot should her "hunter" be getting closer, really try her best not to be caught, and the male partner should use lots of physical energy to find her.

When she is caught, he should ask: "Lady, will you accept me here tonight?"

She then has a choice: to pass on or to accept him.

Accept him!

Should you not have this much space, make do in your house or you may choose to do a stationary version by using guided visualization or with really athletic sex outdoors.

Now ask of the Goddess/God before you reach orgasm:

> Goddess and God: we wish to be refreshed and renewed.
> Allow our relationship (or love) to continue to grow and
> be reborn into something even more satisfying and magical!

Feel how desired you are, how much the feminine or masculine draws you, how energetic and vital you are. Take your time and enjoy this.

Allow yourself to feel the absolute pleasure of making love/having sex. There is so much power in Spring. Feel the power in the fertility and creativity—this power can be directed toward what you desire.

Feel how this sexual power is now racing through your body and that of your partner. Accept these gifts in your own body. Feel your own strength and that of the Goddess/God course through you. Now focus on the feeling of that power coursing through you.

In a loud, firm voice begin a chant about your intention if you have prepared one, or are an advanced practitioner.

Release Your Intention

When you are both near or at the point of orgasm begin to verbalize your intention, if you haven't already. At the point of orgasm, yell out your intention loudly, projecting it out into the Universe. You may wish to express the release of your intention by shouting: "Yes!" or a word or two that expresses your intention. Imagine the power of the release of sexual energy propelling your intention toward the Goddess and God.

You should feel a huge surge of energy and of heat. Ensure that you are lying on the earth/grass without the blanket at the point of orgasm. If possible allow any bodily fluids you may express to integrate into the soil. If you are practicing safe sex you may wish to do this manually.

Allow yourself to express with abandon: shout, laugh, or whatever else you may feel.

Offer Your Gratitude

Know that the Goddess and God of Spring have heard your intention, and are speeding your intention through your body and mind.

Thank the Goddess and God in your own way. Be grateful in the knowledge that all is as you have asked it to be, if it be their will and for the greatest good of all.

Know your mind and body is already responding.

Complete the Ritual

Enjoy some quiet breathing time together. Listen to Mother Nature and know she sings with you both.

Put on your robes if you wish.

Extinguish and bury any remaining charcoal and herbs/incense in the garden or yard. Leave nothing behind in nature. Ground yourself by eating or drinking something else, or perhaps sharing what happened during the ritual with your partner.

Blow out your candle.

You might like to relight the candle during some quiet time over the next few nights to remind you of your intention.

Participation

Sit down together and agree on three participatory points toward achieving your intention. Act on at least one of these within the next forty-eight hours.

Book of Shadows Entries

Record your feelings, behaviors, actions, and results. Share these with your partner if you wish.

Building Instant Sensual Connection: The Spot

I have always loved the idea of a magic wand that changed everything that it touched. Witches have used a variety of wands in their magical workings to focus energy, and in particular the Faery traditions are most well known for this.

Wouldn't it be useful then to have a place on our bodies that changed everything when we touched it? Some of the more sarcastic among you would say you already have that, but what if I suggested it wasn't the place you thought, and you could touch it happily in public, yet get an intense and intimate connection with your partner?

I remember as a very young woman lying next to my boyfriend in bed. I recall looking at the body next to me, drinking it in. I remember looking at a small cleft in the center of his chest and thinking it was the most beautiful thing I'd ever seen. Not really sure why, but just that it was. This is not to say the rest of his body wasn't beautiful, it was just that there was something awesome about that particular spot. Ever since, with every partner I have really been deeply attracted to, a spot has revealed itself, and its inherent power to focus sensual/sexual energy.

What is "The Spot"?

This is the specific part of your lover's/partner's body that—just by thinking about it or touching it—sends you straight to intense desire! It is also something that you can grant to them and on their body, claim as your own, and that your lover can claim as his or her own. It's a bodily exchange of an admission of lust and an acceptance of the fact that you are desired.

Adopting this practice has a hundred percent success rate. I have never met a couple that this did not work for, but it must be a mutual project. Both partners must identify and claim the spot on the other. This spot must be kept totally private by both parties—not only the location must remain secret, but even the fact that you have these spots. This maximizes the intimacy between you both and the illicitness of the idea.

How to Identify the Spot: If you are anything like me you have possibly identified a number of truly delicious parts of your partner's body, any of which initially could be your spot. However, if you had to choose that one place, that one piece of territory that truly makes your boat float, what would it be? Usually there is one standout favorite.

Here are some real-life examples to get you thinking:

- "There is this small upturned triangle of hair that pokes out of the collar of my husband's open-necked shirt. It just says he is a real man to me. When I look at it I get jealous that any other woman would even be able to see it!" —Sue

- "There is this spot where her legs join on to her bottom. It's so soft. It just kills me!" —Jeremy

- "There's this muscle, don't know what it's called, it's on the inside of his elbow. I can't keep from touching it." —Diana

- "I remember the first time we went out I noticed how smooth the skin on her shoulder was, just where it met her neck. It was the first place I kissed her. I couldn't help myself." —Dean.

What the Spot Isn't: When I first advise men about the spot, normally they go big picture and automatically think about either the obvious "Oh, I'm a breast man so it would be her breasts," or the genitalia. When I first advise some women they tend to choose large areas of the body such as legs, chest, or back. The spot is just that: a spot. It is a small piece of real estate on your lover's body that evokes such desire in you that it is truly yours!

How to Use the Spot: Maria tells her story: "Stacey suggested the idea of the spot and I was intrigued. I thought why not? I was lying in bed with my husband one Sunday morning and began to stroke his cheekbone. He has gorgeous high cheekbones. I told him how much I loved his cheekbones and that I had decided that they were mine and were my spot. I told him about the idea and asked him whether he had a spot too.

"Michael smiled and didn't hesitate. He told me that there was this spot on the side of my neck that he loved, just below my ear. And he declared that his spot. Just talking with such passion about a tiny spot on each other's body led to a great lovemaking session, so even if the idea didn't work, well, I still had a fab start!"

Life, of course, goes on, and Maria and Michael have a big fortnight of work. They are like ships passing in the night but they manage to tee up a movie night. Maria explains:

"We are right in the middle of this film. I'm pretty much engrossed in it, but all of a sudden, Michael lifts my hair up and softly but passionately kisses my spot. I instantly know he isn't thinking of the movie, he is thinking about how much he wants me! It's such a turn on! Stacey, we didn't see the rest of the film and we barely made it home that night!"

Thom has an equally rewarding story to tell:

"Julie and I loved the idea of the spot as soon as we heard it. It was pretty easy for me to think about what my spot was: her wrists! She is one gorgeous woman, but she has these amazingly tiny wrists that have always struck me as elegant. She chose as her spot this small place below my belly button. We even did a little ritual around our spots!

"As Julie got bigger in her pregnancy she didn't feel like her usual svelte self and really wasn't feeling too sexy. I loved her new shape and told her, but she really felt big. Let me tell you though, if I played with her spot she always felt good about herself and felt more secure even through all those great hormonal roller coasters!"

Claiming and Invoking the Spot: You can do this in a more formal way later and create a ritual around the spot if you choose but I always think the nicest and most real way to bring up the idea of the spot is to be in a physical position close to your partner, such as in bed or cuddled on the couch, and tell them about their spot and why it's special.

For example: While stroking their spot, "You know I have always loved this spot on you. It's so sexy/soft/coarse/different, etc. I remember the first time I noticed it and this is how I felt . . ."

Then you may get into some discussion about it.

Then you might ask if he or she has an equivalent spot on you. They may know one straightaway, or they may need some thinking time (as you may have had prior). Be patient with this and have fun!

Ensure you are eventually both clear about your spot and how you like it to be touched.

Remember: you may not understand the spot your partner has chosen. Perhaps you feel other parts of you are sexier, more beautiful, or worthy. Alternatively you may feel that the spot they have chosen is ugly or silly. This is not up to you! Do not negate their choice. You don't really need to understand why they desire this part of you in particular, just that *you truly accept that they feel nothing but love and desire for it*—so much so that you will grant it to them!

Then agree that the spots on each of your bodies belong to the other as long as you are together.

To do this you might say something as simple as " You know, I'll give this to you. This is your spot now!"

Or as formal as dedicating the spot to each other perhaps by using a little essential oil and placing your partner's fingers on the spot and saying, *"This spot is dedicated to desire and it is yours as long as we are together."*

Once you have mutually agreed, use your spot regularly but innovatively! Surprise and comfort each other with this—after all, it's your guaranteed personal hot button that changes everything!

Pain: Cutting the Cords

As common as it is for witches to be called upon to assist people with attracting love, we also are asked to help heal the pain when love goes wrong. As there are the myriad ways of joyfully falling in love, there are the million cuts of a relationship breakdown or parting.

There is enormous power in learning to say good-bye well, no matter what the circumstances. If not grieved properly or healed well, lessons inherent in the experience are not only not learned, but the pain continues, and our behavior can affect how we handle future encounters.

So what happens when, for one reason or another, we say goodbye?

Normally we experience pain of some kind. A grieving and perhaps an examination of what went wrong, which is healthy. At times though, we may feel anger, rage, regret, and disappointment, which also may be healthy depending upon degree and intent. Sometimes, though, the pain is extreme and trauma may be involved. The bond we have with this person or ex-partner may be so strong, yet toxic, that it is not easily broken.

So witches can offer some pain relief. This is normally done by first building up our core of personal power so that we can move on naturally. However, if the relationship has been so damaging that it's extremely hard to move on, we may stagnate in our grief or trauma. We begin to be bound by this, leaving no room for the creation of something new and beneficial. It is here that we may choose to cut the cords.

This work is to be undertaken mindfully. I personally consider the process of cutting cords one of the most powerful tools witches have at their disposal to create momentum and healing. I have found it particularly effective for clients who have suffered sexual, physical, or emotional abuse.

I do favor invoking particular goddesses to assist in cord cutting, in addition to having your own personal patron goddess or god present. The goddesses and gods that I have had particularly powerful results with have been Sekhmet, Kali, Durga, and Anubis, the Jackal-headed god. Although these deities seem to be the destroyer or aggressive in their natures, this is exactly the energy you need to purify and cut through ties that no longer serve you.

Cutting the cords must be undertaken only when you are indeed ready to move on to a different kind of relationship, as this profound ritual is not easy to reverse. Cutting the cords by no means indicates that this person will be cut out of your life completely (although this may in fact happen). What it will mean is that the part of the relationship that no longer serves you will be cut and will disappear. Nothing negative from that time forward will bind you to this individual.

This process creates change that is far reaching and highly beneficial, however it normally has attached to emotional processes such as grief, which is not considered a pleasant or desired state. States such as this are a natural and necessary part of healing and moving on, better than before.

Unless you are an experienced witch or extremely confident in magical work, I suggest you do this in consultation with someone who is, or at least with a friend who believes in the concept and can facilitate this journey.

I would also encourage the person with you to ensure that they do a simple ritual of grounding and protection (see later in this section) prior to beginning the cord cutting ritual with you, so that they can be a true anchor and guide without getting involved in what is, in fact, a highly emotional experience. They can also witness what you have chosen, and help keep you to your intentions and moving forward.

Witches in the Bedroom

Sophia is a talented businesswoman in the publishing industry in the United States. She met a man, Michael, through her work with a client in Australia. Their long-distance relationship flourished quickly and they established a genuine closeness via the phone and then in person when Sophia traveled to Sydney. The relationship was an intense one, full of passion and promises. Sophia fell in love and believed Michael when he promised her a different and new life in his country. She was to immigrate with her children. When she met him though, Michael lived a different life than what he had represented. He was still hung up on his previous girlfriend and did not know how to welcome Sophia into his life. Although it was difficult, Sophia tried to keep the relationship alive, but it probably wasn't the best thing to do in hindsight.

They broke up once Sophia had returned from her holiday with Michael. It was a cruel break up and one that had deep consequences for Sophia over a lengthy period of time. Sophia came to me wanting to reduce the pain and shame around this relationship and to finally clear herself of its influence so she could make room for something new and healthy.

This is a passage from Sophia's actual Book of Shadows (she uses the template I suggest on page 79) and I will let her tell her own story:

Cutting the Cords Ritual

As discussed, you need to be very clear that you wish to cut the cords fully with someone. Take your time with this decision. Cutting the cords does not necessarily mean you will never have a relationship with this person ever again (but it may be so), it means that you will not have the same kind of relationship with them. It will transform into something that serves you better. I like either a dark moon or a waning moon phase to cut cords.

Gather

Glass of wine or moon water to open the ritual

White candle to represent the Goddess and a red or black candle to burn
through the cord if you choose to burn through

Sharp knife for cutting the cord if you choose to cut rather than burn

Cord long enough to go around your waist with enough room to fit your
fist between your waist and the cord (choose the size cord that feels right
for you—I favor silver or gold cords)

Personal item from the relationship that you are willing to get rid of

Bowl in which to place the cord after it is cut

Tongs for picking up the cord after it is cut

Lighter to burn cord after cutting

Small spade for burying the cord and personal item

Comfortable robe to put on after the ritual if doing the ritual skyclad

And, of course, your support person, who, if need be, can facilitate you
through the ritual.

Opening and Purpose and Intention

Open a Circle in whatever manner you choose.

Light your two candles with intent.

Take a sip of wine or moonwater.

Ask for your patron goddess and possibly a goddess of purification such
as Sekhmet to be present. Offer them something they may like on your altar.
(Sekhmet loves the color red, beer, or even a statue of a lion.)

Make sure the room is warm and comfortable. Disrobe if you are doing
the ritual skyclad.

State what it is that you are here to do:

"Goddess, I am here before you tonight to cut the cords with _____.
I wish to transform the relationship I have with them into something that
serves me. I ask for your help and protection tonight."

Now lie down or kneel down. Relax. Breathe in the power of the universe. Begin to imagine yourself floating in darkness. It's very quiet. It's very
beautiful. You are not afraid, nor are you alone completely, as the God-
dess(es) are there with you. Look around if you choose and see them in
whatever form they may take.

Look around you. Many points of light now appear, almost like stars. Move closer toward them and you realize that these light points are becoming people you know, past and present.

Search now for the person with whom you wish to cut the cords. When you find them, open your eyes and tie your cord around your waist, leaving it loose, so that it is not big enough to step out of, but big enough at least to put your fist under. Leave room enough that you can cut it or burn it easily and safely.

Raising Power

Close your eyes and sit upright, or better still, stand up firmly—do not lie down. This is a time for action.

Think in sensual detail (touch, taste, vision, aural, feeling) about your interactions with this person. Do not dwell on the good or romantic bits if these are what comes to mind first. Be slightly detached around these as if we are still feeling pain in these areas. It is very easy to romanticize or enlarge these as bigger experiences than those that are more unpleasant. Similarly, if you are only thinking of the bad experiences, become slightly detached.

When you believe you are feeling what it is to be connected to this person with all your senses, imagine them in front of you. Look at them—all of them—not just their eyes, or face. See them in three dimensions in space. Spin them around if need be so you can take in all of them.

Now imagine that there are fine cords linking you to them. They can be as they are, so do not edit how they look. Sometimes they appear like fine spider webs, sometimes like thick cords, sometimes plaited and perfect, sometimes rough or fleshy. Notice this, look at the detail, and notice where you are joined on your bodies and how.

You may feel sensations at the location of these joinings. If you are afraid or worried here, ask for your facilitator's help or for your patron goddesses to be closer.

Decide now whether you will cut or burn through the cords—it's up to you. Imagine that you have a sacred knife or scissors or flame in your hand. It is now time to sever/burn the cords that bind you. (This does not mean that you will not see the person, will love them, or feel any other emotion. It just means that the nature of the relationship you have now with them will be severed. It will end, or transform into something new.)

In your mind or out loud, thank the person you will be cutting the cords with for the lessons that they offered and taught you. It is now time to let this relationship, in its current form, go.

Ask for your goddesses to protect you and to be with you.

Release and Grounding

In real life now, open your eyes, hold the cord in one hand and your cutting/burning implement in the other.

State plainly and strongly:"I wish to cut the cords with _____. I want the old connection that does not serve me to be severed/burned away, and for me to be free and renewed."

Now again recall the person and the relationship in its detail. When you are ready, cut the cords.

Say, "I cut the cords that bind me! I let you go with love and honor!"

Breathe deeply, feel the cords drop from your body (in real life and in the metaphysical world). Close your eyes and watch as those cords that connected you earlier fall away. If there are any left, cut them in your mind or ask that your patron goddess assists you with the cutting. Take your time with this. Ensure you cut or burn them all.

Now breathe again deeply and relax.

All is new and will be better. Be supported if necessary. Allow yourself to feel what you feel.

Closing the Ritual

Give thanks to your goddesses and perhaps leave them a special gift in recognition of their assistance on your altar.

Now take special care here in grounding yourself. Take another sip of wine or water and debrief your experience in your Book of Shadows or with your facilitator. Then ensure you are completely grounded by changing your state through dancing, eating a big meal, or having a bath. Try not to sleep right away, even if you feel tired.

Now take special care to destroy or bury the cords. Pick them up with your tongs and try not to touch them with your bare hands. Take the item that represents the relationship and bury it or destroy it along with the cords.

Participation

Things will be different with this person. This is the time to surrender to any messages you have been given or any realizations that may come forward. Ensure that you allow yourself plenty of time to express any further emotions after this ritual, whether they be joy, anger, grief, or relief. Be very present in your body, and if it is sore or stiff, seek massage or other body work to relieve it.

Results

Track your ongoing participation and change in your BOS. Take particular note of how things have changed with your own feelings with this person, and with the person themselves in their situation. Remember, there are no coincidences.

Sophia's Cutting the Cords Ritual

Date: 11/02/04, 11:00 P.M.

Focus

What do I want and why, opening circle, collecting tools.

What do I want?

Cutting the cords. As discussed, you need to be very clear that you wish to cut the cords fully.

I want to cut the cords that bind me to Michael in a negative, co-dependent, enmeshed way.

Why do I want this?

The connection to Michael is painful and debilitating and I desire to be free of this unhealthy connection.

When do I want this? What is my time frame?

Determine if this is important for me.

I want this now. I have spent time over the last tri-lunar cycle preparing for this important ritual. I have walked through my emotions surrounding the beginning, middle, and end of the relationship. I have remembered the good and the bad. I feel good about having given myself this time to prepare and know that I am now fully ready.

A good result for me would look like:

Being able to treasure the good memories from a more detached point of view while also remembering the bad times realistically. I want to be able to speak of this man without tears, be able to think of this man without tears, be able to learn from this experience so that I see the inappropriate signals when they appear, but not find something wrong where nothing exists.

I want to be able to believe that there will be another man who will indeed be all that I desire to have in a relationship. Who will give as well as take. Who will adore and cherish me, warts and all!

What Magical Supplies Do I Need?

Glass of Shiraz-Cabernet

White, red, and black candles with holders

Gold cord long enough to go around waist with enough room to fit your fist between your waist and the cord

Sharp scissors for cutting the cord

Personal item from the relationship that you are willing to get rid of (I chose a heart-shaped rock that sat beside a light blue candle each evening that Michael and I spoke on the phone)

Bowl in which to place the cord after it is cut

Tongs for picking up the cord after it is cut

Lighter to burn cord after cutting

Small spade for burying the cord and personal item

Comfortable robe to put on prior to going to the yard to bury the items

I chose the waning moon several days after the full moon on October 28 to indicate something I wish to leave behind, yet still have the moon bright enough to see.

How Do I Intend to Open the Circle or Create Sacred Space?

Light candle with intent.

Ask for your patron Goddess and probably Sekhmet.

I made sure the room was very warm and comfortable as I did this ritual skyclad.

Because I was in a completely dark room, I lit the white candle to represent the Goddess prior to opening the Circle so that I could see where I was and not run into anything.

I took my maple wand and opened the Circle clockwise, inviting the Goddess, Sekhmet, and Artemis. As I invited Sekhmet for the first time, I felt sharp pins and needles tingling in my arms. I then lit the black candle, stating the intent of this ritual, and the red candle inviting Sekhmet with her color.

I then drank some of the wine as a sacred communion with the Goddess and her aspects.

Raising Power

Generating powerful energy will propel my intention out to the Universe / Divine. Methods for doing this include: chants, movement, ritual action, and recalling past emotions.

Ritual Actions

Preparing for ritual, tie your cord around your waist, leaving it loose, so that it is not big enough to step out of, but big enough to at least put your fist under.

Decide to cut or burn through the cords—it's up to you. I decided to cut my cord because during the flame test the cord did indeed flame!

Close your eyes and sit upright, or better, still stand up firmly. Do not lie down.

I chose to stand up during this part.

Think in sensual detail (touch, taste, vision, aural, kinesthetic) about your interactions with this person. Do not dwell on the good or romantic bits. Be slightly detached around these as if we are still feeling pain in these areas. It is very easy to romanticize or enlarge these as bigger experiences rather than those that are more unpleasant. When you believe you are feeling what it is to be connected to this person, imagine them in front of you. Look at them—all of them, not just their eyes. Now imagine that there are fine cords linking you to them—they can be as they are. Sometimes they appear like spider webs, sometimes like thick cords, Notice this and look at the detail and where you are joined and how.

This part was *very* difficult for me. I worked on picturing Michael standing in front of me, nude, as I was. I could see him for a flash and then he was gone. I worked on looking at a "movie reel" series of memory pictures, good and bad. Then I tried again to bring a vision of him in front of me. I never could do it.

I called for Sekhmet's and Artemis' help.

What I did notice were places on my body that felt warm, swollen, or painful. Therefore, I allowed that to be my indicators of connections to Michael.

Other

Now imagine that you have a sacred knife or scissors flaming in your hand. It is time to sever/burn the cords that bind you. (This does not mean that you will not see the person, will love them, or feel any other emotion. It just means that the nature of relationship you have now with them will be severed. It will end, or transform into something new.)

Release and Grounding

How am I going to release the powerful energy I have raised and my intention at its climax point? How am I going to get back to my normal space/ time world afterward?

This spell/ritual calls for me to (smash, pour, exclaim, etc.):

In real life now, open your eyes, hold the cord in one hand, and your cutting/burning implement in the other. Ask for assistance from your patron and Sekhmet.

State plainly and strongly, "I wish to cut the cords with _____." I want the old connection that does not serve me to be severed/burned away, and for me to be free and renewed.

"I wish to cut the cords with Michael! I want the old connection that does not serve me to be severed and for me to be free and renewed!"

Now again recall the person and the relationship. and when you are ready cut the cords. Say, "I cut the cords that bind me! I let you go with love and honor."

Breathe deeply, feel the cords drop from your body (in real life and in the metaphysical world). Close your eyes and watch as those cords that connected you earlier have fallen or do fall away. If there are any left, cut them in your mind.

I really did not feel anything very powerful at this point, but I continued with the ritual with solid intent.

Now breathe again deeply and relax. All is new and will be better.

Closing the Ritual

I left the candles burning because I wanted to do scrying after the Cord Cutting Ritual.

I picked the cord up with the tongs and placed it in the silver bowl. I also removed the heart-shaped rock from the sacred Circle and placed it in the bowl.

Ground yourself—important with this ritual.

I then drank another draught of the wine to help ground myself.

What did begin to happen was I began to notice all the parts of my body that were in pain. I had been finding it very difficult to take deep breaths during the ritual. It was now almost impossible. Even my eyes stung and hurt.

I stretched and tried to relax and breathe. Every breath brought more pain. I had pain in my eyes, under my ribs, in my abdomen, my back suffered excruciating pain, my hips hurt, my right index finger hurt. I have felt like this for weeks but the pain really interfered tonight.

Give Thanks to Your Goddesses

I closed the Circle by taking my maple wand and walking counterclockwise. I thanked the goddess Artemis and Sekhmet for being with me during my ritual.

Destroy or bury the cords. Try not to touch them with your bare hands.

After closing the Circle and blowing out the candles, I turned on the lights and put on my robe.

I made sure I had a lighter in my pocket and picked up the silver bowl with the cord and rock in it. I also took the tongs and the glass of wine with me to go outside and finish the Cord Cutting Ritual.

I went to the sacred burial area in the front yard. Placing the glass of wine to the side, I took the tongs and grasped the golden cord, lifting it from the bowl and holding it above the earth.

I lit both ends of the cord and the ends hanging from the knot. As the cord flamed and the bits melted and fell to the ground, I felt the closure I had been seeking. It took some time for the cord to burn completely, but the flame was just right. Not too high, yet not so low that it required tending. I was able to simply gaze at the process and feel the power of the fire burning everything away.

After the cord finished burning, I placed the heart-shaped rock on top of the melted bits and buried them under the fertile, dark earth.

I poured the last of the wine on the burial site as an offering to Gaia.

Participation

What are the first steps toward achieving my purpose and intention? I need to think of two or three and be specific.

I see my participation in this process as continuing to straighten any crooked thoughts that come my way and remember that the first "I love you" means "I don't want to hurt you," and the second "I'm not in love with you" means "I'm not in love with you."

"I love you, but I'm not in love with you."

No matter how much that may have hurt in the past.

I also see my participation as opening myself to new possibilities and continuing to work on my self-care and self-esteem in order to be ready for it when it comes along.

After completing my spell/ritual, I felt very sleepy and more relaxed than earlier in the evening. I did not feel like thinking about how I felt about the Cord Cutting Ritual. I was disappointed in the scrying attempt.

Results

I continue tracking my ongoing participation and success, recording all that is happening in regard to this purpose and intention over time.

11/11/04 STACEY

Oh, Sophia, this is excellent work, really detailed, and the flow of your ritual was great. I so wish I could have been with you.

A couple of things—do not be worried about your failure at your scrying attempt. Scrying takes practice—lots of it for some of us. A good way of practicing is with those funny pictures that appear only after you stare at them for a while. We have them printed in magazines over here. Another way is to try to scry when you are tired. Your eyes tend to trance more easily then. On the other hand, perhaps visuals are not your thing. Oracles appear in many ways, as you know. You know you are quite kinesthetic so perhaps things *appear* to you through your body. Consider where those pains were, in particular around your eyes, stinging, etc. Any intuitive flashes when you were experiencing this that you can remember?

Also, I noticed you got closure after you completely burned the cord. This is common. To watch the connection completely disappear from both ends is great and powerful.

Also some feedback—I've noticed a big change in energy in you since then. Look at how you are sending stuff out re the books; people have been attracted to you regarding work. Remember, *there are no coincidences*. Something is no longer in your way. You have created a big opening.

11/11/04 SOPHIA

Since then I have been much more in tune to the pain in my body and it is great. In addition, I have read two books for review that address this topic.

I almost waited until the next morning to burn the cords because I was so warm and comfortable and I knew it would be chilly outside. But, alas, I put on my robe and went out to finish the ritual properly. It was quietly powerful. Very quiet. Not even a sound of sizzling. Very peaceful. No tears.

I feel the change beginning but I am in it all the time. I can see where it would be more apparent from the outside. Even before the ritual, I think because I had spent the Tri-lunar preparing for the changes, I had begun to feel differently about myself.

07/12/05

As I look back on the last eight months since I performed this ritual, it has been amazing. Almost immediately, I no longer cried when dealing with thoughts of this man. Also, it took quite a while but I finally felt at home in my home—not as if something was missing. Moreover, this summer I am once again wearing the clothes that I wore when I was with this man and I have reclaimed the energy of the clothes. They have no memory energy clinging to them. I am making new memories in them. Along this same vein, I have been using my deck this year without the fog of grief hanging over it. Last year, I do not think I went out on my deck twice and I absolutely could not wear any of the clothes that I wore when with this man.

Ironically, this man has been back in touch with me over the last couple of months and my heart did not skip or miss a beat. We exchange pleasant emails concerning our own children, our families, and our mutual friends. I find that I do not feel any extreme emotions anymore regarding this relationship and I can take or leave the communication as it comes."

Corinna's Experience

Similarly, Corinna, a brilliant multilingual coach and trainer, felt the effects of cutting the cords went far beyond her initial intention.

"I had been separated from Rick for over two years, divorced for almost a year, and I was still receiving letters and phone calls from various banks asking me to balance overdrawn accounts that were no longer in joint names. No matter how much I wanted to disconnect my life from my ex-husband's, I felt as if I was continuously drawn into his financial affairs. Thoroughly frustrated after yet another phone call, I asked Stacey to do a cutting the ties ritual with me.

"During the ritual I intensely felt how much I was still connected with Rick and how angry I was at this man, even though we had separated under the most amicable of circumstances. When Stacey and I cut the cords I felt as if a heavy burden was being lifted off my shoulders and I felt calm and centered in my deepest core.

"The next day I received a call from Rick telling me that he had instructed the banks again to remove me from the accounts. This time it worked. I never heard from them again, nor have I had any involvement with Rick about money since then. We still talk every now and then about what is going on in our lives, and I know that I communicate from a place of peace and acceptance that is only possible because I truly let go of binding ties.

"What I hadn't considered, however, was the flow-on effect of the ritual. As I cut the financial cords with Rick, on a higher level I also agreed to end these patterns with anybody else with whom I had them.

"Two weeks after the ritual, my working relationship with Tom, who I had subcontracted for on several large projects, rapidly started falling apart. I had just started working on another project when I felt for the first time how much his way of doing business was actually costing me. He owed me money from a previous project, and had defaulted on a payment when I found out that he had miscalculated the new project and wouldn't be able to pay me even part of the money he owed me for the work I had done and was still doing. It suddenly dawned on me that the man I held to be one of my best friends was financing his doubtful business on my back. While I was struggling to pay my bills he was going off to other countries to supposedly to raise more business—business that never materialized.

"The emotional impact this realization had on me was tremendous. I had been supporting Tom for over a year by consenting to not be paid until he could afford it—without any consideration of the effect this had on me. It was painful to realize and admit that this was the same pattern I had acted out with Rick. Now I was no longer willing to play the game. Needless to say, Tom has found it difficult to deal with my new boundaries and I no longer work for him.

"Many things have changed since then, some effects are rather unexpected: Where before I often worked as the only woman on the team, convinced that my value was dependent on the men I worked with, I now work mostly with women. They reflect back to me my new-found appreciation of my worth and the contribution I make. "

Making room for the relationships that will serve you and make you happy is one of the most important processes that anyone, witch or non-witch, can perform.

Ritual of Grounding and Protection

Open a Circle if you wish. Stand strongly in the warrior pose (feet firm on the ground; feet shoulder width apart, knees slightly bent, back straight. Arms slightly away from the body, hands may face up or down).

Breathe deeply. Imagine now that your feet are connecting with the earth like roots in a tree. With each breath, they receive the Goddess-given power from the earth knowing that this power is unlimited and protective. If you like you could imagine that this power has a color and a texture and it is running up your body like an electric current or a slow-moving vapor (whatever you prefer. It is permeating every cell, renewing, protecting you. If you have a patron goddess or god, now is the time to call upon them for extra protection and to be with you during any magical working that you may choose to undertake.

Fertility

Being a Moon-Powered Mammal

Our family has a female Siberian Husky called Skaya. Huskies are considered one of the most original breeds of dog. That is, breeds that have a direct bloodline lineage with their ancient dog ancestors, including wolves. One only has to look into those strange, blue Husky eyes to experience a distinct otherness and a deep wildness few other dog breeds exhibit.

Huskies, like other canines, have a period of ovulation or heat twice a year. At this time the female's behavior changes and she becomes receptive to advances made by male dogs. I would watch with interest how my mild-mannered, aloof, and shy girl would change into an eyelash fluttering, prancing furry fatale. However, it was her behavior around the moon that really struck me as different.

The most fertile part of her heat always occurred around a full moon, and I only noticed this because she would often sit near me as I celebrated my full moon ritual, literally howling by my side as we both raised our eyes to that silvery light. She would only do this when in heat. The first time I noticed it, I thought it was a happy and exciting coincidence. The next time after that, I realized there was some pattern to her cycle and it was certainly linked to the moon.

I spoke of this to my veterinarian, who said that although he knew of no research done involving domestic dogs, his own personal experience was that owners often reported their females did go in heat when the light was fullest and complained that the noise in combination with the full moon was, well, spooky!

As I mentioned earlier in this book, ancient societies from prehistory to the more complex have aligned the moon with fertility, growth, creativity, and, in particular, the cycles of women. Modern biodynamic farming methods incorporate the ancient learning of traditional societies and planting by the waxing moon when the energy is conducive to growth, and harvesting and pruning on a waning moon when the energy is restful. Many witches even choose to cut their hair on a similar moon cycle. Scientists have studied marine life that spawns only when the full moon phases signal it, and there have been many studies hoping to increase the fertility yields on commercial domesticated animals such as beef and dairy cattle and pigs by linking fertility with moon cycles.

When it comes to humans, though, it seems there are two firmly entrenched camps on this issue. One camp says that moon cycles (around twenty-nine days) have no influence or correlation to the female menstrual cycle of roughly twenty-eight to twenty-nine days. The other believes that there is an ancient and strong correlation and that those links begin as far back as birth.

No matter what science does or does not think, most women find it an easy leap of faith to say that they are highly connected with the moon. At the very least you can make the direct connection between your cycle and the lunar cycle and at the most you can choose to realign your menstrual cycles with the moon and have greater control over your reproductive health and fertility.

By now most of you can see that I am quite a down-to-earth type of witch, and tend to like to have some evidence to prove a theory before putting it forward. I certainly would not bother collecting case studies if I didn't. What you need to realize here is that science is not always right. Scientists once thought the earth was flat but eventually proved it was not. To its credit, modern science now seems to be swinging back to admitting that it does not know everything and that there is room for possibilities not thought of before. The following information about moon cycles may sound a little far-fetched to some of you, it but has a wealth of data and experiences to back it up. At the time of writing (2004–05), new data backing up this concept has been released with more studies to be undertaken—so open your moon-powered mammalian minds and make up your own mind. Or better still, for those of you wanting to conceive a child, why not give it a go!

The Lunar Link

Most mammals have what scientists refer to as overt ovulation. This is a distinct period of time when the female displays overt symptoms easily noticed by the male, dependent on the species of animal. If you have a dog or cat, you may commonly call this being in heat. Often, there are visual cues such as a change in shape and color of the genitalia or coat, and more commonly, special smells (pheromones) generated by the female that are highly attractive to a suitor.

Up until fairly recently, although there has been some evidence to the contrary, scientists believed that humans have a unique cycle of ovulation and that it is covert or concealed.

Most women would be familiar with being told that you should have a standard twenty-eight-day menstrual cycle (although the lunar cycle is closer to twenty-nine days and most women experience a cycle closer to twenty-nine days). Within this twenty-eight to twenty-nine-day cycle, the woman bleeds, then ripens the next set of eggs. One is released by the follicle at around mid-cycle, and carefully passed into the fallopian tube, where it waits to be fertilized. If it is fertilized, it embeds itself in the uterus. If not, the process of menstruation sheds the unfertilized egg.

So what science is saying here is that there is only one ovulation per cycle, normally happening at mid-cycle, around the fourteen-day mark.

Many primitive societies, including the ancient Sumerians, believed that a woman's cycles were linked to the moon so closely that it was easy to determine her most fertile time. Records of Sumerian beliefs indicate that women are most fertile when the moon is at the same phase as when they were born. Ancient Celt Wise Women also recorded the phase of the moon at the birth of a female child—this was told to her around the time of her first bleed. The Egyptians recorded both female and male infants' moon phases at birth. In astrological terms this is called a lunar return.

Modern medicine would probably liken this to biorhythms—a natural body cycle that repeats at set intervals. Ancient people clearly had learned of a link between the moon phases at birth, the start of the fertile cycle, and ongoing fertility peaks and troughs. This then leads to the assumption that women could in fact have two fertile times a month—therefore more than one chance at ovulation. This has been treated as superstition by the scientific community as a whole, with one exception in the 1950s, backed up recently by a study recorded in the 2004 *Journal of Fertility and Sterility* in the United States.

In the 1950s, staunchly Catholic Dr. Eugene Jonas was dismayed at the inability of his mainly Catholic patients to control their fertility successfully. Many unwanted pregnancies were occurring, even though his patients seemed to be following the rhythm method to the letter. These women, whose cycles were around the 28-day mark, were refraining from intercourse around the mid-part of their cycles, yet still getting pregnant.

Strangely for such a religious man, Jonas had a deep interest in astrology, and also enjoyed reading ancient history. He read of the ancient Sumerian theory, and, well-versed in astrological methodology, calculated each patient's lunar return. He found that often these fertile days fell outside the traditional mid-cycle time frame. He tried out this rediscovered theory and over a number of years recorded data. He was amazed at the jump in the women's success rate when they began to avoid sex during these more fertile times.

This was a highly controversial theory, even today, and another physician independent of Jonas, Dr. Kurt Rechnitz, found that the rhythm method alone had a success rate of up to 80 percent if followed correctly, but the combination of the rhythm method and the lunar return boosted the success rate to around 98 percent.

Today, clinics around the world that use the lunar return method and the more accurate Sympto-Thermal model (taking the place of the rhythm method) has a success rate equaling or exceeding that 98 percent rate of successful fertility management, if followed correctly. Even though literally tens of thousands of women have found renewed confidence and success with this more natural way of managing their fertility, the scientific community as a whole continues to demonstrate its inability to accept that women may indeed have two fertile cycles and that spontaneous ovulation is in fact a real phenomena. Well maybe, until now.

In 2004, writing in the *Journal of Fertility and Sterility*, a diverse group of physicians backed up the facts about spontaneous ovulation. In the study, Dr. Pierson, veterinarian Dr. Gregg Adams, and graduate student Angela Baerwald did daily, high-resolution ultrasound scans on sixty-three women for a month, which allowed them to see the follicles very clearly. They found only fifty of the sixty-three had what they termed normal cycles.

Thirteen of the women ovulated multiple times, in various different ways. And of the other fifty, 40 percent had up to three waves of activity by the follicles, any one of which could result in the production of an egg. The women's measurable hormonal activity did not match the activity of the eggs.

In a phone interview reported internationally by Reuters, Pierson states: "We weren't expecting this. We really weren't. The hormones do what they are going to do and the ovaries just follow their merry path. We always thought that menstrual cycles and ovarian cycles were one and the same. It turns out they are just like two political parties—sometimes they go along hand in hand for the good of the country and sometimes they go along their separate ways.

"We don't know what's causing it—we don't know if it is the weather or exposure to men or grapefruit juice or what. Hopefully this will help women explain how they got pregnant when they really didn't want to be pregnant, and it certainly will help us design better fertility therapies."

Pierson's team plans longer-term studies to see if the women's patterns are consistent from month to month.

Personally, I do not think the reason this is happening is due to grapefruit juice, but a combination of the lunar return and exposure to men. Rationally, sex should trigger ovulation. After all, why would you think you are that much different from other mammals such as my dog Skaya, who exudes hormones that I cannot detect but that drive boy dogs wild? And finally, almost to back this up, after reading the research, I pondered why the veterinarian is involved. The findings were apparently first seen in cattle and horses and the team was curious to see whether humans, as just another mammal, also did the same thing. It makes you feel either really humbled or really connected!

Alice, twenty-eight, is the mother of a one-year-old daughter and newborn twins, and was retrospectively looking at the concept of lunar cycles for contraception while she was breast feeding. Alice did not want to become pregnant as quickly after the birth of her twins as she had after the birth of her first child, Sylvie.

She laughed when she discovered the way the two cycles work. "Ah, that explains it!" she said. "That's how we get fraternal twins with different conception days."

Alice said, "When I got my first ultrasound my technician looked at the babies and said that one was at least two weeks more developed than the other. I told him I did not understand what he meant. He told me that 'clinically, we see this all the time. We see women come in with twins and when we do an ultrasound we see one is at ten weeks development and another at seven or eight.' I was amazed this was not common knowledge outside the medical community."

This is backed up by a number of studies and certainly from the hands-on experience of those medical personnel working with ultrasound.

The Consequences

So, if you take this theory about lunar returns and spontaneous ovulation as long-held wisdom, how can you, as a modern witch, use it to your advantage?

First, you can better control your fertility whether you are avoiding or welcoming conception. All you need to know is the timing of your lunar peak, the fertile times around that point, and your traditional ovulation time.

Second, by aligning closer with the moon, you can correct a badly performing cycle that is too long or too short and restore the balance to your body.

Third, you can rejoice in the fact that women's wisdom, born of millions of years, is right, yet again. Have confidence that your body knows what it is doing!

Monitoring Your Cycle by the Moon

If you do have a cycle that is radically less than twenty-eight to twenty-nine days (e.g., fourteen to twenty-one) or more (thirty-two plus), you may consider trying to balance your moon cycle. There are two ways to do this.

The first is to employ a diagnostic approach and visit a natural therapist. Natural Western and Chinese herbal medicine is particularly useful here. Ancient witch remedies such as damiana, golden seal, black cohosh, evening primrose oil, motherwort, passiflora, and raspberry leaf are still used today to assist various conditions adverse to conception and a regular cycle. Chart your cycle over time with a moon cycle chart (downloadable free from my site) and track your progress.

The second is to connect with the Goddess and literally watch the moon for a minimum period of five minutes each night. If you cannot see her, still be aware of her phase and imagine that in your mind's eye for those five minutes. Ask that your cycle be one with hers. Breathe deeply and know that you are connecting with the female collective consciousness of millennia. Ensure you spend longer outside during full moons and your lunar return.

Increasing Your Chances of Conception the Lunar Way

Since this chapter primarily deals with fertility and getting pregnant, I will concentrate on that side of things rather than coming from the contraception point of view. If you do want to avoid getting pregnant, simply reverse much of what I am saying and avoid sex on days that are lunar cycle fertile days.

Let us be clear on what I have been discussing.

You have a moon cycle that runs around twenty-eight to twenty-nine days, where ovulation occurs around mid-cycle. Your cycle may be slightly longer or shorter.

You also have a lunar cycle that is based on the phase of the moon that existed at your birth, which is also a fertile time. Having frequent sex at this time of lunar return is likely to trigger spontaneous ovulation.

Having sex at these times optimizes your chances of achieving a pregnancy. Better still, if you can align and combine these two phases, you get a lunar hot spot!

Finding Your Moon

How, then, do you determine when your lunar return falls each month?

Start by finding out your birth date, location, and, if possible, the time of birth, but if you do not have your time of birth it does not matter. Some women choose to take this information to an astrologer and get a detailed printout of where the moon phases were and exact timings for the current months ahead. However many women I interviewed and some case studies chose to find out the phase through simple cost-free channels like the Internet, and then watch out for their moon in the sky each month. I like this idea because it has the double benefit of keeping aligned physically with the moon, which tends to regulate your twenty-eight-day moon cycle, and links us more closely as goddesses with the Divine Feminine.

I highly recommend the U.S. Navy's website. This site gives a fantastically accurate moon calendar to which you simply plug in any date, time, and geographical place, and you get a wonderful view of the moon phase that existed at your chosen time.

Once you know your personal moon phase, your lunar return occurs every time your moon is in this position in the sky. For example, my birth moon is the dark moon. I actually was not surprised at this as I have always loved this rich, dark time and found my magical workings were always extra powerful. I remember a teacher telling me that I should never cast on a dark moon because the energies were so dark and unpredictable, but I disregarded this because I always felt an intuitively calm confidence about this time. So I know that at each dark moon, my lunar return is potentially a highly fertile time for me.

Let us say, purely for example purposes, that the dark moon for the month of March falls on the tenth. Research shows that in order to trigger ovulation during the lunar return, sexual activity needs to be frequent within that twenty-four-hour period. Having sex may trigger the kind of spontaneous ovulation that scientists are just beginning to discover.

Something to remember, though. Sperm are resilient! They can live up to seventy-two hours in the female's body, so take care! Your fertile time during a lunar cycle will include the two days prior to your moon phase. Sex should be avoided on the eighth and ninth days as well, if you do not wish to become pregnant. If you do, here is your chance.

The regular menstrual moon cycle will still take place and you will have yet another chance there. However, optimum fertility will take place if you can combine the two cycles, and you will not have to abstain or use barrier contraception so often!

For example, when I first started to experiment with the idea of lunar returns, my twenty-eight-day cycle was exactly opposite my lunar return. This meant I generally bled at dark moon and ovulated at full moon. Ovulation at full moon is generally considered a very favorable combination and there are many anthropological studies of primitive tribes that showed whole villages of women ovulated at full moon when it was most light. For me however, it just meant a few more days I had to be careful! The idea for me therefore was to realign my twenty-eight-day cycle so that my lunar return and my ovulation days were one and the same. After four months of focused alignment mediations, I had achieved my wish of creating one lunar hotspot. They have continued to align now for over five years.

How Can You Create This Lunar Hotspot?

Your lunar cycle is immovable. Whatever the phase was at your birth is your moon. However, your twenty-eight-day menstrual moon cycle can be altered and changed. Most women know this, as at one time or another they have had cycles of varying lengths, and if especially stressed, sick, or traveling, their moon cycle may be seriously out of sync or not come at all.

So the focus and intention here is to move the ovulation point of your twenty-eight-day cycle to your lunar return date, thus creating your lunar hotspot.

You can see here how both cycles can overlap, creating those few amazing days of moon-driven hot spot fertility.

The best way to realign your twenty-eight-day cycle is by guided meditation and spell work. If you research this process further you will find this same technique is referred to as self-hypnosis or auto suggestion, but for those of you who do not have your magic legs yet, feel free to refer to this process the scientific way. The bottom line, though, is that it is the very same thing; it is just that witches have been doing it a lot longer!

The Alignment Meditation for Women that follows will assist your realignment process. You may want to tape it in your own voice and replay it a few times a week while in a relaxed state, just before bedtime, so that you process while you sleep.

Male readers have not been forgotten—we also have an Alignment Meditation for Men. You may think this is strange since you do not have a moon cycle—or do they?

Although male fertility does not depend on such a complex cyclic process as a female, there is a growing body of evidence to suggest that the quality and number of sperm produced does rise and fall in a wave-like pattern.

It was thought that men experience a constant fertility, and in a way this is true. Men naturally produce sperm constantly, and as such are fertile all the time, unlike women who are either fertile or infertile—there is no in-between. Research is now showing that men do have a regular rise and fall in sperm production and that it increases minimally three-fold on a man's lunar return. The ancient Egyptians knew this and would often try and arrange wedding nights on the lunar return of the groom to ensure a first encounter full of energy and fertility.

If a man has a healthy sperm count, a normal range of about 350–400,000 million per ejaculation, three times this amount may seem a little superfluous, but it really can be an obstacle course once the sperm enters the partner's body. Nature has provided this many sperm to ensure conception in an environment where many factors weed out the weak and unprepared! For example, many sperm simply die or run out of mitochondria (or life energy) before they get started, some that do make it farther on the journey may enter the wrong fallopian tube, get eroded by the yoni's natural acidity, or simply lose their way. Sperm are much smaller and therefore less resilient than the egg, so never take a boost to production lightly. However, if a man has a low sperm count, knowing his lunar return time comes in handy. Tripling a low sperm count could be the only chance of naturally conceiving.

Leon, a twenty-eight-year-old journalist, recorded a low sperm count while his partner Julie, also twenty-eight, seemed fine physically. Specialists considered Leon's problem the reason they had not conceived after eighteen months of intermittent attempts.

Julie explains: "I say intermittent, because after twelve months flew by Leon was tested and we found out his low sperm count was probably the reason. After that Leon just lost hope, and frankly, the sex was not too hot after that!"

Leon explains: "I just felt like less of a man somehow, knowing that I was shooting pretty close to blanks. I was devastated."

Leon and Julie followed the lunar return method and Julie aligned her lunar hotspot to Leon's lunar return. Four lunar months after alignment, Julie conceived.

Combining a male lunar return with a female's fertile time will give conception an even greater likelihood. Current accepted scientific statistics show that men are responsible for 40 percent of infertility, women are also at 40 percent, and 20 percent is unexplained.

If you are a same-sex couple who is undergoing assisted conception techniques and do not know the identity or lunar return of your donor, do not fret. Use the lunar return of your partner. You are a united couple under the eyes of the Goddess and the energies of the Universe will respond the same way.

Alignment Meditation for Women

This meditation is for those women whose lunar return date is not the same as their twenty-eight-day moon cycle ovulation midpoint and they wish to combine them to identify a lunar hotspot.

The best results are achieved at night, right before sleep. I recommend lying in bed alone, relaxing, and simply falling into sleep once the ritual is complete.

Preparation

Know your lunar return phase and have a clear picture of what the phase looks like in your mind.

Know your estimated twenty-eight-day cycle ovulation point—roughly thirteen-fourteen days before day one of your moon bleed this month, or if you chart your cycle, when symptoms and temperature suggests ovulation occurs.

Tape this mediation until you have memorized it.

Perform this spell on any night on a regular basis, being certain to perform it in your lunar return phase.

Ensure that you will be undisturbed. I like to turn off all the lights and do the meditation in darkness, but candlelight can also be beautiful and relaxing. Just ensure you extinguish the flame before sleeping.

Open a Circle around your bed if you wish, although this is not necessary. Light your candle if you are using one and relax.

Breathe in and out deeply. On the in breath begin to take deep into your body the sweet energy of Mother Earth—green, nourishing, and never-ending healing. On your out breath exhale any negativity or problems that the day you've experienced has brought. The day is over, and it is time to breathe out any thoughts or circumstances that do not serve your needs right now. Blow them out and allow them to be recycled by the Mother. There is time enough tomorrow to look again with fresh eyes and wisdom at these. Continue to do this until you feel at ease and at peace on every level. Allow this. Take your time.

When you are ready, begin to imagine that there is no ceiling above you, but it is now the deep, comforting midnight blue of the night sky.

The stars are twinkling and they are everywhere, not just on top of you, but now around you. You are floating on a sea of stars, indescribably beautiful. You are totally relaxed and connected.

You look down at yourself reflected in the star's silvery light, and you know that yes, you are a goddess and creator. You now begin to look deeper through your yoni, which softly twinkles in the starlight. You now look inside yourself at your yoni and your creative system. You see how your ovaries look like a dandelion, full of healthy and growing eggs. They look just like the seeds on the dandelion, perfect and full of potential.

Now you communicate with your body and ovaries.

My eggs are my essence. They are perfect and fertile.
They will unite with the spark and create.

Now look into the night sky. There in front of you is your personal moon phase. It is getting larger in the sky as you look at it. It is all-encompassing, and you feel a great love of your own body and power as a woman looking at it. This is a symbol of power for you.

Now again turn to your dandelion-like ovaries and eggs.

Communicate:

> *When the moon looks like this in the sky, the time is right to be ripe and to release. The date for this to happen is* (insert your lunar return date for that month). *Union is certain as I am irresistibly fertile.*

Now imagine one egg being born from the ovary (like a seed blowing from the dandelion) and it looks just like your moon. Watch it travel gently down the fallopian tubes where it glows even more brightly. Suddenly there are many tiny sperm surrounding your egg. You know these have come healthy and masculine from your partner (or donor) and one burrows into your egg. You watch as both the Divine Feminine and Divine Masculine combine to create a glowing spark full of life and energy. You watch as this form attaches itself to your womb and is enveloped there. Communicate:

> *I welcome this baby of the moon. It is the best of both of us and will be born easily into this world. It will be healthy and happy as we will.*

Hold on to this pleasurable feeling as you joyously move through the night sky basking in your moon.

Know that conception is close.

The Goddess and God are close and will assist you.

Now and only when you are ready, come back to the comfort of your bed and let the room become more concrete.

Breathe deeply and settle down to sleep.

Offer Your Gratitude

Know that the Goddess and the God have heard your desire to align cycles.

Thank the Goddess and the God for being here with you tonight. Be grateful in the knowledge that all is as you have asked it to be, if it be their will and for the greatest good of all.

Know that your mind and body are already responding. Your cycles are aligning.

Complete the Ritual

Close your Circle. Extinguish the candles. Sleep!

Participation

Begin to live what you have experienced. Ensure you share your progress with your partner, particularly if they are aligning with you. Record your progress on your moon chart or in your BOS.

Book of Shadows Entries

Chart your progress by recording your feelings, behaviors, actions, and results, paying close attention to coincidences and details, even if they seem insignificant or unrelated at the time. Remember to date all your entries and review over time.

Alignment Meditation for Men

This alignment is for those men who wish to either align their lunar return with their wife's lunar return or twenty-eight-day cycle, or for boosting the sperm count and motility of sperm on your own lunar return.

Best results are done at night right before sleep, lying in bed alone and relaxing, and simply falling into sleep once the ritual is complete.

Preparation

Know your lunar return phase and have a clear picture of what the phase looks like in your mind. Know your partner's estimated twenty-eight-day cycle ovulation or lunar return date and phase.

Tape this meditation until you can remember it yourself.

Perform this spell on any night on a regular basis and be certain to perform it on your lunar return phase.

Ensure that you will be undisturbed. I like to turn off all the lights and do the meditation in darkness, but candlelight can also be beautiful and relaxing. Just ensure you extinguish the flame before sleeping.

Open a Circle around your bed if you wish although this is not necessary. Light your candle if you are using one and relax.

Breathe in and out deeply. On the in breath begin to take deep into your body the sweet energy of Mother Earth—green, nourishing, and never-ending healing. On your out breath exhale any negativity or problems that the day you have experienced has brought. The day is over now, and it is time to breathe out any thoughts or circumstances that do not serve your needs right now. Blow them out and allow them to be recycled by the Mother. There is time enough tomorrow to look again with fresh eyes and wisdom at these. Think now also of the God, he who is protector and ruler of masculine fertility. He assists you to let go of issues that really are not important and to focus on your wish for a child.

Continue to do this until you feel at ease and at peace on every level. Allow this. Take your time.

When you are ready, begin to imagine that there is no ceiling above you, but it is now the deep, comforting midnight blue of the night sky.

The stars are twinkling and they are everywhere. Not just on top of you but now around you. You are floating on a sea of stars, indescribably beautiful. You are totally relaxed and connected.

You look down at yourself reflected in the stars' silvery light and you know that yes, you are a God and Creator. You are strong and virile, and you feel powerful in your masculinity. You now begin to look at your lingham as it glows in the starlight. It is erect and hard. You now look inside yourself through your testicles at your creative system. You see how millions of sperm are being made every second. Take a closer look. They are all healthy and strong. Every second as you watch, more are created, more than you could ever imagine, all strong with tails that kick energetically. They are perfect, each and every one, and full of potential.

Now you communicate with your body and testicles:

My sperm are my essence. They are perfect and fertile. They are ready to unite.

Now look into the night sky. There in front of you is your moon phase.

It is getting larger in the sky as you look at it. It is all encompassing and you feel a great love of your own body and power as a man looking at it. This is a symbol of power for you.

(If you do wish to align your cycle with your partner's now, watch as the moon now transforms itself into her lunar return.)

Now again turn to your body and sperm. Communicate:

When the moon looks like this in the sky, the time is right to be ripe, perfect and plenty. This will be the time to release. The date for this to happen is (insert your lunar return date for that month, or the day you will try to conceive). *Union is certain as I am irresistibly fertile and purposeful.*

Now imagine your sperm being released with complete ecstasy, all traveling toward your partner's moon-like egg. Watch and be filled with wonder as many of your sperm, wave after wave, surround the egg, which is the essence of her. Now one of your sperm burrows into her egg. You watch as both the Divine Feminine and Divine Masculine combine to create a glowing spark, full of life and energy. You watch as this form attaches itself to your partner's womb and is enveloped there. Communicate:

In the name of the God, I welcome this baby of the moon.
It is the best of both of us and will be born easily into this world.
It will be healthy and happy as we will.

Hold on to this pleasurable feeling as you joyously move through the night sky, basking in your moon. Know that conception is close. The Goddess and God are close and will assist you.

Now and only when you are ready, come back to the comfort of your bed and let the room become more concrete. Breathe deeply and settle down to sleep.

Offer Your Gratitude

Know that the Goddess and the God have heard your desire to align cycles.

Thank the Goddess and the God for being here with you tonight. Be grateful in the knowledge that all is as you have asked it to be, if it be their will and for the greatest good of all.

Know that your mind and body are already responding. Your cycles are aligning or strengthening.

Complete the Ritual

Close your Circle. Extinguish the candles. Sleep!

Participation

Begin to live what you have experienced. Ensure that you share your progress with your partner, particularly if they are aligning with you.

Book of Shadows Entries

Chart your progress by recording your feelings, behaviors, actions, and results, paying close attention to coincidences and details, even if they seem insignificant or unrelated at the time.

Remember to date all your entries and review over time.

Preparing the Ancient Witches' Way

There are many naturalists, pagans, and witches who simply draw the line at technology-based assisted conception techniques. On first view, I can see their point, with the unknown, long-term impact of drugs, the complete overriding of the natural process, and the variety of natural healing techniques that have a strong history of effectiveness readily available to choose from as an alternative. I can even sympathize with the idea that if you cannot conceive the natural way then it is the Universe's way of telling you that the road to parenthood is not for you.

However, it is my personal view that witches are here to be of service, to assist people in getting clear about what they want, empowering them, and giving them the support to attain it. Denying help to those who choose to tackle the problem with the aid of modern science seems short sighted. The Witches Way is one that deeply honors the natural cycles of all things and, as such, the invasive techniques should only be used as a last resort and not as a shortcut or as the easy way out, because it truly isn't.

The industry quickly built up to offer in vitro fertilization (IVF) and assisted conception programs make literally billions of dollars. Although most clinics now have clearly defined goals and ethics statements as well as counselors, it is still a business that actively advertises and solicits clients. When a couple desperate to have a child, their time running out due to age, combined with a business that needs to reach its own performance and financial goals, what can result is something quite divorced from the caring, honest, and life-affirming experience that one would expect.

Caryss' Experience

Take the experience of Caryss, thirty-nine-years old, for example. Caryss had no medical history that would indicate infertility. Healthy, a yoga practitioner, and a non-smoker, the infertility seemed unexplained. Her husband Rusty had already had tests to check the motility and count of his sperm and all was well.

Caryss explains:

"I decided upon a well-regarded infertility doctor connected to the leading IVF clinic in my state. I chose a female specialist because I felt more comfortable with female doctors. I explained to her that we had been trying unsuccessfully for seven months after going through a natural preconception program. I knew diet, exercise, and pollutants were not factors. I had been tracking my cycle closely. I was puzzled why we hadn't conceived yet and, because of my age, I guess I wanted to know my options.

"After asking one question about whether my husband had been tested, the doctor quickly told me that IVF was my solution. She then began to give me a quick outline of the way IVF worked. I must say I was pretty shocked that straight up IVF would be the way to go. I asked to her to clarify some of the more general statements she made like, 'We will give you drugs that will stimulate your follicles,' which, in reality, meant: 'You will inject yourself twice daily with drugs that will stimulate your follicles.' Big difference! She seemed quite amused that I really would need anymore information to make a decision.

"I was pretty shell-shocked so I asked her, 'Is there anything else we could try first that's less invasive, since I have no reason to believe right now that there is anything radically wrong?'

"She said to me 'Well, I guess we could do an ultrasound to see if your tubes are blocked, and if they're not, we could go a few trials of intrauterine insemination (IUI).'

"I liked the sound of this far more. Ultrasound and IUI seemed good, gentle options. IUI would be less expensive, although if it didn't work, of course, we would perhaps have the cost of IVF in addition to the IUI trials.

"The whole experience was quite unnerving. I felt like I was part of a big production line in a factory with one solution. I thought afterward how women that are, let's say, a little less questioning or confident, would so easily just go for the more invasive procedure because this is what they were told."

Caryss' story is typical of many of the women interviewed over three continents for this book. On the one hand, women need clear advice and solid recommendations so that they can make an educated decision about their own bodies, and, on the other hand, it seems that there is a culture of over-prescribing techniques likes IVF.

Caryss became pregnant on her second round of IUI, but was prepared to go for IVF if a third cycle of IUI with super-ovulation drugs added to the third trial had not been successful.

The Witches Way, although ancient in origin, can guide and support any couple deciding to engage in cutting-edge technology to help them conceive. The Witches Way concentrates the laws of attraction and the keys to power building (page 39) so that the couple is in the best state they can be, spiritually, mentally, and physically. It removes many obstacles to their conceiving, naturally or with assistance, from the equation.

The following factors offer a guide to starting the kind of natural changes you can make yourself in order to be in the best condition you can be and to increase your chances of attracting a child. The bottom line here is to be willing to make these changes and utilize the spellcraft and ritual that can support you if this is difficult. The Spell for Health and Vitality earlier in the book is a great place to start.

Diet

You cannot expect a plant to grow in poor soil and so it is with conception and later with a baby growing inside of you. Many women I've encountered only started paying attention to their diet when they became pregnant, rather than at least a few months prior to that time. Researchers now have strong evidence that the diet of the father has a direct correlation with the quality and motility of his sperm. Certain vitamins such as selenium and zinc are vital to the production of good quality sperm. More than 60 percent of Australian men have a selenium deficiency and 50 percent of American men have a zinc deficiency. So, as soon as you are thinking of becoming pregnant, both of you need to consciously begin to adopt extreme self-care and extend this to your diet. Suggestions for an improved diet that are easy to implement:

- Eat organic. Choose organic produce and meat instead of the usual. Organic food can cost a little more, but it is certainly worth it in taste and nourishment! (When you cut out all those coffees and chocolates, you can spend your money on organics instead!)
- Eat whole foods—those that are as close to their natural state as possible (for example: fresh meat, vegetables, fruits, and herbs). Cut out processed foods, especially those high in sugar and salt—for example: cakes, biscuits, packet sauces.
- Eat more fresh fish, but avoid large fish at the top of the food chain because of higher levels of mercury.
- Vitamins. Take a good quality pregnancy vitamin with the RDA of folic acid for at least three moon cycles prior to plans for conception.
- Cut out caffeine. There is much conflicting research about the safe level of caffeine for pre-pregnancy and pregnancy, but it seems the less the better. Do not take chances. Wean yourself off your daily latte! Reduce your intake of chocolate. Notice I said reduce, not cut out completely.
- Drink filtered or high-quality bottled water, a minimum of six glasses per day.
- Drink herbal teas. Make an appointment with your herbalist who can recommend the kind of nourishing teas that are sure to get your fertility levels up and your reproductive organs toned.
- Prescription drugs. Speak to your doctor about any prescription drugs you or your partner may be taking, and assess the risks to fertility.

Addictions

Do choose life and a clean body for your child. Get the assistance you need to overcome any addictions before you plan to conceive. If you need professional help seek it well before you wish to become pregnant.

- Smoking. There is nothing here I can say that you have not heard a thousand times before. Do not smoke.

- Alcohol. Again you have heard the facts. Give it up *prior* to plans for conception.

- Drugs. Avoid all recreational drugs well prior to conception as some drug residue can stay in the body for long periods of time before being eliminated.

Stress

This book emphasizes the importance of reintroducing pleasure back into your lives, and making a baby should, ideally, be a highly pleasurable process! However, if you do not conceive as quickly as you would like, that pleasure can soon be left behind and in its place can enter perfunctory sex, tension, anxiety, and depression.

Many partners live busy lives, juggling the demands of a career and home life. Stress seems inevitable. When stress builds up to an uncomfortable level it can affect the ability to conceive and, later, the development and health of the unborn child. The National Institutes of Health in the United States have found that high pre-pregnancy stress not only affects rates of fertility in indirect ways, such as overeating, but directly impacts the woman's coping and health behavior during pregnancy. According to psychiatrist Professor Bryanne Barnett of the National Australian Post Natal Depression Program, depression of the mother during pregnancy was an important but seemingly unrecognized factor in the health of a newborn. "Before you are born, the way your brain develops is affected by the person who is providing you with your experiences."

A number of U.S. studies have suggested that very high levels of stress may increase the risk of preterm labor and low birth weight. A 1999 study at the University of California Los Angeles School of Medicine found that women who reported high levels of stress at eighteen to twenty weeks of pregnancy were more likely to have high levels of a hormone called corticotropin-releasing hormone (CRH) in their blood. This and other studies have found a potential link between high levels of CRH and preterm labor. CRH, which is produced by the brain and the placenta, is closely tied to labor. It prompts the body to release chemicals called prostaglandins, which trigger uterine contractions. CRH is also the first hormone your brains secrete when you are under stress. Researchers continue to explore the possibility that women who experience high levels of stress early in pregnancy have elevated levels of CRH that set their placental clock for early delivery.

Some easily adaptable ways of lowering your stress levels prior to pregnancy are:

- Identify stressors. Discover where stress is originating and reduce it. That sounds easier than it is, but this must be a priority in your life. Make yourselves and conception a priority.

- Exercise. This does not need to mean slogging every day at the gym, but perhaps a period of half an hour, three times a week. Yoga and pilates are great destressors but so is walking briskly around the block with your dog. When you do get pregnant being fitter certainly keeps you in good stead to cope with any pregnancy-related discomforts like backache, headache, and fatigue.

- Meditation and ritual. Having a dedicated time to yourselves to reconnect with your "beingness" and the Goddess is vital to maintaining resilience and calmness through difficult situations. Learning to let go and let the Goddess handle things is a sure way to reduce your ego and stress levels at the same time! Some of the beautiful preparatory rituals and guided meditations in this book are a great start, even for beginners. Book appointments for yourself in your day planner. Even if you are very busy, honor those appointments, no matter what. And do not forget full moons!

- Sleep. Get adequate rest and ensure your bedroom is conducive to getting that rest. Get rid of the television if you have one and buy yourself a new mattress if you know the old one has seen its best days. Refresh the sanctuary of the bedroom by purchasing some beautiful new sheets and pillows. There's nothing like fresh crisp sheets to usher in a good night's sleep!

- Support. You are no longer an "alone ranger"! Do not be afraid to ask for help and start to delegate tasks that you know can be done by someone else. Start now! When you do have a child, you will certainly need to be in the habit of asking for support because you will need it!

- Breathe. Sounds obvious, but when you are stressed you tend to hold your breath and constrict your breathing. Be more aware of the life-giving, rejuvenating power of bringing enough oxygen to your system and learn to recognize the constricting feeling of not relaxing the muscles around both the in and out breaths.

Pollutants

You no longer live in a world that is in balance, and Mother Earth is heavy with all kinds of pollutants that damage her fertility. This is reflected in your own fertility. As within, so without. Prospective parents need to be alerted to the warnings about high levels of mercury in some fish, that the water in your taps can be contaminated with all kinds of heavy metals including copper, and that pesticides in your food can have long-term detrimental effects to your bodies.

Hair analysis and blood tests are two noninvasive ways to check for levels of pollutants and toxicity in the body. If infertility is unexplained, these levels may give some insight. Visit your naturopath who can recommend high doses of elements that can flush some unwanted pollutants out of your system naturally.

Adopt these ways of reducing pollution in your body and environment:

- Stop smoking and stay away from smoky environments.
- Drink plenty of filtered or bottled water.
- Wash all fruit and vegetables thoroughly and choose organic whenever possible.
- Try natural alternatives to commercial household cleaners. A little vinegar and lemon or baking soda and water will tend to clean up most stains in your kitchen!
- Use the air-conditioning in your car in heavy traffic.
- Be more aware of any chemical exposure, especially at work, such as cleaning chemicals and photocopy toner.

Moon Cycles

As you have read, it is important for both sexes to discover and align your cycle with your lunar peak to increase your chances of becoming pregnant. The closer your cycle is aligned with the lunar cycle of twenty-nine days, the easier it is to maintain a healthy and regular cycle with good quality, mature eggs, and to more easily select the optimum time for conception.

Making Room for a Baby Ritual

The Witches Way is one of balance and rebirth. When you perform powerful rituals and spells around removing obstacles you acknowledge that once these obstacles are removed there is a hole or void created. Think of this like pulling out weeds in a garden. If you decide to remove the weed there is a hole in the earth. This hole is a place of possibility and anything can grow there. This hole, this void, can be refilled by weeds or with something that will benefit the garden more.

I speak to you about the concept of the void because often our lives are like gardens: so full of plants and weeds that there is no room for any new seeds. Time and time again, I have looked at the lives of my clients and the lives of some of the talented people I have been lucky enough to work with as part of my case studies and truly there is no room for anything new—no room for further creation.

Elana, a business development manager for a large pharmaceutical company, came to me asking for help to conceive. I normally take a full history of any fertility clients, including what they do in an average week. Elana's week was completely jam-packed, including weekly interstate travel, being a part-time caregiver to her elderly parent, going to the gym, and taking a language class, among other things. She also admitted that due to her extensive travel schedule it was difficult for her husband and her to get together at the right time to even try for a child. Her husband was also an extremely busy corporate executive, and although he did not travel, he did work long hours.

I asked Elana outright what she was willing to give up to make room for a child.

"I have to do all of these things. I have no choice. It is just the way my life is set up."

After some initial resistance, we worked together on discovering smarter ways to use her time and to identify which activities in her week were flowers and which were weeds.

"I can see that I could negotiate perhaps traveling every fortnight and not every week, and maybe I could ask my sister to take a more active role in the care of my mother. This would give me more free time. I do enjoy the language classes though, as it is so social, so I would like to keep that in!"

Yet seeing the possibilities and actually doing something about them are two different things. At the time of this writing, Elana has not given up anything except a few gym classes. Not surprisingly, she has not become pregnant either.

By allowing room for a baby in your lives, you are preparing both the mind and the body for change. Make room and fill that void with a new soul!

Ritual for Preparation

You will be invoking both the God and the Goddess tonight. You may like to choose a specific aspect of the God and Goddess. You will not be raising any energy here, just connecting with the energy of male and female and asking to be opened to conception. Ideally, perform this ritual where you can see the moon and/or nature. If you have a spot that is totally secure, private, and safe outdoors you may prefer to undertake it there.

Preparation

Perform this ritual on any night prior to the procedure. Perform on a regular basis prior to any procedure especially around a full or dark moon for best results. Ensure the room is warm. Ensure that you will be undisturbed.

Welcome the God and Goddess and thank them for being here with you tonight in this beautiful place.

Gather

An orange or gold candle to represent the God
A silver or white candle to represent the Goddess

Matches

A few drops of rose or rose geranium essential oil blended with two tablespoons of carrier oil such as jojoba, avocado, or olive

A small, shallow bowl to hold the oil

Charcoal

Sandalwood chips or frankincense to burn on the charcoal

A comfortable robe that you can slip out of easily for the skyclad elements
of the ritual

Focus

Cast and open a Circle if you wish. Face the moon if you can. Light the sil-
ver/white candle and relax. Take several deep breaths.

Welcome the Goddess to your Circle:

I welcome you Goddess, my Mother.
I know you are all things and create all things in unity with the God.
You are the Goddess of the moon, of all of its cycles.
As it is born, as it grows, and as it diminishes across the sky.
You are the Goddess of healing, of compassion, of cooperation, of wisdom,
of death and rebirth, of fertility, of the water, of the earth beneath my feet,
of the air that I breathe. You show me that we are all connected
and without the feminine aspect we are incomplete.

Gaze at the candle or close your eyes and go within.

Visualize the Goddess, the Divine Feminine, before you. She can look as
you wish—there is no wrong image.

Meditate on some of the aspects of the Goddess around fertility, cycles,
and plenty that you may like to bring forward tonight or that appeal to you
at this moment.

Open your eyes. Light the orange/gold candle and relax. Take several
deep breaths.

Welcome the God to your Circle:

I welcome you, God.
I know you are all things and create all things in unity with the Goddess.

You are the God of the Sun, blazing for all to see, and spreading your
life-giving warmth for all to feel. You are the God of protection,
of wild animals, of fertility in all its forms, of the life-giving fire,
of hunting, of the earth beneath my feet, and of the air that I breathe.
You show me that we are all connected and without
the masculine aspect we are incomplete.

Gaze at the candle or close your eyes and go within. Visualize the God, the Divine Masculine, before you. He can look as you wish—there is no wrong image.

Meditate on some of the aspects of the God around fertility and protection that you may like to bring forward tonight or that appeal to you at this moment.

Now light your herbs and incense. Breathe in deeply. As you breathe, you are inhaling even more support and energy from the earth, the trees, the moon, and the sky.

Think about your life as it is now, and how a child would positively impact it. Think about your partner and your relationship and in particular how each of you will combine in masculine and feminine energy to make a new creation, your baby. Feel anticipation of what is to come!

The God and the Goddess are now reaching out to you. They are telling you that you are a God and a Goddess also. You are a creator too.

Disrobe.

Say, with feeling:

I call upon you, Great Goddess, to open my body and my womb and
help me to be all woman. I ask that you prepare my body
for the ultimate act of creation, no matter where creation occurs.
Allow me to feel the power of being fertile, prepared, and lush with life!

Now with the oil, gently anoint your womb, your breasts, your heart, and your forehead. You, too, are Goddess!

I call upon you, Great God, to assist my body and spirit to accept
the Divine Masculine and help me balance any imbalances in my body.

I call upon you to protect and watch over our seed, no matter where creation
may occur. Prepare me to feel the joy of life within me!

State here, out loud, any particular fears or worries you may have. Tell the Goddess and the God about the obstacles, real or feared, that you are encountering. Take your time. They will hear you and begin to act on your behalf if it be for the good of all.

Release Your Intention

Now take out a few more drops of your essential oil.

Anoint your left shoulder with the oil, saying:

I honor the Divine Feminine power in me.

Anoint your right shoulder with the oil, saying:

I honor the Divine Masculine power in me.

Anoint your genitalia with the oil, saying:

I honor my potential to create.

Anoint your forehead with the oil, saying:

I am the unity of the God and the Goddess and I will unite the
masculine and feminine within me to create life. I am open
and prepared. I am a creator! I am life!

The God and the Goddess are still with you and sharing with you their support. Accept these gifts in your own body. Feel the power of *yes*. This is pleasurable, healing, and uplifting.

Offer Your Gratitude

Know that the Goddess and the God have heard your desire to be prepared to accept a child in your life.

Thank the Goddess and the God for being here with you tonight.

Be grateful in the knowledge that all is as you have asked it to be, if it be their will and for the greatest good of all. Know that your mind and body are already responding. You are being prepared.

Complete the Ritual

Close your Circle. Extinguish the candles. Extinguish and bury any remaining charcoal or herbs/incense in the garden or yard.

Participation

Begin to live what you have experienced. Be confident that you are ready and prepared to accept the gift of life within yourself. Do not dwell on your obstacles or fears. Surrender!

Book of Shadows Entries

Chart your progress by recording your feelings, behaviors, actions, and results. Take note of any resistance you feel to welcoming the child. Discuss this with your partner with a solutions mindset. Share your feelings of confidence with your partner and physicians if you feel so inclined. Remember to date all your entries.

Artificial Insemination or Intrauterine Insemination (IUI)

This is probably the least invasive of all the modern assisted-conception techniques, as it involves no surgery or drugs. The procedure involves insemination of sperm via a thin catheter into the cervix or into the uterine cavity around the time of ovulation. Both blood samples and ultrasound are used to confirm the window of ovulation in order to ensure that the ovulation time is not missed.

Intrauterine insemination is most often performed if the couple's problem with fertility appears to be the inability to complete intercourse, hostile mucus, or unexplained infertility. It is not recommended for those couples experiencing very low sperm count or blocked fallopian tubes. The technique is often a couple's first foray into the technology and it is normally suggested that a few trials be tried prior to more invasive techniques like in vitro fertilization (IVF). The success rate is similar to that of a natural conception. It is between 5 and 10 percent successful, age dependent. Research is demonstrating that combinations of low doses of drugs used to hyperstimulate the ovaries and intrauterine insemination is generally recognized to give a higher rate of success than IUI alone. This is commonly called super or hyper ovulation. However, these drugs do have side effects (including a higher incidence of multiple births) and the decision to take them should not be taken lightly without being fully informed.

How the Witches Way Can Assist

IUI sounded deceptively simple to me and I wondered what factors within the process limited its effectiveness. One such process involves the treatment of the man's sperm.

Whether or not ovarian hyperstimulation is chosen, IUI and IVF procedures require that the sperm be washed prior to placement in the woman's body. Washing struck me as a strange term when there should ideally be nothing present that such a perfectly natural substance would need to be washed free of. Washing separates the sperm from the semen since semen contains molecules called prostaglandins that cause painful contractions of the uterus if placed into the uterine cavity. Additionally, the sperm may contain oxygen-reactive molecules that can interfere with fertilization and there may be unwanted bacteria in the sample. Sperm washing techniques almost always involve centrifugation and suspension in an inert medium. The problem with this process is that centrifugation, which is spinning at high speed to separate out the different elements, creates dizzy sperm. Imagine this, normal fresh sperm are mobile and purposeful but spinning them at high speed confuses them. The process also leeches much of the calcium from the sperm that is integral to motility. When viewing footage of two petri dishes of sperm, one washed, one not, even to the untrained eye there was certainly a difference.

What can you do to assist these dizzy washed sperm to swim straight and hit the target? In sperm with seriously decreased motility, chemical agents similar to caffeine have been used to enhance the motility. Thankfully, the use of these agents has been significantly reduced over the past several years due to concerns of possible embryo toxicity. Shooting a substance into the female womb that is poisonous to the very life you are attempting to create is not a great idea.

So can we look to the Witches Way for more natural assistance? Of course. It is called the Supercharging Sperm Spell. A funny name, but a serious intention!

One small serendipitous story before I share the spell with you. I completed this spell and had sent it to a doctor friend for reading. Feeling it was a great spell, I passed it on to a couple who agreed to use it prior to their IUI the following week. The next day on the morning news, an IVF doctor in the United States announced a breakthrough treatment for dizzy sperm. According to the white-lab-coated doctor on the television screen, the new technique involves treating the sperm with a calcium-rich serum, which "supercharges them!"

The Supercharging Sperm Spell is for the male to do, or it can be altered slightly if you are a woman and receiving donor sperm.

Simultaneously, or the night before the procedure, the female partner should perform the Siren Call of the Egg Spell, which is a spell of attraction. This spell draws the sperm to your egg, calling them so they cannot resist! If you are having two IUIs a day apart (which research shows also improves your chances of success) ensure you perform the Siren Call Spell the night in between. Finally, if at all possible, you can try to align the procedure with your lunar peak. Although this may prove difficult, it multiplies your chances of conception.

Supercharging Sperm Ritual

This spell is specifically written for a male partner. However, if you are female and are undertaking IUI or IVF with sperm from an unknown donor, the meditation still works beautifully. I recommend that you work with Pele (or your patron goddess or god) no matter what your gender. She will provide the explosiveness and action orientation that you need!

Just a word here of warning to men. You may feel like you wish to ejaculate at the height of your energy, which normally is absolutely natural and fine. However, it is not advisable within a few days of the IUI procedure. It is imperative that your sperm count is at its maximum and the sperm of good quality, not too old or immature, to boost your chances of conception.

Please channel your energy into the movements or sounds suggested instead.

Preparation

Preferably perform this spell on any night where the moon is full or on a waxing moon. However, performing this ritual every night, beginning a few nights before the IUI procedure will take place, is much more important than the phase of the moon.

Ensure the room is warm. Ensure that you will be undisturbed.

Have your intention clearly in mind. For example, that your sperm will not only reach the egg but that they will do it in a purposeful and super-speedy manner.

Have a visual image of the female egg. For some people this is a traditional egg shape, a dandelion, a seed, a glowing circle, or a spark . . . whatever appeals to you.

Welcome the Goddess and thank her for being with you here tonight in this beautiful place.

Gather

Large pillar candle with a large flame in white, yellow, or green

Large red candle for Pele

Matches

Charcoal

Your favorite incense or frankincense, damiana, dill, mandrake, and snake root

Music that has a drumming beat or rhythm that gets faster and faster

A comfortable robe that you can slip out of easily for the skyclad elements of the ritual

Focus

Cast and open a Circle if you wish. Light the first candle and dim the lights. Turn on the music.

Now invoke the Goddess Pele, who is the goddess of volcanoes and regenerative power:

I call you, Pele, great Goddess of Fire and Volcanoes.
You, who demonstrates to all that power can build and be unleashed
with mighty force. Tonight I call upon you to assist me
to release my seed like a glowing eruption in days henceforth.
I ask that you be here tonight to bless the union that will soon take part.

Now light the red candle representing Pele, saying:

Pele! Assist me tonight!

Light your herbs or incense.

Now relax and go within. Slip out of your robe and lay on your back, arms and legs outstretched like a star. Ensure your head and back are supported as you need to feel completely comfortable and safe. Take several deep breaths, breathing out all stress and tension. Listen to the drumbeat.

Building Power

First, begin to imagine the egg. You should have a symbolic or visual image already in your mind. Really see the detail in this image, how beautiful it is and how desirable. She begins to call to you, a siren call of wanting and desire. Feel how desired you are, how much the feminine draws you. Take your time and enjoy this.

Now imagine your sperm. Imagine what they look like especially their shape. Notice the seed-shaped head, all perfect. Notice their muscular tails, sensuously moving from side to side. Notice how many there are, thousands, millions, all pulsing with life, all perfect, all healthy, all alive!

Allow yourself to feel the excitement of this, the miracle of it! There is so much power in each one and they belong to you. They *are* you.

Feel them now in your body, tingling, growing hotter, and becoming restless. Sense how good each part of your body feels in that soft warmth being generated from your genitals. You feel alive!

Feel how the heat and activity rises just like lava and pressure in a volcano. Pele is there encouraging you to awaken to your masculine creative power!

Accept these gifts in your own body. Feel your own strength and that of the Goddess course through you. Now focus on the feeling of that power coursing through you.

In a loud, firm voice, chant:

> *I am life! Stronger and stronger!*
> *I am life! Faster and faster!*

Repeat the chant faster and faster, feeling your strength, health, vitality, and energy grow.

Release Your Intention

Now imagine the sperm are kicking faster and faster, growing hotter and hotter, and now they are racing, absolutely unstoppably, toward the egg. You should feel a huge surge of energy.

If you cannot stay still, get up and jump, run, or dance to the beat of your own life!

Move! Feel your aliveness! Your speed, your energy!

At the height of your energy, imagine the explosion of life just like a volcano's explosive eruption. Imagine your sperm colliding with the egg, causing a river of sparks and light. An explosion of fire and heat!

Allow yourself to express with abandon: shout, laugh or whatever else you may feel. You may wish to express the union by shouting:

> *Yes!*
> *I am life!*
> *I am unstoppable!*

Offer Your Gratitude

Know that the Goddess has heard your intention, and Pele is speeding your intention through your body.

Thank the Goddess. Be grateful in the knowledge that all is as you have asked it to be, if it be her will and for the greatest good of all.

Know your mind and body is already responding.

Complete the Ritual

Close your Circle. Put on your robe.

Extinguish and bury any remaining charcoal and herbs/incense in the garden or yard.

Ground yourself by eating or drinking something, or perhaps sharing what happened during the ritual with your partner.

You may like to light the candles during some quiet time over the next few nights to remind you of your intention.

Participation

You are now supercharged! Feel confident when you visit your doctor or clinic and are asked to provide your sample. Know that your sperm will be extra charged, extra fast, extra strong, and that more will survive the freezing process (if this is part of the procedure). You may even wish to imagine the same visualization as the ritual just prior, after, or during your donation.

Book of Shadows Entries

Record your feelings, behaviors, actions, and results. Share these with your partner if you wish. Remember to date all your entries.

Siren Call of the Egg Spell

This spell is dedicated to the Sirens of Greek mythology that lured sailors to them with their irresistible song. Except this time, you will be wishing to call the male energy into the egg so that there is a definite fertilization! Although some versions of the story spoke of sailors being lured to their deaths, this may have been based on scare stories from lonely wives not wanting their sea sailing husbands' eyes to wander! I would also highly recommend invoking the power of one of the goddesses of sexuality, for example Freya, if you do not feel aligned to the Sirens. If you do call Freya, ensure that you wear something she likes, such as amber or feathers.

Preparation

Perform this spell on any night when the moon is full.

Ensure the room is warm. Ensure that you will be undisturbed.

Decide on the location for the spellcraft. Have your intention clearly in mind or written down.

Welcome the Goddess and thank her for being with you here tonight in this beautiful place.

Gather

Red candle

Matches

Jasmine or rose petals

Potion: three drops each of essential oils of ylang ylang, rose, and sandalwood, mixed in 10 mls of carrier oil; place in a small glass bottle

Moon-charged water

A comfortable robe that you can slip out of easily for the skyclad elements of the ritual

Sea salt

Focus

Cast and open a Circle if you wish. Light the red candle, dim the lights, and relax. Take several deep breaths.

Run a bath. Add some of the potion to the bath: no more than a teaspoon, and add the rest to a bath sachet. Add a dash of moon water, the jasmine and/or rose petals, and a handful of salt. Soak and relax for a minimum of fifteen minutes.

Visualize how good each part of your body feels in that soft warmth. As you come out of the bath, gently towel off.

Then take almost all the remaining oil and massage your body from the feet up, leaving a few drops in the bottle. Massage your body slowly and lovingly. Pay special attention to your breasts, thighs, and belly area. Breathe in the rich scent of aphrodisiac oils. As you massage your body, say this to each part of your body as you massage and move up:

I am a Goddess. I am beautiful. Men have desired me
since the beginning of time. Each part of me is loved and is irresistible.

Use your own words as you move forward. The idea here is to infuse positive qualities to each part. If you feel a hesitation somewhere, notice it, but still say something positive.

Slip into your robe or dress comfortably and go somewhere right away to do your spell.

Building Power

Bring your candle and the bottle with the remaining oil into another room or outside, if it is warm enough. Face the moon if you can. Ask that you receive the Goddess, she who embodies love, lust, and sexuality.

Call in the Sirens or the goddess of your choice by name. For example:

> *I invoke you, Sirens of the sea! Your voices called men so strongly*
> *that they heard nothing else. I ask that your powers of attraction be*
> *focused on my egg so that the seed draws inevitably to her. I call you now!*

Look back in your mind now. Look back to a time where you felt sexually confident or sexual pleasure. (If this is difficult for you, you can even imagine your favorite sexy scene in a movie.)

See this and *feel* this time clearly in your mind and body. Feel your personal, vital sexual energy. Feel it warm you, pulse through you. Notice how you feel and what thoughts enter your mind. If your thoughts or feelings are negative, note this, but decide you will put this aside until a later time. Take some of the remaining oil from the bottle and anoint and massage your yoni. (Be careful not to put oil inside, concentrate on the fun bits on the outside!)

The Goddess is still with you and sharing with you her attributes of sensuality, pleasure, and sexual power.

Accept these gifts in your own body. Allow these energies to begin to mingle—yours and those of the Goddess. Feel your own sexual strength and that of the Goddess course through you. Now focus on the feeling of that power in your hands.

In a loud, firm voice, chant:

> *Come to me*
> *Come to me*
> *I am beauty and light*

Come to me
Come to me
Goddess let us unite!

Repeat the chant faster and faster at least three times, feeling your strength, health, vitality, and energy grow.

Release Your Intention

Here you have a choice. You can bring yourself to climax and yell your intent or continue to hold and channel the sexual power back into your body. If you hold and channel, place your hands around your hips where your eggs would be and imagine them being charged with sexual energy. Both are a form of release.

You may wish to yell: *Unite!* or *Come to me!*

Offer Your Gratitude

Know that the Goddess has heard your intention and that you are now a virtual magnet for masculine energy, including sperm. Your egg is now charged and calling her suitors!

Thank the Goddess. Be grateful in the knowledge that all is as you have asked it to be, if it be her will and for the greatest good of all.

Know your mind and body is already responding.

Complete the Ritual

Close your Circle. Ground yourself by eating or drinking something, exercising, or dancing!

Participation

Take the energized oil with you and feel free to use the leftover drops just before your procedure. You may wish to make a symbolic anointing of your yoni and womb.

Feel confident that your egg will be attracting the sperm and that fertilization will occur. Carry this confidence with you into the procedure.

Book of Shadows Entries

If you wish, chart your progress by recording your feelings, behaviors, actions, and results. Share your feelings with your partner if you wish, paying close attention to coincidences and details even if they seem insignificant or unrelated at the time.

Remember to date all your entries.

In Vitro Fertilization (IVF)

OK, let's get real about the process of in vitro fertilization (IVF). It is not fun by any stretch of the imagination for either partner, but obviously less so for the woman having the treatment. She will have enough blood samples taken on such a regular basis that she will believe a vampire has come a-calling. She will be prescribed drugs that will hyperstimulate the follicles in her ovaries, which will, at the least, make her feel hormonal (read the worst PMS you will ever have), bloated, or, at worst, if the dose is not controlled correctly, she can suffer from hyper ovarian syndrome which can be life threatening. She will inject herself (or if squeamish ask her partner to) twice daily for almost two weeks, which leaves her pelvic area looking like target practice for a squad of very large mosquitoes. She will have regular ultrasounds and minor surgery to extract the eggs, and all the while trying not to get too stressed about it all.

All this is extremely tough going, but the results are truly worthwhile if a pregnancy is achieved. IVF has come a long way from its beginnings and truly is miraculous in the hope and results it gives to thousands of infertile couples each year.

In order for pregnancy to occur, an egg must be released from the ovary (ovulation) and unite with the sperm within a woman's body. If nature takes its course, this initial fertilization will be followed by development of an embryo. IVF differs from the natural process in that the natural process of ovulation is taken out of the control of the body and the egg and sperm are collected from each partner and united in the laboratory to produce an embryo. This embryo is then transferred back to the uterus for continued growth.

So what do I mean by the "process of ovulation is taken out of control of the body"? The objective of IVF is to harvest enough mature, good-quality eggs to have a number of fertilized embryos to transfer. A woman's body generally releases a single egg per moon cycle. Therefore, science steps in and controls nature.

To control the timing of the egg's release (ovulation) and to increase the number of eggs collected, the woman will receive drugs to both stimulate the growth of more than one egg that moon cycle and another drug to stop her from releasing any eggs naturally before harvesting can take place. Throughout this process, she will be continually monitored by ultrasound scans of her ovaries to see images of the enlarging follicles, which contain the eggs. Taking a series of blood samples also checks hormone levels. When the time is right, the IVF doctor determines when to administer an injection to cause final ripening of the eggs and when to schedule the egg retrieval.

During a thirty-minute surgical procedure, the egg retrieval is performed using a needle through the vaginal wall guided by transvaginal ultrasound. During this procedure the follicles in the ovary are visualized by placing an ultrasound probe into the woman's vagina. Fluid from the grape-sized follicle, which presumably contains the egg, is then withdrawn. This is called follicular aspiration.

Again, timing is crucial. Too early, and the eggs won't fertilize when they meet the sperm. Too late, the eggs may again not fertilize or may actually be released naturally from each ovary. The woman is then sent home, while her eggs are isolated in the lab and washed sperm is added. This mixture is placed in incubators to allow fertilization to take place. The eggs are observed for fertilization twelve to sixteen hours later, and placed in a fresh culture medium for continued growth. Once cell division occurs in the fertilized egg, it is then referred to as an embryo. The rest of the process involves one or two embryos being placed in the woman's uterus three to five days after egg retrieval.

How the Witches Way Can Assist

It occurs to me that there are three major obstacles for those women going through IVF:

- The Spiritual Stress. The acceptance of the body and spirit to the complete overriding of the strong rhythm of the natural moon cycle.

- The Physical Stress. Being poked, prodded, and injected on almost a daily basis in such an intense period of time is incredibly stressful on the body, as is any surgical procedure. The powerful drugs interrupt, magnify, and change many processes in the body, some of which are not even linked to reproduction.

- The Mental Stress. A cycle of IVF is also not cheap, and there are often real fears about finances. In some of my case studies both partners have expressed worries such as "We are borrowing to do this, and if we fail, we can't afford any more," or "I am taking off a week from work to give myself the best chance, but that is a week off without pay." Mental stressors such as guilt and anxiety are stressful to both partners, often over the long term. Ironically, stress is considered a major factor in infertility and in unexplained miscarriages.

The Witches Way is always linked to change and cycles, and it is always better to work with one's natural cycle. IVF is a cycle, although it is an unnatural one for the body. Alerting the unconscious of your intent to change things, albeit for the better, is a necessary way to prepare the spirit, body, and mind for this overriding process. By gently informing the body and the Universe of your good intention, you effectively block any overprotective defenses that both may throw up covertly or overtly. For years, witches and other psychic counselors have been advising patients preparing to undergo surgery to let the body and mind know that they are giving permission for the procedure before they go under anesthetic. The body is therefore less stressed and the mind better understands the intention of what it sees as violence. Healing of both body and mind is far faster. By performing the Ritual to Increase Your Success with IVF, you are programming and reassuring the body and spirit to accept man's involvement in what is a truly feminine cycle.

Witches in the Bedroom

Jodie, a thirty-six-year old software programmer from London, speaks of her initial experience of IVF.

"I consider myself an intelligent woman but I truly did not realize the extent to which my body would be turned upside down. At the time on one level I did not mind because I thought, well if it works I will have a baby and it will be all worth it. On another level, though, I kind of got the creeps that my doctor would be controlling my cycle. I felt it was really invasive and I certainly resisted the idea secretly."

Although her eggs were harvested and fertilized successfully, this cycle was unsuccessful for Jodie, and pregnancy was not achieved at all.

"The clinic I went to seemed quite unconcerned by the failure and just automatically assumed I would be in for another attempt the next month. I was pretty rocked by the whole process and I wasn't sure whether I wanted to try again at all, let alone next month!"

Jodie decided to try the preparation meditation a few months later to see if it made her feel any better. Jodie performed the meditation three nights in a row around her lunar peak. "I felt like less of a failure and that my body could work with the IVF cycle and not against it."

She decided to try again over the following moon cycle, and combined it with the Acceptance Ritual after the procedure.

"I felt much more assured and confident, and realized I was actually quite ashamed at having to go to these lengths to get pregnant. I had been hiding this from even my best friends. I told them after the procedure this time and they all took me out a few days later to welcome the little frog (My husband is French!). I just knew I would be pregnant or at least, I wouldn't be so unhappy this time if I wasn't."

Jodie is, at time of writing, just about to give birth to a baby boy.

George and Linda had been trying for five years to conceive a child and decided that IVF would give them the best chance. The couple had been diagnosed with "unexplained infertility," and according to their specialists had no physically traceable reason that pregnancy had not occurred.

Linda revealed "We decided to try IVF because we felt we had explored all the other options. We went through the first cycle, which was very stressful for both of us. It was unsuccessful. The second time, I think, was less stressful for me, but heartbreaking when it didn't take and this brought our level of stress right up.

"I kept thinking that stress was a real factor in things not working for us and I didn't want to keep doing the same things, spending more money for the same result."

George and Linda did the Spell for Health and Vitality, the Siren Call of the Egg Spell, the Supercharging Sperm Ritual and the Ritual to increase your Success with IVF over a two lunar-cycle period. They skipped one month of IVF to enable themselves to integrate these energies. The third IVF cycle, they conceived.

"I was more relaxed this time, as was George. I felt confident that things would work!"

George called me with the good news "We got pregnant first go. We were not fearful, we just trusted our own bodies far more after the spell work."

Caren and Karl had one beautiful three-year-old boy, but wanted to extend their family by one more. Both were in their early 40s and so decided to go straight to IVF after Caren's failure to conceive after six months of trying. It was discovered that Karl had a low sperm count, which seemed to make things even harder.

"Technology is fantastic but after all the bells and whistles we only managed to get two viable embryos. This meant we had two chances. And we wanted to give this our best shot."

Caren and Karl decided to reduce their physical and mental stressors as much as possible prior to the procedures and so delayed the IVF cycle for almost two months. They built their levels of confidence and self-care through Power Circles, and when the time drew near, performed the Siren Call of the Egg Spell and the Ritual to Increase Your Success with IVF.

Physical Stress

Physical stress should be handled by exercising extreme self-care for a minimum of three months prior to an IVF procedure and throughout the process. Please re-read page 46 where I describe how self-care is one of the keys to building resilience and personal power. Some suggestions you may wish to adopt are:

- Clean up your act: Stop smoking, drinking, and limit your intake of caffeine. All these are scientifically proven stressors on your body and on your reproductive system, let alone your blossoming embryo.

- Chill out: Actually build time into your schedule to meditate, do yoga, do your spellcraft, and other gentle exercise—all activities that will rest you, facilitate recuperation within your body, and focus it on something other than the drugs and tests it is going through.

- Nourish yourself: I have a number of clients who, when stressed, began to eat stress trigger foods like fried food and cakes high in sugar. Make it your intention to eat nourishing foods most of the time and perhaps undertake the Health and Vitality Ritual to motivate you.

- Pleasure is important: Treat your body! Give it a luxurious massage, go get your hair done, get a manicure and pedicure, or go shopping for a new fragrance or some clothes that make you feel like a woman. Do not forget to do the things that make your heart sing (see section on Pleasure).

- Physical support from your partner: If you are exhausted, hormonal, in pain, or just going through the rigors of too much adrenaline, ask your partner for some physical support. This may be as simple as a back rub, running you a bath, kissing the bruise from your latest injection to doing the shopping or cooking the dinner. Tell them what you need—they are not psychic.

Mental Stress

This can be the most debilitating of all, but if you are prepared and resilient, your personal power will certainly get you through with flying colors.

- Have a mental framework of curiosity, anticipation, and discovery rather than close-mindedness, hopelessness, or a victim mentality. Treat this experience as something you have chosen to do, and every part of it is one of discovery. The outcome is vitally important, and you put an intention there certainly, but this is a journey. By seeing the process this way, and being in the moment, you reduce your stress.

- Meditate or undertake an activity that feels like it rests the mind—for example, walking, painting, listening to music, or dancing freely.

- Get plenty of uninterrupted sleep and go to bed early, particularly if you need to report to the IVF clinic early in the morning for monitoring.

- Ensure that you and your partner have thoroughly investigated the costs of the procedure up front and know that there are no further surprises. What I am going to say next may seem harsh, but it is better to be relaxed about finances and wait a few months than to stress out over money and undertake IVF now. It is very easy to get caught up in paying for cycle after cycle. If you can at all avoid it, do not stretch yourselves too thinly financially to try for a child. Stress chemicals make the body more acidic, which does not pose a great environment for an embryo, in addition to putting a wedge between you both. If it makes things easier, wait a little.

- Connect with the Goddess: Now is the time you need the Goddess' love and support. Simply ask. Invoke your patron goddesses or gods regularly, and basically tell them what you want and how you are feeling. You are never ever alone in this endeavor, and the Goddess is always ready to assist.

Ritual to Increase Your Success with IVF

You will not be raising any energy to release but you certainly will be connecting with the Goddess and God energy. This is a ritual written to perform with the two partners involved, however you can perform variations. If you are a female and your partner is a female, allow the partner that is not actually going to carry the baby to take the God's role on behalf of the sperm donor. If you are performing the spell yourself, simply imagine your partner or the god of your choice next to you. The spell works equally well with or without a live partner.

The meditation section is written as if the female partner who is having the IVF procedure is leading. Just rewrite to fit if the non-IVF partner is leading.

Preparation

Perform this spell on any night, but definitely within a few days before the IVF cycle commences. Ensure the room is warm. Ensure that you both will be undisturbed. Decide ahead of time which one of you will lead the meditation and guide the other out loud.

Welcome the God and Goddess, and thank them for being with you here tonight in this beautiful place.

Gather

An orange or gold candle to represent the God
A silver or white candle to represent the Goddess
A third candle of your chosen color to represent the baby
Matches
Charcoal
Some sandalwood chips or frankincense to burn on the charcoal
Comfortable robes that you can slip out of easily for the skyclad elements of
    the ritual

Focus

Cast and open a Circle if you wish.

Face each other. The female lights the silver/white candle. Relax. Take several deep breaths. Welcome the Goddess to your Circle:

> *We welcome you, Goddess, Maiden, Mother, Crone. We know you are*
> *all things and create all things in unity with the God. You are the Goddess*
> *of the moon, of all of its cycles, as it is born, as it grows, and as it diminishes*
> *across the sky. We ask your help here tonight to overcome any barriers*
> *to a successful pregnancy of a child conceived outside our physical body.*
> *We ask that you extend our connection and body limits so that life*
> *is created within us, even though man would see it differently.*
> *You are the Goddess who made us from your own spark, your own womb,*
> *so we ask that you create our child in the same way.*

Gaze at the candle or close your eyes and go within. Visualize the Goddess, the Divine Feminine, before you. She can look as you wish—there is no wrong image. Meditate on some of the aspects of the Goddess that you might like to bring forward tonight or that appeal to you at this moment.

Open your eyes. The male lights the orange/gold candle. Relax. Take several deep breaths.

Welcome the God to your Circle:

> *I light this in honor of the God. I know you are all things and*
> *create all things in unity with the Goddess. Be with us tonight.*

Now light your herbs and incense, and both disrobe. Look into your partner's eyes. See them. The female says:

> *I honor you. You are a God and a Creator.*

Look into your partner's eyes. See them. The male says:

> *I honor you. You are a Goddess and a Creator.*

Both say as you hold hands:

> *We unite to bring life.*
> *Bring us a child that will be the best of both of us.*
> *As above so below.*

Now both lay down on your backs, in a subtle star shape—legs apart, arms outside your body, and link the nearest hand touching yours. You should look like two touching stars.

Relax. Breathe in deeply. This is a time for just the two of you.

Whoever is leading the meditation begins to speak.

Imagine now that you are lying on the softest, freshest green grass. So soft, so green. Above you is the night sky. Stars twinkle and glisten. The breeze is warm and you can feel the hair on your head stirring just a little. Your skin feels so alive and sensitive. It is almost like you can feel the starlight kissing your body.

Now, feel the skin on your back laying heavily against the grass, which slowly yields to the weight of your bodies. You both begin to sink through the grass. Breathe deeply as you pass through the grass and fragrant, moist earth until you find yourselves lying on heaps of red satin.

You are in a red room. The room has no corners and is curved. It is softly glowing. You are lying on the softest, silkiest red fabric. It warms to the touch of your skin and you are infinitely comfortable.

Mmmmmm, this feels sooo good. Slowly become more aware of the red room. There is a curtained door at one end. You sit up, still holding hands and look at the magnificence of each other. How beautiful you look. How perfect. Full of love and potential.

Now you stand, and you ask that the Goddess come forward. (Call however you wish, but do not go beyond the curtain—wait for her to come through the curtains.)

The Goddess is now with you. She steps forward and greets you both with love and laughter. The Goddess is holding out to you a gift.

It is a deep pink flower bud. She touches the skin of your lower belly and the bud now glows softly pink on you and in my womb. The Goddess smiles and steps away. There is a heat, a shimmer of light that begins to spread over your body. Your partner can feel it too, its warmth, its ripeness. The bud within your womb begins to flower, and each exquisite petal begins to open, petal by petal. It is beautiful. There is a shiver of light and you can now smell the heady fragrance of the flower in full bloom, in full sweetness and ripeness. The Goddess then steps forward and reverently takes the flower in her hands.

She beckons for you to step forward (the male partner). She asks you to add your essence to the glowing ripe flower. Do this your way. (For example some visualizations have included kissing the flower or transferring a golden orb from the lingham.) As the flower and essence combine, the flower begins to glow more brightly and transform into an incredibly bright form.

The Goddess says warmly:

It matters not where life is created. It matters only that life is created.

She then places the glowing form back into your womb, where it reduces in size, but feels anchored there. The glow is still visible and you know it won't be extinguished.

You now both offer the Goddess a gift. She accepts it and she is gone. You lie back down in that red softness, and begin to float back up through the red ceiling, until you have passed back through the earth onto the grass.

Now begin to place your awareness back into this room. Feel your hand in your partner's, and slowly begin to open your eyes. Welcome back!

Now light the third candle that represents your union.

The God and the Goddess are still with you and sharing with you their gift of fertility and creativity. Stay in the Circle for a while and share your experiences and ground yourself by perhaps eating, having a glass of wine, or even dancing. I would normally even recommend having sex, but if your procedure is close please refrain. Know that your mind and body are already responding to your intentions.

Complete the Ritual

Close your Circle. Extinguish the candles. However, you may wish to keep the one representing your union alight for a little longer.

Extinguish and bury any remaining charcoal or herbs/incense in the garden or yard.

Participation

Commit to the IVF cycle in full confidence that you are both prepared and that you have increased your chances. The process will be easy and painless. The fertilization will be successful and the embryo strong. It will be implanted and it will anchor to your womb strongly. Begin to live what you have experienced. When you are feeling worried or low, light the candle representing your union and talk about things between you.

Book of Shadows Entries

Chart your progress by recording your feelings, behaviors, actions, and results. Share your feelings and experiences also with your partner in particular as you go through the cycle, paying close attention to coincidences and details even if they seem insignificant or unrelated at the time. Remember to date all your entries.

Acceptance Ritual

This ritual is especially for those who have had a pregnancy confirmed, are pregnant, and have a history of miscarriages, or if you have had in vitro fertilization (IVF) and want to increase your chances of becoming pregnant after the implantation procedure.

You may choose to invoke your patron goddess here and if you are pregnant you may wish to invoke a particular goddess to look after your growing baby. There are many goddesses who specialize in looking after children, so do your research and find one that resonates with you. I highly recommend Artemis, Lady of Beasts, Demeter, Gaia, Oya, and Brigid.

Preparation

Perform this spell on any night but particularly when the moon is full or on your lunar return phase.

Ensure the room is warm. Ensure that you will be undisturbed.

Gather

Three candles: one in your favorite color, representing you, one in a color you choose to represent your baby (avoid red), and a silver or white candle to represent the Goddess

Matches

Something to represent the four elements of the witches' Universe: Air, Fire, Water, Earth—for example: a feather for air, some incense for fire, some moon-charged water for water, and perhaps a favorite crystal for earth; place these on your altar

Focus

Cast and open a Circle if you wish.

Please stand for this ritual. Face the moon if you can.

Light the silver/white candle and relax. Take several deep breaths.

Welcome the Goddess to your Circle:

I welcome you Goddess: Maiden, Mother, and Crone.
I know You are all things and create all things in unity with the God.

You are the Goddess of the moon, of all of its cycles,
and I now ask that you assist me as I transform my cycle
from maiden to mother. I wish to share in your deep
and unending fertility as is my birthright.

If you are going to call in a particular patron or aspect of the Goddess, do so here. For example:

I invoke you, Artemis, Moon Goddess and protector of women and children.
You who are free yet connected, focused yet wild, fierce yet loving.
I ask that you lend your energies to my intent tonight.

Now light the candle representing you. Say:

I light this candle in honor of my creative female power.
It is unmatched. It is unending.

Gaze at the candle or close your eyes and go within. Visualize yourself naked, beautiful and glowing. The Goddess, the Divine Feminine, stands directly before you. She can look as you wish—there is no wrong image, or you may have an image, particularly if she is your patron goddess.

The Goddess asks what is your request of her.

Tell her about the child within your womb or the child that has been placed within your womb. Tell her all about your hopes and dreams for this child. Do this in great detail. Feel your joy and hope grow.

The Goddess steps forward and places her hands upon your womb.

Breathe deeply, feeling the power of millennia of women pulse through you. This energizes you and is highly pleasurable and you feel the stirrings of your child. It is content and healthy in your watery womb.

She asks:

Do you accept this child fully?

Answer her truthfully. I am assuming here that you will answer to the positive, but if you have any fears or any obstacles pop into your mind, tell her about them. She will assist you to move through your fears.

When you have finished this exchange, the Goddess says:

I am life as are you. Accept this gift of life. So be it.

Answer her:

I am life. I accept this gift of life. So be it.

Now open your eyes and light the third candle representing your baby. As you light the candle, place one hand on your womb and say:

May the element of fire give me courage and laughter that I can share with you.

Then continue:

May the element of air allow me to communicate positively with you. May the element of water keep you content and protected, and may the element of Earth keep us healthy and growing.

Now thank the Goddess for her help and offer her a gift, which she graciously accepts. Know that she will be with you any time you wish and then part from her.

Offer Your Gratitude

Know that the Goddess has heard your desire for full acceptance of this baby and your intention to have a strong and successful pregnancy.

Thank the Goddess for being here with you tonight. Be grateful in the knowledge that all is as you have asked it to be, if it be her will and for the greatest good of all. Know that your mind and body are already responding and your baby is consciously aware of your love and wishes for her or him.

Complete the Ritual

Close your Circle. Extinguish the candles. You may wish to keep them all burning for a while after the ritual has completed. Be sure to extinguish them after your quiet time.

Participation

Begin to live what you have experienced. Be confident that your baby is totally connected to the nourishment of your womb. Share your joy and hopes with your partner.

If you did bring up some objections to acceptance of the baby to the Goddess, take care now to work through these. Seek professional medical help or counseling if necessary.

If you do feel any fear you might like to light the three candles for some reassurance, or repeat the ritual on a regular basis.

Book of Shadows Entries

Chart your progress by recording your feelings, behaviors, actions, and results even if they seem negative, paying close attention to coincidences and details even if they seem insignificant or unrelated at the time. Remember to date all your entries.

Bonding with Baby Meditation

This is an ideal meditation to do when you have a spare fifteen minutes. It is designed to be done several times a week, and although simple and short, it is highly beneficial for you and your little goddess or god.

The bonding process is enhanced by the music, your voice, and your touch. Babies are aware of noise outside the womb at a surprisingly early stage, so know with confidence that he or she is very aware of what you are up to and choose that music carefully.

Anne Marie, a thirty-four-year-old nurse from Sydney, began to use this meditation almost from conception. She chose an unusual piece of music for this kind of meditation, some really hard rock. A big heavy metal fan, she found that the idea of playing classical or "That boring new age garbage" would not be pleasurable for her, just "downright annoying." Anne Marie would do this meditation while both massaging her growing belly and having a bit of a jiggle to the music.

All fine, but there is a catch. Babies learn to associate this music with contentment and their happy life within the womb *after* they are born. If the same piece or pieces of music are played after they are born, they noticeably settle and become quiet and content. So when Anne Marie's baby would wake at three in the morning, crying and upset, the ideal thing to do would be to play their song. However, even for a dedicated metal fan like Anne

Marie, playing that kind of music after no sleep at that hour is a big thing to ask!

You can make up the Blossoming Belly Balm and use this in your ritual, or some rich massage oil such as jojoba, macadamia, or peach. Do not add any essential oils except tangerine as most are contraindicated for the early and middle stages of pregnancy.

Preparation

Ensure you are wearing something that you can expose your belly in. Ensure that you will be undisturbed—this is your time with your baby.

Have your piece of music or song picked out. Have fun with this! Right now there are women all over the world playing jazz, opera, soul and R&B and dancing with their baby goddesses or gods!

Gather

Your music

Your massage oil or Blossoming Belly Balm (page 262)

Focus

Cast and open a Circle if you wish, but it is not really necessary.

Take a few deep breaths and place your hands on your belly and womb. Breathe in the power of the Universe, the healthy fertile energy from the earth and trees, the fresh air from the sky. Know that there is an unending supply of this love and nourishment from the Goddess.

Breathe out any tension in your body. Notice where it is and breathe it out. Imagine any pain just being flushed from that place in your body and replaced with that green nourishing earth energy. Exhale any fears or worries you have. Notice what they are, but you have no need for them during the next fifteen minutes. Breathe them out completely.

Take your time with this process. When you are feeling connected with the Divine Goddess and your own Self, begin to focus your attention on your hands and the child within you. Now turn on your music.

Get a clear picture of your baby love, growing and floating peacefully in your watery womb. Tell your baby how much you love him or her and tell him or her that he or she is the best of both of you.

Now take some Belly Balm or massage oil in your hands and begin to massage your belly clockwise with firm round strokes that start in the center (your navel) and work out again like a spiral. Enjoy this! It feels good! Plus it is great for your skin!

Now say out loud your intention. Feel free to have a different one each time you do this, or share one for a while. It can be around both of you, or one of you.

For example: Early pregnancy:

Grow healthy and with love! or *My morning sickness is decreasing daily!*

Mid-pregnancy:

I am a great mother! or *We grow together every day!*

Late Pregnancy:

We will both experience a safe and joyous full-term delivery!

Complete your massage and feel free to use the excess oil or balm on your breasts or thighs. Remember if you do feel like moving to your music, feel free, but no all-night dance parties please!

Book of Shadows Entries

Chart your progress by recording your feelings, behaviors, actions, and results even if they seem negative, paying close attention to coincidences and details even if they seem insignificant or unrelated at the time. Remember to date all your entries.

Blossoming Belly Balm

This is a rich, nourishing, and almost fragrance-free balm perfect for protecting and soothing the belly and thighs during pregnancy. Remnants of similar balms have been found in Mayan and ancient European archaeological sites. Combining this creamy balm with witches' traditional methods of relaxation and growth will encourage stretch mark-free skin and a strong prenatal bond. Primarily, I believe that touch and sound alerts the baby in all sorts of ways to your presence and love, so do yourself a favor, make up a batch, and enjoy the difference.

Gather

1 tablespoon jojoba oil
1 tablespoon of olive oil
2 tablespoons of cocoa butter
2 teaspoons of natural beeswax
4 tablespoons of distilled or spring water
1 teaspoon of borax
½ teaspoon of vegetable glycerin
Whisk or hand-held beater
Sterilized jar
Music that you love and that relaxes you
Candle

Method

1. Mix butter, oils, and wax in a heat-proof bowl. Put bowl inside a pan of boiling water and melt slowly. Stir, and once wax is completely melted, remove from heat.

2. Place water, borax, and glycerin in a separate heat-proof cup. Place the cup inside a pan of boiling water until the borax dissolves. Stir for a minute or so. Remove from heat.

3. Using a hand-held electric mixer or whisk, begin mixing the oils and waxes. Add water mixture and blend on medium speed until a thick balm begins to form. This should take 3–4 minutes.

4. Pour into jars. Cap after a skin forms on the top. This mixture has no preservatives so store in the refrigerator.

5. When jar is cool and fully set, sit comfortably on a pillow or on a chair and expose your gorgeous growing belly. Light a rosy or white candle to signify your creative power as a woman. Take a deep breath and relax. Take another one and relax. As you breathe in the third time imagine breathing in the goodness and gentle power of the earth. This refreshes and relaxes you further. Breathe out all that is

worrying you and any pain or discomfort that you may be feeling. Keep doing this until you feel balanced and relaxed.

6. Put on your favorite music.

7. Now take some of your Belly Balm and begin to massage it in a clockwise direction around your belly. Do not forget the sides of your belly and your thighs. This will feel very good and very nourishing.

8. As you massage, repeat in your mind or out loud:

As my belly grows,
My body knows,
To grow with ease,
My baby sees.

You may wish to make up your own chant, which is even better! Make sure your message is positive to both your baby and your body.

Do this as long as you like, and ensure you make time to have this sacred space several times a week, if not daily!

The Pregnant Postscript

In the eighteen months that I was conducting case studies, I am happy to report that there were:

- Ten natural or unassisted conceptions out of fourteen participants
- Seven conceptions out of seven assisted techniques, with four of those having previously gone through multiple IVF cycles
- No known miscarriages
- Every participant recorded a decrease in her stress levels and recognized that the increased levels of meditation/ritual work assisted in controlling stressors
- Only one couple would label themselves pagan

I wish you love and luck in creating your own new life!

Section Four

Passing On and Extending Your Tradition

If you have ventured this far into this book, I hope you are interested and perhaps inspired enough to move forward toward your desires the Witches Way. Whether or not you are an experienced witch or this is your first foray into the Craft, you have wisdom to offer others.

Witches were always considered the "wise" of the village. They could be relied upon for healing and good counsel. Very few leaders in ancient times made major decisions without first consulting the wise of their country or those who were able to translate oracles. Oracles such as that at Delphi were famous for hundreds of years and gave guidance to kings and those who would be kings.

Our problem, of course, was to find ways to continue or evolve our traditions during the long periods of persecution in later times. Happily, attitudes have changed somewhat and there is a noticeable resurgence in bringing back some of the old traditions and celebrations, especially those that mark significant moments in our personal timeline.

Witches believe the sharing of wisdom is one of the most enduring ways to connect and reconnect with those closest to us and to the wider world. Most of the ways we choose to share our traditions involve either education or celebration, or both. Allow me to introduce to you some of the simple, complex, and perhaps surprising ways that we pass on and extend our traditions in relation to love, creation, and relationships.

Traditional/Modern Ceremonies

As the cycle of the seasons and the balance of light and dark changes, so do the stages of our lives. You don't have to be a witch or Pagan to put one of these great ceremonies together. Pagans really know how to celebrate, so why not join in the fun and connect the Witches Way.

Births

As the Goddess is a creative force, the birth of a baby is celebrated with great joy by witches. As you have read earlier, witches were often the mid-wives of the area and brought many children into the world through their birthing skills and spiritual remedies.

As the Christian faith has rituals, namely christenings, that welcome and initiate the baby into the family of their God, Wicca has Wiccanings. Many Wiccans, though, prefer to allow the child to choose a faith when he or she is older, instead of initiating the child with the parents' choice. As such, these parents choose Wiccan blessings or simple spiritual ceremonies that ask the community to join together to guide and bless their child.

I have included below a simple ceremony with exactly this intention. Enjoy!

Baby Blessing Ceremony

Ahead of Time: Invite your friends to think of a non-material gift for the child. This gift should be represented in some symbolic way. For example, the last gift I gave was the gift of a great sense of humor. I represented this with a little card with a montage of things that make me laugh on it. The friend that accompanied me gave the gift of integrity, representing this with a white feather, the symbol of Maat, Goddess of truth and justice.

On the Day: three candles should be lit: one for the Goddess, one for the child, and one for the life they will co-create together.

The child should be held by the parents and a bowl held by the God/dess parents to hold all the gifts. One by one guests come forward and offer the gift to the baby and the parents accept the gift on his or her behalf.

The gifts will then be catalogued in the family Book of Shadows and items may be kept or photographed.

Each guest is given a small token gift of thanks from the baby. This may be a simple flower, seed, or the baby's footprint on a card.

Coming of Age

One of the most rewarding things about being part of a witch community is that I am often invited to join in various ceremonies that mark special times in the lives around me. Pagan traditions, like many others throughout the world, welcome the transition between children. For example, in the Jewish faith, when a boy reaches the age of manhood at thirteen, he is welcomed into manhood through his Bar Mitzva. For girls the ceremony is her Bat Mitzva. In many Goddess traditions such as Wicca, the time a girl experiences her first moon bleed is marked and honored. I have been to a number of these ceremonies and they are incredibly empowering and life affirming for the young woman.

I remember as a young girl how confusing the whole menstrual thing was. There was no celebration as such, but a lot of uncertainty and fear around the pain. I was lucky in that there was little shame attached to my moon bleed experience, but for the majority of women there is.

The idea that this blood is dirty and undesirable has been propagated by many societies and cultures, and the belief that the bleed makes us unhealthy or weak is still a popular one. In contrast, within many Wiccan and Goddess religions, menstrual blood is considered a highly magical substance, and permeating all is the knowledge that a woman's moon time is a perfectly natural and powerful one. I believe it is every woman's duty to encourage the young to see how intrinsically special our moon blood is and to celebrate its presence rather than teach them that it is something to be avoided or dreaded.

Here are a number of ideas for coming-of-age ceremonies, witch-style:

- To celebrate a first moon bleed you might wish to have a special women-only celebration. Perhaps it's a very special dinner in a "grownup" restaurant, a beautiful hotel, or an overnight stay in nature. The important thing here is the company—she is now a woman and should see that she can share in the glories of womanhood. Allow her to hear and be part of great conversation and have her questions about womanhood answered. To mark the occasion you may want to give her a piece of good jewelry that you have blessed with moon water. When she is old enough she may wish to pass this jewelry on to another young woman at her first bleed, thus passing on the wisdom.

- Take your daughter/young woman to a bookstore and buy her books that show the world in its infinite variety, and humans at their most creative. These books may be the start of her gaining wisdom.

- Introduce the idea of lunar returns to her and explain her special moon.

- Bringing up your boys to appreciate the magical differences between the sexes should include discussing the moon cycles with them. Boys that are brought up to honor the feminine and with a strong appreciation for their own strengths in being masculine are often more balanced men.

Handfasting

Handfasting is the term given to traditional Pagan wedding ceremonies. Originally, the two partners were joined for a period of one year and agreed to be faithful to one another for this time ("no other hands but yours"), and then they would be free to decide whether they wished to be joined ever after. Sometimes the ceremony would involve the couple jumping over the woman's broom, signifying the joining of the two homes. Other actions, such as tying the hands together with a beautiful fabric woven by the family or even the feeding of blessed food to each other, are symbols of being joined body and soul.

Today, many Pagan folk like to combine some of the rituals of handfasting into a marriage sanctioned by law. In most countries Pagan celebrants can legally marry couples through handfasting ceremonies, or you could write your own ceremony and ask a civil marriage celebrant to incorporate it into the legal requirements. There are a number of handfasting ceremonies on my website if you are interested in using them. These elements are common among the ceremonies:

- There is a celebration of the uniqueness of the individuals: this gives a highly personalized quality to the ceremony.
- There is a dedication of freedom of expression during the marriage yet of Harm None.
- There is equal time given to the male and female energies, and the chalice and athame are often used to symbolize this.
- Promises are made by the couple to each other that are valid as long as their love should last.
- Although there is some binding symbology (like the joining of hands with the fabric or the drinking from a common chalice of wine), the couple are reminded that they will always be individuals and should grow strong together by being apart.

Croning

Our youth-obsessed Western culture has little time or honor for age. Age truly is a dark taboo and one where women are particular victims. In pagan societies, all ages were honored for different reasons, but those women who had the life experiences in gathering and growing wisdom were most venerated. These were the people from whom one could learn skills, take counsel, and even take sanctuary.

The most powerful witches in such societies were naturally the older women, the crones (elder women) of the area. Once these women reached a certain age, normally around sixty, or when their menstrual blood ceased to flow completely, a special ceremony would take place, called a croning. The croning ceremony would celebrate their abundance of wisdom now that their moon blood was kept within them. The bloom of youthful beauty might have passed, but these women were particularly skilled and powerful, and therefore the most dangerous to the new religion. The idea of the ugly old crone as the evil witch was an easy leap to make for the storytellers of the new ways. Unfortunately, the word "crone" became something that no woman would want to be labeled, and the idea of venerating such a creature fell away, until perhaps the last twenty or so years.

Here is what three women had to say about their own modern cronings:

- "I felt honored and exhilarated to be the age that I am." —Eda, 60, USA

- "I must say I was feeling quite unconfident before the croning. Worse, I was feeling invisible. The croning clearly made me see again what I had to offer, and it was plenty!" —Susan, 62, Australia

- "This was one of the best days of my life. So many amazing women there and they honored me by asking me to share my wisdom. It left me feeling very vital and useful." —Abbey, 72, Australia

There are as many ways to celebrate a croning as there are ways to cook eggs, but allow me to share a format that I like.

You can hold a croning for yourself or for someone else.

Choose a great outdoors venue, and put aside a whole day, at least. Some of the best cronings I have been to have been a weekend away in nature, but if time does not permit a day will do.

The venue should be private enough that you will not be disturbed and open enough that it gives you some room. Invite all age groups. The more generations the better!

Choose a facilitator or priestess to run the show—they need not be witches, of course.

Prepare a feast of the favorite foods of the crone.

Prepare a decorated throne (chair) for your crone. Everyone should help decorate the throne with flowers, tinsel, or whatever you like!

When the time comes, play the crone's favorite music and carry the throne into the center of the space you are using. Dance around and sing along with the music. Bang drums if you have them.

Place the decorated chair in the center of the circle.

Call in your crone! Give her a huge round of applause and cheers as she sits in the center of you all!

Light a candle for her, one for the Goddess, and one for the combined wisdom.

Your facilitator then will explain to all present the process of everyone speaking in turn and sharing stories of wisdom and love for the crone. Then the crone will speak to each and all about her life, and answer any questions those in the circle may want to ask.

One by one, the circle members will speak of the crone. They may even have pictures or objects as evidence of her good deeds and great wisdom.

Then the crone speaks to each person individually, commenting on their words and sharing a piece of her wisdom especially for them. Then the crone opens the floor to questions and problems. The circle normally throws up some current vexing problems, and whether they are about love, relationships, children, spirituality, or work, the crone passes on her wisdom and calls on others to assist if necessary.

I have never been to a croning where there wasn't a belly laugh, many tears, and some amazing wisdom passed on. Someone may also want to make a record of what is said or take photographs to mark the croning.

Close the circle when you are ready by offering a glass of fine wine or champagne to each, a final intention, and much applause and dancing!

Sensual Circles

In my earlier book about business magic, I discussed how important it was that we don't try to change everything ourselves without support. As a fiercely independent person, I thought that I would be able to make the differences I sought just by my skills and force of will, and I soon became exhausted and disillusioned at not being able to share the wisdom and the load.

At the time, I looked around me and saw how many talented, yet isolated, people there were in the business world, and I knew that to stay that way meant that not only was any change going to take longer, but that this lack of collaboration was actually against my witch's principles. I nicknamed those of us who were bravely trying to go it solo "Alone Rangers."

I used to be one. You can tell an Alone Ranger by the huge hours they put in, the lack of delegation (just in case someone else gets the credit), and the lack of having any other opinion or mentor, and a big black chip of seething resentment on the shoulder for having to do it all alone.

It seemed to me that it would be a smart idea to have a bunch of people to support me. It also seemed a good idea to have a number of folks around who could give me a variety of opinions and advice, and that I might have something to offer them too. I didn't even have to know them, but that we shared some common values. I thought laterally about the witches' covens and how they supported and raised power for each other, and it finally dawned on me that we could utilize this ancient tradition in a modern way.

The concept of Career Covens was born. A Career Coven (CC) is a group of people, as few as two or as many as you feel comfortable with, who get together on a regular basis to support each other in their career and business goals. Career Covens are always free and totally confidential.

The concept of Career Covens has expanded internally very quickly. Career Covens started off in small face-to-face groups, but now most models combine monthly or bi-monthly face-to-face meetings, with email circles in between. The growth of the online email Career Covens has been especially rapid, and often there are participants from as many as eight countries in one CC, all assisting each other with their business and career obstacles and celebrating successes.

To learn more about CC just visit www.themodernwitch.com.

It seemed a natural progression to try a similar method of assisting those who wish to achieve new relationship goals for themselves. Relationship and love transitions and changes are perhaps some of the deepest, most frightening yet exhilarating experiences that we as humans can undertake.

I did hesitate before I tried this though—after all, we were dealing with sensitive subjects and sometimes high emotion. However, the concept of Sensual Circles is as powerful as that of Career Covens in that support and the support we can give back is synergistic and changes lives. Sensual Circles can:

- Be a safe and strictly confidential place to discuss your relationship/love/sensual problems or obstacles.
- Be a forum to discuss and discover ideas and solutions.
- Be a non-aggressive, non-committal place to meet like-minded people.
- Offer support to individuals looking to transition from one relationship or state to another.
- Be free and non-profit.
- Have mutually agreed-upon guidelines for behavior and format.

- Facilitate the raising of energy to accomplish individual and group intentions.
- Follow guidelines in ethics (Witches' Rede), although members certainly do not have to be witches or even interested in Witchcraft to participate.

Sensual circles do not:

- Take the place of professional assistance, such as medical or psychological advisors.
- Become a place where members gossip.
- Become a place where any sexual activity whatsoever is initiated or become a matchmaking service.
- Make anyone feel uncomfortable about their sexual choices or preferences.

Sensual Circles are like Career Covens in that they have a central core of collaboration. Members are dedicated to offering real and honest support in a collaborative, circular way. There are no leaders, although there will always be a facilitator who will direct the energies, ensuring that no one person dominates the group. Again, no Sensual Circle should ever take the place of professional advice, however they are an extremely good accompaniment.

A Sensual Circle can be started easily by simply finding another person to discuss your issues with within the filters of the Witches Power Keys and the Laws as they relate to love and relationships (page 39). You will find that they grow from there. Alternatively you might like to check my site for Circles near you or to register to start one.

Sharing Your Personal Book of Shadows

Once there was a beautiful book. It had crisp, creamy parchment pages. It had a butter soft, brown leather cover. It smelled earthy and green, and the girl who owned it loved it. She placed it on the shelf in her bedroom, high enough that dirty fingers could not stain it and covered it so that the dust could not accumulate on it, for it was a precious thing and should not be ruined.

Let's stop right there.

This all sounds very nice doesn't it? Having a gorgeous special book that you have bought to create your Book of Shadows? Now let's go on with the story so you can see what many of us did with such a book.

The beautiful book sadly had no writing in it, even though the magnificent ostrich feather quill with the gold nib sat enticingly adjacent. The girl loved the book so much that she dared not write in it, lest she make a mistake and damage its perfection. And so it sat, unused, yet admired.

Ah, yes. I bought something so lovely that I just couldn't bear to use it, and so many of my first experiences with Witchcraft and the results and methods I used were lost. There are a few scraps. In the early days I sometimes wrote my spells, techniques, and experiences on crumpled slips of paper and later in some old exercise books, but I lost a huge amount of wisdom by not recording it.

I learned how important it was to record my own traditions, not only to track my own successes (and failures!) and growth, but to use them to assist others. I remember having a heated conversation with someone at a dinner party who asked me to prove how this stuff worked and to give them a technique for a particular problem. I knew I had overcome this particular problem myself through a spell I had developed, but as I had not written it down nor tracked the timeline of results, I had little to share.

Traditionally, wisdom, whether it be spells, rituals, or redes, was shared within a closed group only after certain levels of initiation had been reached. This is still the process in many Wiccan Covens. For those of us who are solitary or who may not even label themselves witch, it is important still that we have a legacy of magical work that we can choose to share with others. Imagine sharing your wisdom tradition with your children or closest friend, or with your grandchildren. Here is your chance to lead by example, which is truly the Witches Way when it comes to life, especially with bedroom magic!

This book that you are reading is part of my Book of Shadows and is part of my wisdom tradition. I can even see this as part of my legacy. For me, it's a way of succinctly seeing how the Goddess is active in my life and how I can be of service. It matters not how many people share these pages, but how deeply they are affected by them.

I invite you to connect deeply with your own great wisdom, no matter how it manifests, and pass this on. This book covers a wide variety of topics as encompassed by the broad term of sensual magic, but its primary function is to wake you up to your own unbelievable power and to use this to get you moving toward what you desire.

My sisters and brothers, learn how to be sensual, how to experience the most exquisite pleasure, to love profoundly, and surrender completely. You are here for a divine purpose and to share your purpose with others in ways deep and broad. Your body knows instinctively how to find bliss through attraction, to focus on connection, and to even co-create another being.

You know, you have always known, and the Goddess is here to remind you of your own great wisdom.

Recommended Resources

Pagan/Witchcraft Resources

Australia: The Pagan Awareness Network www.paganawareness.net.au

UK: The Pagan Federation www.paganfed.org

US: Witchvox www.witchvox.com

The Wiccan and Pagan Times: www.twpt.com

General Spirituality: www.beliefnet.com

I have an updated and growing list on my site: www.themodernwitch.com

Books

Ah! So many books, so little space! These are books or authors that I would recommend for your library if you are interested in exploring a pagan path. I would also suggest you go to specialty publishers' websites, such as Llewellyn Worldwide, who have large, quality catalogues.

Scott Cunningham (Llewellyn Worldwide)

Raymond Buckland (Llewellyn Worldwide)

The Spiral Path & Twelve White Swans by Starhawk

A Witches Bible, Janet Farrar / Gavin Bone

Doreen Valiente

Erica Jong, *Witches*

Sacred Contracts, Caroline Myss

Drawing Down the Moon, Margot Adler

The Feminine Face of God, Sherry Ruth Anderson

Fertility Resources

Foresight Foundation www.foresight-preconception.org.uk

For good information on natural fertility www.mensturation.com

To get in touch with other women going through the conception journey: www.tryingtoconcieve.com

Moon Charts: www.themodernwitch.com

A note regarding assisted conception programs such as IVF: Please consult your health-care professional for a referral. Go prepared. Ask as many questions as you need to, and do not make a decision on the spot no matter how tempting. Go home and talk about it and then decide. Consider seeing a variety of doctors and IVF Centers before making a decision on who may serve you best.

Aphrodisiacs

I recommend (and clinic studies do too) Femi-X for women
www.femi-x.com.au

Consult your herbalist/witch for specific formulas for men.

Other Handy Resources

To find your lunar return or to keep track of the moon phases:
http://tycho.usno.navy.mil/vphase.html

For handy Pagan shopping online: herb supplies, Books of Shadows, etc., try:

www.whitemagic.com.au

www.morganaschamber.com

www.enchantmèntsnyc.com

www.seventhousepublishing.com

For information and assistance with co-dependency, I recommend:

Shirley Smith www.theradiantgroup.com

Co-Dependents Anonymous (CODA) for free support for those who are choosing to break free from co-dependency. For locations in your state, contact Alcoholics Anonymous in your area or simply use a search engine.

Glossary

Aphrodisiac: A substance that affects the mental and or physical state for the stimulation of the libido in either sex. Can be herbal or food based.

BCE: Before Common Era. Referring to period of time after the birth of Christ.

Beltaine/Beltane: One of the seasonal witches' holidays and part of the traditional Wheel of the Year. Traditional fertility festival. Around May 1 in the Northern Hemisphere, October 31 in the Southern Hemisphere. One of the two major holidays that divide the year into the Dark Part (shorter days) and the Light Part (longer days).

Besom: Broom. A ritual tool traditionally made by tying the twigs of a birch tree around a handle made of ash.

Candle Colors: The various colors of candles are said to assist in focusing on the particular intention that you seek in spell craft. For example: a silver or white candle is traditionally used as a sign of the Goddess; green for money, flow, and growth; red for passion.

Charcoal: Flat, round briquette of charcoal, often wrapped in foil and used as a base when lighting herbs or incense.

Charisma: From the Greek *Charis- Ma*. Meaning literally allowing the "spirit to run through."

Co-dependency: Psychology term for a dysfunctional relationship between people that typically involves an over-reliance or over-dependency between the two parties. There is little independence or growth within the relationship.

Cord Cutting: Ancient technique used to break an unwanted or unhealthy connection between people.

Craft of the Wise: Phrase that refers to Witchcraft.

Croning: Witch-based ceremony that celebrates a woman's substantial wisdom. Normally conducted after the woman has completed menopause.

Delphi, Delphic Oracle: Holy place in ancient Greece. Said to be the place where Apollo directly communicated with humans through his priestesses. Able to be visited today.

Delphic Maxims: Sixteen Guidelines for Good Living as passed from Apollo's priestesses at Delphi.

Dizzy Sperm: Sperm that are treated for IVF/IUI are affected by the centrifuge process and may lose motility because of this. This is a descriptive term for their behavior.

Drawing Down the Moon: Drawing down the power of the moon for a direct connection to the Goddess, who is represented by the moon. A beautiful ritual commonly used in many different Wiccan Traditions.

Endorphins: Pain-killing and pleasure, delivering chemicals within the body. Triggered during stress, exercise, "falling in love," and sex.

Esbat: Full moon Sabbaths.

Familiars: Animals who lend their energies to magic and have a direct and intimate connection with the Wiccan practitioner.

Free Will: The idea that everyone is responsible for making their own choices freely. Witches will not interfere with the free will of another.

Handfasting: Traditional pagan marriage ceremony.. Partners agree to forsake all others for a period of one year (or more).

IUI: Intra Uterine Insemination (artificial insemination).

IVF: In Vitro Fertilization (and the process of).

Lunar Return: The phase of the moon at your birth. Can be used to calculate a fertile period each lunar month.

Matriarchal: Societal structure in which women are the primary counselors and purveyors of wisdom.

May Day: Beltaine in the Northern Hemisphere.

Monotheism: Worship of a single divinity.

Ostara: One of the seasonal witches' holidays and part of the traditional Wheel of the Year. During Ostara, witches focus on renewal and rebirth. Celebrated approximately March 21, the Spring Equinox in the Northern Hemisphere, September 21 in the Southern Hemisphere.

Pagan: Umbrella term for earth-worshipping spiritual practices.

Pantheistic: Worship of various aspects of the Divine.

Pantheon: The group of gods and goddesses that represent different aspects of the Divine in a particular region of the world.

Patriarchal: Societal structure in which men are the primary decision makers.

Poppets: A doll used as a charm, only more powerful. Often stuffed with a variety of herbs and flowers. Known traditionally as an item with which to curse, it is actually more often used to promote positive attributes such as health, love, and protection.

Quantum Physics: Branch of physics based on Quantum Theory. Looks at the structure and behavior of atoms and molecules.

Solitary Witch: A witch who has chosen to conduct her craft without alliance with a particular Wiccan Tradition or a particular coven.

Swahili: Popular language of Northern Africa. Also can be a term referring to certain Arab-influenced areas of Kenya such as Lamu.

Synergy: Two or more energies working to mutual advantage. The power of the two working together exceeds the power of the individuals involved.

Tri-Lunar Spells: Spells for a specific intention that are conducted three times in succession, one per lunar cycle for greater effectiveness. They may be altered slightly as the circumstances change over the time frame.

Unconscious Competence: The step of learning where we are able to unconsciously perform an activity easily and correctly.

Wiccaning: Ceremony to welcome a child into the Wiccan faith. Could be likened to the Christian practice of Christening.

Yule: One of the seasonal witches' holidays and part of the traditional Wheel of the Year. Signifies the coming of light and hope. December 22, Winter Solstice in the Northern Hemisphere

Witch in the Boardroom
Proven Business Magic

STACEY DEMARCO

Must cutthroat tactics and backstabbing be synonymous with "getting ahead?" Does success in the corporate world equal spiritless, energy-draining drudgery? Successful business leader and experienced Witch Stacey Demarco insists that spirituality and business are not mutually exclusive. Combining Wiccan principles with down-to-earth business techniques, *Witch in the Boardroom* demonstrates how to rejuvenate your career and your spiritual life.

Demarco illustrates how to achieve material and spiritual fulfillment in the workplace by applying Witchcraft laws, spellworking, and magical thinking. Inspiring stories from the author's own case studies confirm the potency of the rituals and spells outlined in this Wiccan-based guide to business success.

0-7387-0840-2, 312 pp., 6 x 9   **$14.95**

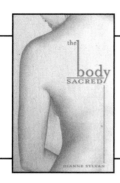

The Body Sacred

DIANNE SYLVAN

When you look in the mirror, do you see a Goddess?

For anyone who's experienced a "fat day" or wished a doctor could make them younger, Wiccan Dianne Sylvan speaks candidly about overcoming body hatred and offers a spiritual path back to Divine femininity.

Sharing her own struggles with poor body image and self-acceptance, Sylvan explores how the impossible standard of female beauty has developed and endured. Emphasizing the Mother, the Healer, the Lover, and other archetypes of one's relationship with the sacred body, the author provides a uniquely Wiccan approach to achieving a healthy, new self-perception as Goddess.

0-7387-0761-9, 312 pp., 6 x 9 $14.95

To order, call 1-877-NEW-WRLD
Prices subject to change without notice

Modern Sex Magick
Secrets of Erotic Spirituality

Donald Michael Kraig

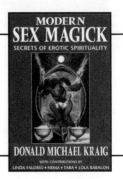

(Contributions by Linda Falorio, Nema, Tara, and Lola Babalon)

Deep within you is a center of power so potent and strong it defies imagination. Now you can learn to control and direct it when it's at its most intense and explosive moment—during sexual arousal. *Modern Sex Magick* provides easy and precise exercises that prepare you to use the magical energy raised during sexual activity, and then it shows you how to work with that energy to create positive changes in your life.

This is the first book to clearly reveal the secrets of western sex magick without relying on Tantric theory. It explores the latest scientific discoveries in the field of human sexuality. This unique mixture of science and magick produces a simple fact: practicing these techniques will help you increase and extend your sexual pleasure! You will uncover depths of ecstasy experienced by only a few, and the results can enhance and deepen your relationships. Four powerful women sex magicians also contribute articles to this book.

1-56718-394-8, 400 pp., 6 x 9, illus.   **$17.95**